A PRACTITIONERS' GUIDE TO THE EC–TURKEY ASSOCIATION AGREEMENT

A PRACTITIONERS' GUIDE TO THE EC–TURKEY ASSOCIATION AGREEMENT

By

Nicola Rogers

On behalf of the
Immigration Law Practitioners' Association

Kluwer Law International
The Hague / London / Boston

A C.I.P. Catalogue record for this book is available from the Library of Congress.

ISBN 90-411-1281-2 (hardback)
ISBN 90-411-1282-0 (paperback)

Published by Kluwer Law International,
P.O. Box 85889, 2508 CN The Hague, The Netherlands.

Sold and distributed in North, Central and South America
by Kluwer Law International
675 Massachusetts Avenue, Cambridge, MA 02139, USA

In all other countries, sold and distributed
by Kluwer Law International, Distribution Centre
P.O. Box 322, 3300 AH Dordrecht, The Netherlands

Printed on acid-free paper

Printed and bound in Great Britain by Anthony Rowe Limited.

Table of Contents

Acknowledgements

I would like to thank ILPA, and particularly Susan Rowlands, for all their assistance and for asking me to write this guide. I am extremely grateful to Elspeth Guild for her support and guidance and Kees Groenendijk for his comments on drafts. Any errors or omissions are, however, entirely my own fault. I am also indebted to Joanna Skates for tirelessly formatting and scanning documents.

Writing a book on a subject such as this is never an easy task and I am very grateful for the people around me for giving me the support that I needed, particularly the Immigration Team at my present Chambers, 1 Pump Court. I would also like to thank Lamb Building for giving me time during my pupillage to write this, particularly the clerks. Finally I am always indebted to the people who have encouraged me to expand my horizons, Nuala Mole and my ever-supportive parents.

Foreword

In 1990 a dozen or so immigration solicitors met in the reception area of a legal aid firm in London in the context of the regular monthly meetings of the Refugee Legal Support Group. With amazement and incredulity they listen to a rather garbled account of the decision of the European Court of Justice in *Sevince* which had just been handed down and which was the starting point of the importance of the EEC Turkey Association Agreement ("the Ankara Agreement") for work and residence rights of Turkish nationals in Europe. Most of the lawyers in the room had never heard of the Ankara Agreement. The few who had discounted it as valueless for Turkish workers in the UK in the same way as the Court of Appeal had done earlier that year. The possibility that Community law could give rights of immediate and direct value which took precedence over the Immigration Rules to Turkish residents in the UK seemed incredible.

Eight years on, Association Council Decision 1/80, the critical piece of subsidiary legislation of the Ankara Agreement which gives rights to individual Turkish workers in the Member States has become part of the furniture of immigration lawyers in the UK. Although the Immigration Rules have still not been amended to recognise the rights which Community law gives to Turkish workers[1] this has not prevented bold immigration lawyers in the UK from asserting these rights on behalf of their clients and obtaining recognition of those rights from the Home Office. Indeed, last year for the first time a UK court made a reference to the European Court of Justice in Luxembourg on the interpretation of the Ankara Agreement as regards the standstill clause designed to protect Turkish nationals who are self-employed in the Member States from any reduction in their rights as to entry into force of the additional Protocol in 1970.[2] A second reference had now been made from a UK court on the meaning of the transitional period. If one can measure the degree of

---

[1] Notwithstanding an obligation to do so contained in Article 6(3) of the Association Council Decision 1/80.
[2] The effective date for the UK 1.1.1973 when the UK formally aceded to the Community.

acceptance of a provision of Community law in the UK system by the willing-ness of UK judges to acknowledge its potential effects *vis a vis* national law and therefore make a reference to the European Court of Justice on interpreta-tion, the rights of Turkish nationals under the Ankara Agreement have now come of age.

The role of the Immigration Law Practitioners' Association in the process has not been insignificant. The critical subsidiary legislation of the Agreement, Association Council Decision 1/80, although produced in English in 1980 has never been published by an official source. The first time it became available in published form to lawyers and others in the UK was 1994 when ILPA produced the first edition of the Immigration Lawyers' Guide to the EEC/Turkey Association Agreement. The demand for copies of the guide was intense, evidencing the thirst for information about this important part of Community law in the UK. At that time, the state of the jurisprudence on the agreement and its subsidiary legislation was still in its infancy. Only four decisions had been handed down by the European Court of Justice and many aspects of the interpretation of the legislation were deeply unclear.

Now there are fourteen Judgments from the Court of Justice already on the table and numerous references are pending still before it. We now know definitively that Article 6(1) of Decision 1/80 gives a Turkish worker who has worked and resided lawfully in the UK for a period of one year a right to an extension of his or her leave to remain and work provided that his or her position in the labour force is secure and stable. We also now know that after four years lawful employment and residence a Turkish national is entitled to free access to the labour market which in the UK is the immigration status of indefinite leave to remain. These rules apply equally to Turkish workers whose access to lawful employment has arisen through different means such as by virtue of family reunion or because they were granted leave to enter and take employment as trainees.

Many areas of Community legislation protecting Turkish workers still remain to be clarified. One reference currently pending before the Court of Justice relates to the permitted grounds of expulsion of a Turkish worker protected under the Agreement. It is argued that the subsidiary legislation of the Agreement must be interpreted as meaning that a Turkish worker can only be expelled on the same grounds as a Community national, that is to say, public policy, public security or public health. Another area which is still in need of clarification is the right of the children of Turkish workers to equal treatment in access to education. Can such children be refused home student fees and grants? This question has yet to be raised before the Court of Justice.

In view of the current state of the law, ILPA has concluded that the time is right for a new edition of the Immigration Lawyers' Guide to the Ankara Agreement. Notwithstanding eight years of jurisprudence by the European Court of Justice and the appearance of the original guide, too often Turkish nationals in the UK are failing to receive good, concise and comprehensive advice on their rights where they are based on Community law. In order to seek to remedy this situation, Nicola Rogers, a highly talented young Community law barrister at 1 Pump Court, has prepared for ILPA the second edition of the guide. Once again, included in the guide are all of the key texts which an advisor needs in order correctly to advice Turkish nationals on their rights. The important provisions of the Ankara Agreement itself are of course included. However, of equal importance are the provisions relating to workers and the self-employed in the 1970 Additional Protocol of the Agreement and the subsidiary legislation, Decisions 2/76, 1/80 and 3/80 made under the Agreement.

The reader also has to hand in this guide all of the Decisions of the Court of Justice relevant to workers as regards the interpretation of the Agreement and its subsidiary legislation. Only the opinions of the Advocates General have been excluded.

The discursive part of the guide has been completely re-vamped since the first edition. Rogers, in clear and precise language takes the reader through each category of Turkish worker and each right clearly setting out the law, its interpretation by the Court of Justice, Home Office practice and the question marks which still surround aspects of the provisions.

It is hoped that the guide will not only be of value to advisors in the UK but also that it will assist officials both in the Immigration and Nationality Directorates and at Consular posts abroad to understand and give effect to the rights of Turkish workers in the UK or returning here. It is also hoped that Immigration Adjudicators and other Judges will find the guide useful in consolidating in one place the text of the law, the Judgments of the Court and a comprehensive explanation of how Turkish workers' rights must be protected in the UK.

As regards application of the law, not only is it incumbent on the Immigration and Nationality Directorate to amend the Immigration Rules to include and correctly reflect the rights which Turkish workers have by virtue of the Agreement and its legislation[3] but it is also in their interests. Clarity and consistency are virtues of public policy and law which help both those charged with its administration and those seeking to rely on its benefit. The UK government may wish to note that the German Interior Ministry, the government and ministry which has appeared in the largest number of cases before the European Court of Justice to defend its actions as regards Turkish workers, last year finally introduced into its equivalent the Immigration Rules provisions to give effect to the rights of Turkish workers under Community law. It would, therefore, at the very least seem appropriate that a Member State government which prides itself on prompt implementation and transposition of Community law, such as the UK, equally transposes into the Immigration Rules those rights. Only then will it be clear and self-evident to everyone picking up a copy of the Immigration Rules that Turkish workers are entitled to protection of their right to work and residence, as regards the right to commence employment

---

[3] Article 6(3) Decision 1/80.

and residence for their family members and non-discrimination not only for themselves, as regards working conditions, but for their children, as regards education.

Elspeth Guild
Chair, ILPA European Group
March 1999

I. Introduction

1. Historical Context

The Association Agreement with Turkey ("the Ankara Agreement") was signed on 12 September 1963[4] as a preliminary to membership of the Community. It was the second agreement of its type, the first being with Greece and reflected a political will on the part of the Community to be more closely associated with its Mediterranean neighbours.

The Ankara Agreement envisaged the establishment of a customs union, although in stages, and provided for assistance during the preparatory stages for Turkey to strengthen its economy.

In 1970 a Protocol[5] to the Ankara Agreement was signed detailing arrangements and a timescale of between twelve and twenty two years for the establishment of the customs union.[6] Free movement of workers was to be achieved within the same period.

One of the most important provisions in the Ankara Agreement was the establishment of an Association Council, capable of making decisions in relation to the Ankara Agreement.[7] The Association Council decisions have in practice served to provide most guidance in relation to the freedom of movement of workers.

The 1970's oil crisis and economic depression in the rest of the European Community created a negative perception generally towards migrant workers. The 1980's saw a cooling off of political cohesion between Turkey and the Community following the military coup in Turkey in 1980. More recently massive inflation and economic instability in Turkey have placed strain on any economic will on the part of the Community to enjoin Turkey in its membership. Additionally Turkey's human rights record, in relation to the treatment of its Kurdish community, has dampened any political motivation to encourage

---

[4] OJ 1973 C113/2.
[5] Signed on 23 November 1970, OJ 1973 C113/18.
[6] Article 36 to the Protocol.
[7] Articles 22 and 23 of the Ankara Agreement.

1

closer relations. Turkey's position in the Community is certainly not assisted by the Greeks with whom Turkey has long standing disagreement over Cyprus.

As a result of a combination of these factors, Turkey's application to join the Community in 1987 was rejected and the timetable in so far as the free of movement of workers has been long overshot. This in itself has lead to a feeling of distrust on the part of the Ankara Government and tensing of the relationship between Turkey and the Community.

Despite these difficulties, on 31 December 1995 the Decision on the final phase of the customs union came into force, the Association Council having decided to step up co-operation in several sectors, to strengthen institutional co-operation and to intensify political dialogue. It is significant that there is no provision for the free movement of persons included in the customs union decision.

Relations between the EU and Turkey have since deteriorated again. After the Luxembourg European Council in December 1997 Turkey suspended political dialogue with the EU believing that it was receiving discriminatory treatment compared with other countries applying to join the EU. Although Ankara has since showed willingness to co-operate with the EU, the relationship between Turkey and EU is fragile.[8]

In its Report on "Turkey's Progress towards Accession" published at the end of 1998 the Commission pointed to a number of economic and political barriers to accession. Whilst the report contained no surprises, it highlighted the fact that accession to EU will be some time coming.

2. The Turkish Community in Europe

In January 1995 there were 2,668,690 Turkish nationals living in the European Union. In the European Union as a whole the Turkish population represents less than one percent of the total population. However it does represent the largest group of foreign nationals. Significantly there continues to be a large migration flow from Turkey to the EU. Between 1986 and 1995 nearly 1 million Turks immigrated to the EU. Despite a relatively steady decline since 1991, 91,000 Turks emigrated to the EU in 1995.

The vast majority of Turkish nationals resident in the EU live in Germany. In January 1995 there were 1,955,577 Turks living in Germany, representing over 2.3% of the total population in Germany.[9] The majority of Turkish nationals migrating to the EU today migrate to Germany. The large number of Turkish nationals in Germany is a relict of the "*gastarbeiteri*" of the 1960s and 1970s, whilst the majority of migrants today answer not to the call of "*gastarbeiteri*" but to that of family union or formation as well that of asylum.

---

[8] For a more detailed history of relations between the EU and Turkey see European Commission's Regular Report on Turkey's Progress towards Accession (COM (1998) 711, 17.12.1998).

[9] Reunification of Germany reduced this percentage.

In comparison there were only 29,000 Turkish nationals resident in the United Kingdom in 1995, representing less than 0.5% of the total population. In 1995 net immigration of Turkish nationals was 3,000. A large proportion of these are asylum seekers of Kurdish origin.

It is therefore not surprising that the vast majority of cases in the European Court of Justice concerning the Ankara Agreement emanate from Germany and that they increasingly concern the social rights of workers and the rights of their families. To date the European Court of Justice has delivered fourteen judgments directly relating to the Ankara Agreement, whilst many more remain pending before the Court.

II. The community law context

It is essential to the understanding of the Ankara Agreement, its Protocol and the European Court of Justice's jurisprudence in the area, that the Community law context of the Agreement is understood.

1. MIXED AGREEMENTS

The Ankara Agreement is a mixed agreement. In Community law, competence for matters covered by an international agreement may be exclusively with the Community, or shared between the Community and the Member States, or exclusively with the Member States. A mixed agreement is where competence is shared between the Community and the Member States.

There is some argument about whether the concept of the mixed agreement is one which should be recognised in Community law. However there can be no doubt that the Court of Justice recognises such concept and indeed has referred specifically to the Ankara Agreement as such an agreement.

The essential feature of a mixed agreement is that some provisions fall within the competence of the Community, while others fall within the competence of the Member States. However the Court of Justice is reluctant to allocate exact division of competence. Instead it emphasises the need for common action or "close co-operation" thus requiring common standards to be reached and uniform interpretation of provisions contained within the agreements.[10] Accordingly the Court has afforded itself a wide jurisdiction to interpret agreements.

How far the Court can go in determining issues of interpretation in mixed agreements is a source of anguish for Member States, which would rather preserve greater proportions of agreements to their exclusive jurisdiction. In **Demirel**[11] the German and the United Kingdom Governments argued that the Court did not have jurisdiction to rule on the interpretation of a provision in

---

[10] Demirel v Stadt Schwabisch Gmund (C-12/86), 30 September 1987.

[11] Ibid, para.8.

a mixed agreement over which the Member States had exclusive jurisdiction. Even the Commission agreed that it would be 'illogical' to refer for review by the Court of Justice provisions over which the Member States have exclusive jurisdiction. The Court side-stepped the issue by holding that the relevant provisions concerned the free movement of workers which fell within the powers in conferred on the Community by Article 310.[12]

The Court has looked at the question of competence as regards the Ankara Agreement in the light of the EC Treaty. Because the EC Treaty gives the Community exclusive competence over movement of workers under Article 39 of the Treaty, the subject area is one over which the Community has competence in respect of third country agreements. By including in the Ankara Agreement and its Protocol the intention to establish free movement for Turkish workers, the Member States transferred competence to achieve this to the Community.

In addition it has made no difference to the Court, with regard to the right of continued employment that the Agreement provides for member states to lay down rules necessary to give effect to its provisions or the decisions adopted by the Association Council. As the Court stated in **Kupferberg**,[13] the obligation of member states to lay down such rules is a community obligation.[14]

2. THE JURISDICTION OF THE ECJ

(a) *In relation to the Ankara Agreement and the Protocol*

The Ankara Agreement is concluded within the ambit of Article 310 of the Treaty of Rome which provides that

> "The Community may conclude with one or more States or international organisations agreements establishing an association involving reciprocal rights and obligations, common action and special procedures"

Article 300 provides for the procedure within the Community institutions for the conclusion of such agreements. Agreements concluded under this procedure are binding on all Community institutions and Member States.[15] As the Court of Justice has stated in the past[16]

> "an agreement concluded by the Council under Articles 228 and 238[17] of the Treaty, as from entry into force of the Agreement ... forms an integral part of the Community legal system."

---

[12]   Ibid., para. 9, see below. Unless in the context of a direct quote from the Court of Justice, the references to EC Treaty articles follows the post Amsterdam Treaty numbering.

[13]   Hauptzollamt Mainz v Kupferberg (C-104/81) [1982] ECR 3641

[14]   See also Demirel, op. cit., para. 11.

[15]   Article 300(7) of the Treaty of Rome.

[16]   Demirel, op. cit., para.7.

[17]   Now Articles 300 and 310 post Amsterdam.

In fact the question was first decided by the Court of Justice in the context of the Association Agreement with Greece in **Haegeman**[18] when it held that an agreement concluded under Articles 300 and 310 of the Treaty represents a measure adopted by a Community institution. Consequently under Article 234(b) the Court of Justice has jurisdictions to give preliminary rulings concerning an agreement concluded under Articles 300 and 310.

This approach was confirmed by the Court of Justice in relation to the Turkey EC Association Agreement in **Demirel**.[19]

(b) *In Relation to the Decisions of the Association Council*

Articles 22 and 23 of the Ankara Agreement provide for the establishment of a Council of Association comprising members of the governments of the Members States of the Community, of the Council and the Commission and members of the Turkish Government. The Association Council has the power to take decisions in order to attain the objectives laid down by the Agreement.

In the context of the Ankara Agreement the Court has repeated the opinion it held in respect of the Greek Association Agreement that

> "since they are directly connected with the Agreement to which they give effect, the decisions of the Council of Association, in the same way as the Agreement itself, form an integral part, as from their entry into force, of the Community legal system"[20]

The Court considers that it follows that since it has jurisdiction to give preliminary rulings on the Ankara Agreement itself, it must also have jurisdiction to give rulings on the interpretation of the decisions adopted by the authority established by the Agreement and entrusted with responsibility for its implementation.[21]

It is a function of the Article 234 of the EC Treaty to ensure uniform application of all the provisions forming part of the Community legal system, which would include decisions by the Association Council, and thus the Court's jurisdiction is fortified.

Despite the clarity with which the Court of Justice has declared its jurisdiction both in relation to the Ankara Agreement and to the decisions of the Association Council, Member States persisted until 1992[22] in requesting the Court to reconsider its jurisdiction to give rulings pursuant to Article 234. The Court would appear, however, to be adamant.

---

[18]   Haegeman v Belgium (C-181/73) [1974] ECR 449.
[19]   Ibid.
[20]   S Z Sevince v Staatssecretaris Van Justitite (C-192/89) [1990] ECR I-3461, para. 9.
[21]   This is of course comparable with the situation under the Treaty of Rome itself where provisions need specifying through regulations and directives.
[22]   Kazim Kus v Landeshauptstadt Wiesbaden (C-237/91) [1992] ECR I-6781.

3. DIRECT EFFECT

The concept of direct effect has been of fundamental importance in the Community legal system. The Court of Justice has stated on numerous occasions that the EC Treaty created a new and unique legal order. In that legal order Member States have limited their sovereign rights and Community law has primacy over the law of Member States and many of the provisions of Community law have direct effect.

In basic terms if a provision of an agreement is directly effective, as a matter of Community law, then it grants rights to natural and legal persons that must be upheld by the national courts of the Member States regardless of any other provisions in domestic law.

The general test for direct effect, as set out by the Court of Justice in **Van Gend En Loos**,[23] is three fold:

(a)   The provision must be clear and unambiguous
(b)   It must be unconditional
(c)   Its operation must not be dependent on further action being taken by the Community or the national authorities or any other body.

In relation to international agreements, including Association Agreements, the Court of Justice has stated that its provisions are certainly capable of direct effect. The general approach of the Court has been to examine the provisions of an agreement in the light of the general structure of the agreement as well as the general aims of the Agreement in order to establish whether its provisions have direct effect.

In fact the Court of Justice has not often found international agreements to have direct effect and likewise it has not found the provisions of many Association Agreements to have direct effect. In the context of the Ankara Agreement the Court has found some of its essential provisions to be programmatic and not sufficiently precise and unconditional to be capable of direct effect. This is explained by the fact that

> "in structure, and content, the Agreement is characterised by the fact that, in general, it sets out the aims of the association and lays down guidelines for the attainment of those aims without itself establishing the detailed rules for doing so. Only in respect of certain specific matters are detailed rules laid down."[24]

Thus so far the provisions of the Ankara Agreement have not been found to be directly effective because of their structure and lack of specific rules but this does not mean that no provision of the Agreement is capable of direct effect.

It is of great significance, however, that the Court has found that many of the decisions of the Council of Association, which give effect to the programmes

---

[23]   (C-26/62) [1963] ECR 1.
[24]   Demirel, op. cit., para. 16.

envisaged by the Ankara Agreement are capable of direct effect. In **Sevince**[25] it stated

> "Decisions 2/76 and 1/80 were adopted by the Council of Association in order to implement Article 12 of the Agreement and Article 36 of the Additional Protocol which, in its judgment in Demirel the Court recognised as being intended essentially to set out a programme. ... The fact that the above mentioned provisions of the Agreement and the Additional Protocol essentially set out a programme does not prevent the decisions of the Council of Association which give effect in specific respects to the programmes envisaged in the Agreement from having direct effect."

This conclusion is not altered by the fact that the Decisions of the Association Council provide that the procedures for applying the rights conferred on Turkish workers are to be established under national rules.

> "Those provisions merely clarify the obligation of the Member States to take such administrative measures as may be necessary for the implementation of those provisions, without empowering the Member States to make conditional or restrict the application of the precise and unconditional right which the decisions of the Council of Association grant to Turkish workers"[26]

Furthermore the Court has stated that the fact that a decision of the Association Council is not officially published in the Official Journals of the European Communities does not deprive the individual of the rights contained within it.

Finally the existence of 'safeguard clauses' enabling parties to derogate from certain provisions of the agreement is also not in itself sufficient to exclude the possibility of direct effect.

---

[25]   op. cit., para. 21.
[26]   Ibid., para. 22.

III. The Provisions on the Free Movement of Persons

1. THE ANKARA AGREEMENT AND ADDITIONAL PROTOCOL

Of principal importance in the field of free movement of persons is Article 12 of the Agreement which provides that:

> "The Contracting Parties agree to be guided by Articles 48, 49 and 50 of the Treaty establishing the Community for the purpose of progressively securing freedom of movement for workers between them"

This provision follows from the general aim of the Ankara Agreement to promote economic relations between Turkey and the Community and the eventual accession of Turkey to the Community. It outlines an objective of the parties to the Agreement, laying the foundation stone for the free movement of workers. The Court of Justice has held, however, that the general nature of the provision does deprive it of direct effect.[27]

Furthermore Article 36 of the Additional Protocol provides that:

> "Freedom of movement for workers... shall be secured by progressive stages in accordance with the principles set out in Article 12 of the Agreement of Association between the end of the twelfth and the twenty-second year after the entry into force of that Agreement.
>
> The Council of Association shall decide on the rules necessary to that end"

Thus the aim of the free movement of workers was to be achieved between 30 November 1974 and 30 November 1986.

In **Demirel**[28] the Court of Justice held that Article 12 of the Ankara Agreement together with Article 36 of the Additional Protocol were essentially programmatic and not sufficiently precise and unconditional to be capable of governing directly the movement of workers. This is partly justified by the exclusive powers conferred on the Association Council to lay down the detailed rules to achieve the aims of the provisions.

---

[27]   See Demirel, op. cit.
[28]   Ibid, para. 23.

The fact that the time framework set out in Article 36 of the Protocol has now long overrun, has not apparently resulted in any legal measure making the provisions of Article 12 directly effective.[29] This is to be contrasted with the provisions of Article 39 of the EC Treaty on the Free Movement of Workers where the Court of Justice held that the end of the transitional period set out in the Treaty did confer directly on Community workers rights upon which they could rely directly.[30]

Whilst the Court has not yet examined the specific question of the implication of the expiry of the time framework for the transitional stage, Advocate General Darmon suggested in his opinion in **Demirel** that the expiry of that time framework did not create any binding effect.

> "The passage of time, has no legal implications here. Progressive implementation depends on decisions of the Council of Association. The absence of such decisions in this field, reflecting the difficulties experienced by the contracting parties in reaching a consensus, precludes the application of provisions without a clearly circumscribed content. Any other solution would, indeed, be incompatible with the consensual nature of an international convention"[31]

The contrast between implications of the end of the transitional period of the EC Treaty and that of the Ankara Agreement and its Protocol is thus explained by the fact that the provisions of Article 39 of the EC Treaty were sufficiently precise and did not require any further implementation measures to be taken by any Community institution. Article 36 of the Additional Protocol to the Ankara Agreement, on the other hand, specifically provides for the adoption of measures by the Council of Association.

2. The Decisions of the Council of Association

The Council of Association, in conformity with its powers under Article 22 of the Ankara Agreement generally and under Article 36 of the Protocol specifically in relation to the free movement of workers, has adopted a number of decisions in order to achieve the aims of Article 12 of the Agreement.

(a) Decision 2/76

This was the first decision relevant to the question of free movement of workers. Article 2 provided for continued employment for a Turkish worker in the same occupation after three years and free access to any paid employment after 5 years. Article 5 provided for priority to be accorded to Turkish nationals in

---

[29]   Whether the passing of time has any legal effect is the question in Saglam C-370/98.
[30]   Van Duyn v. Home Office (C-41/74) [1974] ECR 1337.
[31]   Ibid, p. 3744.

the offering of employment to non-EC nationals. Article 7 provided a stand-still clause, prohibiting Member States from introducing new restrictions on the conditions of access to employment applicable to workers legally resident and employed in their territory.

However the Association Council adopted this Decision as a first step only; the duration of this first step being four years beginning on 1 December 1976. Although the Decision has been superseded by Decision 1/80, Article 7 containing the stand-still clause, remains relevant.[32]

(b) *Decision 1/80*

In contrast to Decision 2/76, Decision 1/80 has no time limit on its applicability. As far as the free movement of workers is concerned it entered into force on 1 December 1980. The provisions contained within Decision 1/80 are said to constitute "one stage further, guided by Articles 48, 49 and 50 of the Treaty, towards securing freedom of movement for workers".[33] In order to ensure compliance with that objective, the Court of Justice has held it

> "essential to transpose, so far as is possible, the principles enshrined in those articles to Turkish workers who enjoy the rights conferred by Decision 1/80"[34]

The Court of Justice has consistently held that the specific provisions of Decision 1/80 are capable of having direct effect. In **Sevince** it held that the fact that relevant provisions of the Ankara Agreement and the Additional Protocol essentially set out a programme

> "does not prevent the decisions of the Council of Association which give effect in specific respects to the programmes envisaged in the Agreement from having direct effect."[35]

It is therefore not surprising that the decisions of the Association Council and in particular of Decision 1/80 has been the subject of the most litigation to date.

Of specific interest with regard to the free movement of workers is Article 6(1) of Decision 1/80, which provides:

> "1. Subject to Article 7 on free access to employment for members of his family, a Turkish worker duly registered as belonging to the labour force of a Member State:
>
> – shall be entitled in that Member State, after one year's legal employment, to renewal of his permit to work for the same employer, if a job is available;

---

[32] See Chapter V.
[33] Bozkurt v Staatssecretaris van Justitie (C-434/93) [1995] ECR I-1475.
[34] Ibid., para. 20.
[35] Sevince, op. cit., para. 21.

– shall be entitled in that Member State, after three years of legal employment and subject to the priority to be given to workers of Member States of the Community, to respond to another offer of employment, with an employer of his choice, made under normal conditions and registered with the employment services of that State, for the same occupation;

– shall enjoy free access in that Member State to any paid employment of his choice, after four years of legal employment."

The Court of Justice has repeatedly held that Article 6(1) has direct effect.[36] However the rights provided for in Article 6(1) only benefit those workers who fulfil the requirements in terms of legal employment, belonging to the labour force and time. The full implication of this provision is discussed in Chapter IV.

Similarly Articles 6(2), 7(1), 7(2) and 13 have been held by the Court of Justice to have direct effect. Article 6(2) makes provision for annual holiday and short periods of illness being incorporated into periods of legal employment and Article 6(3) provides that the procedures for applying Articles 6(1) and 6(2) being those established under national law.

Article 7 provides for members of the worker's family being able to respond to offers of employment after 3 years, free access to the labour market after 5 years and children who have completed vocational training being able to respond to an offer of employment, irrespective of the length of time they have been resident in the Member State.

Article 13 contains a "standstill" clause regarding the introduction of new restrictions on access to the employment of workers legally resident and employed in the territory of the Contracting States.

(c) *Decision 3/80*

Decision 3/80[37] sets out to co-ordinate Member States' social security schemes with a view to enabling Turkish workers employed or formerly employed in the Community, members of their families and their survivors to qualify for benefits in the traditional branches of social security.

Decision 3/80 refers specifically to Council Regulation No. 1407/71 of 14 June 1971 on the application of social security schemes to employed persons and their families moving within the Community.

There is no specified date of entry into force of Decision 3/80 unlike Decision 1/80. However the Court has held that the date of entry into force is taken as the date on which it was adopted i.e. 19 September 1980.

Whilst Decision 3/80 refers specifically to EEC Regulation 1408/71, the former lacks the cumbersome implementing measures set out in EEC Regulation 574/72 which were deemed necessary for the implementation of

---

[36]   See Sevince and Kus.
[37]   OJ 1983 C 110, p.60.

EEC Regulation 1408/71. It is for this reason that the Court has held that the provisions of Decision 3/80 do not have direct effect.

In its judgment in the case of **Taflan-Met**[38] the Court of Justice referred to the fact that the Commission had in fact submitted a proposal for a Council Regulation implementing Decision 3/80 in 1983, which was based to a large extent on EEC Regulation 574/72.[39] That proposal however has not yet been adopted by the Council depriving Decision 3/80 of much of its impact.

However, the Court of Justice is currently considering whether Article 9 of the Ankara Agreement on social security can remedy the fact that a Council Regulation implementing Decision 3/80 has not yet been adopted.[40]

---

[38] Z. Talfan-Met, S. Altun-Baser, E.Andal-Bugdayci v Bestuur van de Sociale Verzekeringsbank, C- 277/94, 10 September 1996, [1996] ECR I-4085.

[39] OJ, English Special Edition 1972 (I), p.159.

[40] Advocate General La Pergola's opinion of 17 December 1998 in the case of Sema Sürül v Bundesanstalt fur Arbeit, C-262/96, suggests that it does.

IV. Workers

1. The Worker and His Right to Continued Employment

Nothing in the Ankara Agreement itself or the Decisions of the Council of Association confers rights of free movement on workers not already part of the labour force. However Article 6 of Decision 1/80 does provide rights some Turkish nationals. In order to benefit from the rights conferred under Article 6(1) a Turkish national must satisfy three main conditions that:

(a)   He is a worker and legally employed
(b)   He is duly registered as belonging to the labour force
(c)   He has been legally employed for one of three possible time periods.

All three concepts are necessarily interconnected and the Court of Justice has not always considered it necessary to examine each separately. For instance the Court of Justice has stated that legal employment presupposes a stable and secure situation as a member of the labour force, thereby merging the first and second concepts.[41] In many cases it has not been in dispute as to whether or not the national could be considered a "worker" only whether or not the second condition had been fulfilled.

However, each concept does raise specific questions in itself and it is therefore necessary to broadly define each term.

(a) *"He is a worker and legally employed"*

(i) *The Concept of "Worker"*
Just as in the Treaty of Rome there is no definition of a Community "worker", there is no definition of a "Turkish worker" in the Ankara Agreement, its Protocol or the decisions of the Council of Association although the term is repeated. However the reference to Articles 39, 40 and 41[42] of the EC Treaty and the general commitment in the Ankara Agreement towards eventual accession of Turkey to the Community would tend to indicate that the "Turkish worker" should take on the Community law definition.

---

[41]   See Birden v Stadtgemeinde Bremen, C-1/97, 26 November 1998.
[42]   As renumbered by the Amsterdam Treaty, formerly Articles 48, 49 and 50.

The Court of Justice's commitment to providing uniform and objective application of the provisions contained within the Ankara Agreement and the decisions adopted by the Council of Association would tend to support use of a Community law definition, as would its attempts to interpret the decisions of the Association Council, as far as possible, in the light of Treaty provisions on the freedom of movement of workers.

The Court of Justice has put this most explicitly in its recent judgment in **Birden**[43]

> "Reference should ... be made to the interpretation of the concept of worker under Community law for the purposes of determining the scope of the same concept employed in Article 6(1) of Decision No. 1/80".

The basic Community definition of a "worker" is that the individual, for a certain period of time, performs services, for and under the direction of another, in return for which he receives remuneration. The term includes trainees and apprentices, part-time workers and those engaged in employment schemes. The underlying requirement is that the person is engaged in a "genuine and effective economic activity" and that

> "he is entitled to the same conditions of work and pay as those which may be claimed by workers who pursue identical or similar activities, so that his situation is not objectively different from that of those other workers".

In line with its case law on Article 39 of the Treaty of Rome the Court of Justice has recently made clear that

> "A Turkish national such as Mr Birden, who is employed on the basis of a law such as the BSHG, performs, as a subordinate, services for his employer in return for which he receives remuneration, thus satisfying the essential criteria of the employment relationship ... That interpretation is not altered by the fact that the remuneration of the person concerned is provided using public funds since, by analogy with the case-law relating to Article 48 of the Treaty, neither the origin of the funds from which the remuneration is paid, nor the "sui generis" nature of the employment relationship under national law and the level of productivity of the person concerned can have any consequence in regard to whether or not the person is to be regarded as a worker."

(ii) *The Concept of "Legal Employment"*

The requirement that the worker is legally employed within the territory of the Member State does not necessarily presuppose the possession of residence documents or even a work permit.[44] The Court of Justice affirmed in **Birden**

---

[43]   Ibid, para.24.
[44]   See Bozkurt v Staatssecretaris van Justite, C-434/93, [1995] ECR I-1475, paras. 14, 19 and 20.

that the concepts "being duly registered as belonging to the labour force" and "legal employment" are one and the same.[45]

The legality of employment must be determined in the light of the legislation of the Member State governing the conditions under which the Turkish worker entered the national territory and is employed there.

The worker must not, therefore, be working in breach of any legal conditions of stay or have entered on false documentation and thereby entered into employment as the result of fraudulent conduct.[46]

The Court of Justice has repeatedly stated that the legality of employment *"presupposes a stable and secure situation"*. In other words there must be an undisputed right of residence, for any dispute as to that right must lead to an instability in the worker's situation. Therefore the worker, who is only able to work by virtue of making an appeal, for instance, against the refusal of residence permit, will not be considered to fulfill the requirements of legal employment. This is equally the case where a first instance judgment upholds the right of residence but where there is retroactive suspension of the residence permit, order by a court, through the exercise of an appeal.

The Court of Justice has justified its decision in both **Sevince** and **Kus**, to recognise as periods of legal employment the periods during which the person concern benefits from the suspensory effect deriving from an appeal relating to right of residence

> "was to prevent a Turkish worker from contriving to fulfil that condition and consequently from being recognised as being in possession of the right of residence inherent in the freedom of access to any paid employment ... during a period when he had only a provisional right of residence pending the outcome of the dispute".[47]

The justification for the more draconian decision in **Kus**,[48] where it was the authorities which appealed against a first instance decision to grant the residence permit was that if the national court subsequently refused the residence permit,

> "for such refusal would have no effect whatever and the person in question will be enabled to contrive to obtain the rights provided by ... Article 6(1) during a period when he did not fulfil the requisite conditions"[49]

The Court of Justice did, however, acknowledge that if the right of residence was finally granted, then the worker must be deemed retrospectively to have had during the period in question a right of residence which was not provisional but fulfilled the requirement of being "stable and secure".[50]

---

[45] Birden, op. cit., paras. 51-53.
[46] See Kol v Land Berlin, C-285/95, [1997] ECR I-3069.
[47] Kus v Landeshauptstadt Wiesbaden, C-237/91, [1992] ECR I-6781, para. 15.
[48] Ibid.
[49] Ibid, para.16.
[50] Ibid, para.17.

Finally the reasons for a Member State allowing a Turkish national to work and reside in its territory are not relevant to the question of whether the employment was "legal". For instance the fact that work and residence permits were granted to a worker only after his marriage to a German national does not affect the worker's rights under Article 6(1), even where the marriage is subsequently dissolved. Neither does the fact that the worker was allowed to enter into the Member State to fulfil a specific labour requirement there, for example as a specialist chef, deprive him of his rights derived from Article 6(1).[51] Even the fact that a Turkish worker expressly accepted restrictions on his length of stay does not deprive him of the rights acquired under Article 6(1). Thus the Court of Justice has decided that the fact that a Turkish worker declared his intention of returning to Turkey after having been employed in the Member State for the purpose of perfecting his vocational skills does not deprive him of the rights deriving from Article 6(1) unless it is established by a national court that he made that declaration with the sole intention of deceiving the national authorities.[52]

(b) *"He is duly registered as belonging to the labour force"*

This concept is not one referred to in the jurisprudence of the Court of Justice in relation to Article 39 of the Treaty of Rome, unsurprisingly as the concept is not mirrored in Article 39. It introduces an additional element to those who may benefit from the provisions for workers under the Ankara Agreement and the decisions of the Association Council, although the test for "labour force membership" appears to be equitable to that for "worker" under Article 39.

In this connection, it must be determined whether the worker:
(i)   is in an employment relationship or available for employment
(ii)   is engaged in employment which can be located within the territory of the Member State or retains a sufficiently close link with that territory
(iii) has completed the applicable formalities required by national law

(i) *Is the person in an employment relationship or available for employment?*

The Employment Relationship

The Court of Justice has identified that it must be determined

> "whether the worker has been employed on the basis of national legislation derogating from Community law and intended specifically to integrate him into the labour force and whether he receives in return for his services remuneration at the level which is usually paid, by the employer concerned or in the sector in question, to persons pursuing identical or comparable activities".[53]

---

[51]   Ertanir v Land Hessen, C-98/96, [1997] ECR I-5179.
[52]   Gunaydin v Freistaat Bayern, C-36/96, [1997] ECR I-5179.
[53]   Gunaydin, op. cit., para. 34.

In other words a test of whether the Turkish national's situation is objectively different to that of other workers determines whether a true employment relationship exists.

In **Gunaydin**[54] this lead the Court of Justice to the conclusion that the mere fact that the employment in question was solely designed to qualify the worker for work elsewhere in the undertaking, did not deprive it of the character of "employment".

The crucial question is one of comparison with the other workers in the same position and thus the level of pay in itself is not a determining factor. According to Advocate General Fennelly,

> "there is no attempt to distinguish between tasks which are performed in response to the free play of the principle of supply and demand and those which have a public interest content"[55]

> The question narrows down to whether or not the individual is in "genuine and effective employment".[56]

Thus recently in **Birden**[57] the Court of Justice decided that the concept of "being duly registered as belonging to the labour force" can not be interpreted as excluding those persons working under a scheme established with a view to improving the integration of the participants into working life which is funded from the public purse. This position is supported by the objective of Decision No. 1/80 which in its preamble seeks to improve, in the social field, the treatment accorded to workers and members of their families.

This is situation is, however, contrasted to the situation where a person, through some form of physical or mental debilitation is only able to be recruited to a position adapted to his physical and mental possibilities, and is thus unable to work under normal conditions.

Furthermore it is clear that the nature of the employment relationship is not altered by the fact that the contract for employment is only temporary. Member States have no power to make conditional or restrict the application of the rights conferred on Turkish workers and thus a worker who has been permitted to enter a Member State's territory and who has lawfully pursued a genuine and effective economic activity for a continuous period of more than one year with the same employer benefits from the three indents of Article 6(1) regardless of the duration of his contract for employment.

The fact that a Member State may impose restrictions on certain categories of workers as to the duration of their residence and permission to change employers, can not alter the genuine and effective nature of an employment relationship either. In this context, the Court of Justice has stated that such

---

[54]   Ibid.
[55]   Advocate General's Opinion in Birden v Stadtgemende Bremen, C-1/97, 28 May 1998, para.38.
[56]   c.f. Levin v Staatssecretaris van Justitie, C-53/81, [1982] I-1035.
[57]   op.cit.

restrictions are "incompatible" with the rights deriving from Decision No. 1/80 and thus irrelevant for the purposes of its interpretation.

Incapacity and Retirement

In **Bozkurt**[58] the Court stated that underlying Article 6 was the prerequisite that the worker is able to work. It pointed out that whilst Article 6(2) envisages temporary breaks in employment and therefore periods of legal employment will include annual holidays, absences for reason of maternity or an accident at work or short periods of sickness, the provisions of Article 6 presuppose fitness to continue working.

Where a worker is absent from long period on account of sickness, the second sentence of Article 6(2) stipulates that the "inactive" period cannot be treated as a period of legal employment, although the rights of the worker acquired as a result of previous employment cannot be affected. The Court of Justice has stated that this prevents a worker, who recommences work after a long period of illness, from having to "reset the clock" in terms of time periods fulfilled under Article 6(1) as a new arrival would.

In the case of permanent incapacity, the worker can no longer be considered as available for work and there is no objective justification for guaranteeing him the right of access to the labour force and an ancillary right of residence.

The Court of Justice has excluded from benefiting from the provisions of Article 6 any Turkish worker who "*has definitely ceased to belong to the labour force of a Member State*" whether by reason of reaching retirement age or becoming totally or permanently incapacitated for work. In the absence of any other right, the worker thus loses a right of residence.

The Court of Justice has not defined what periods of time are envisaged by Article 6(2) in precise terms and therefore it will be a question degree as to whether time taken off for illness constitutes "*short periods of sickness*" or "*long absences on account of sickness*".

Retirement age will be that defined by the Member State's national legislation, regardless of capacity to work.

Involuntary Unemployment

In the case of involuntary unemployment, Article 6(2) provides that like in the case of long periods of absence due to sickness, the inactive period can not be treated as periods of legal employment for the purposes of Article 6(1) although they do not affect the rights which the worker acquired as the result of preceding employment. Thus a worker who, for instance, had been employed for 3 years and is made involuntarily unemployed for 3 months, will not have the 3 months taken into account when calculating periods of legal employment, but will not have to recommence the periods of employment under Article 6(1) as if he had never previously been employed.

---

[58]   op.cit.

The Court of Justice has stated, *obiter*, that the unemployment must be "*through no fault of his own*" and not attributable to any misbehaviour on the part of the worker himself, which follows from the use of "*unverschuldet*" in the German version of the decision.[59]

Voluntary Unemployment

In **Tetik** the Court of Justice made specific reference to its own jurisprudence under Article 39[60] of the EC Treaty in relation to those seeking employment. By reference to its decision in **Antonissen**[61] it noted that

> "Article 48 … requires that the person concerned be given a reasonable time in which to appraise himself, in the territory of the Member State which he has entered, of offers of employment corresponding to his occupational qualifications and to take, where appropriate, the necessary steps in order to be engaged".[62]

The Court of Justice went on reiterate the relationship between Decision 1/80 and Articles 39 to 41 of the EC Treaty. Whilst Decision 1/80 does not confer a right of entry into a Member State and thus can not confer the right to enter and seek employment analogous to the situation under Article 39 of the EC Treaty, the Court has held that a Turkish worker must be able, for a reasonable period, to seek effectively new employment in the Member State and have a corresponding right of residence. The Court left it to the discretion of the Member State to determine how long a reasonable period for seeking employment would be but it may not deprive Article 6 of its substance by "*jeopardising in fact the Turkish worker's prospects of finding new employment*".[63]

In the Court's opinion it makes no material difference that voluntary unemployment is not specifically envisaged by Article 6(2). Where the time period in question is short, the worker can not be deemed to have left the labour force, provided that he continues to be duly registered as belonging to the labour force of the Member State.

(ii) *Is the worker engaged in employment which can be located within the territory of the Member State or retains a sufficiently close link with that territory?*

The question of whether or not a worker is member of the labour force has arisen in cases where the person in question was an international lorry driver, requiring no residence or work permit in the Member State in question.

The Court of Justice has stated that it is for the national courts to determine

---

[59] Ibid., para.38.

[60] Formerly Article 48.

[61] The Queen v Immigration Appeal Tribunal, ex parte Antonissen, C-292/89, [1991] ECR I-745, paras. 13, 15 and 16.

[62] Recep Tetik v Land Berlin, C-171/95, [1997] ECR I-329, para. 27.

[63] Tetik, op. cit., para. 32.

whether the employment relationship of a worker retains a sufficiently close link with the territory of the Member State. It has, however, held that the following factors should taken into account:-

- where the worker was hired
- the territory on which the paid employment was based
- the applicable national legislation in the field of employment and social security law

(iii)   *Has the worker completed the applicable formalities by national law?*
This would include the payment of income tax, contributions for health, pension and unemployment insurance.

(c) *"He has been legally employed for one of three possible time periods"*

In order to qualify under Article 6(1) of Decision 1/80 specific time periods of legal employment must have been fulfilled.

The first indent of Article 6(1) provides after one year's legal employment, the worker is entitled to a renewal of his work permit "for the same employer". The aim of the first indent is to ensure continuity of employment with the same employer and is therefore only applicable where the worker requests an extension of his work permit in order to continue working for the **same employer** after the initial year.[64]

Furthermore, the Court of Justice has stated that even where the Turkish worker has worked for one year without interruption but for different employers, with the permission of the national authorities, he does not qualify under the first indent of Article 6(1) and will only qualify when he has completed a full year's employment with one employer.[65]

It should be clear from the above that once a worker has fulfilled the first year's legal employment with one employer attempts by the national authorities to limit renewal of contracts are incompatible with Decision 1/80.

The second indent provides that the Turkish worker may, after three years legal employment change employers and respond to any other offer of employment "for the same occupation".[66]

The third indent provides that after four years legal employment, the worker enjoys free access to any paid employment. This will include the right to seek employment for a "reasonable period".

Article 6(2) specifically states that "annual holidays and absences for reasons of maternity or accident at work or short periods of sickness shall be treated as legal employment".

---

[64]   The Transfer of Undertakings Directive would indicate that where there has been a transfer of undertakings, for these purposes the employer remains the same even if the legal entity has changed.

[65]   See Eker v Land Baden-Württenburgh, C-386/95, [1997] ECR I-2697.

[66]   As yet there is no ECJ guidance on the meaning of 'same occupation'.

Furthermore periods of involuntary unemployment and long absences on account of sickness are not to be treated as periods of legal employment but at the same time do not affect rights acquired as the resulting of previous employment.

In **Ertanir**[67] the Court of Justice further clarified that short periods without a valid residence or work permit do not affect the periods of legal employment referred to in Article 6(1).

It should be clear from the discussion on "legal employment" above that the fact that a Turkish worker once expressed the intention to return leave the Member State after a certain time period, does not deprive him of the rights deriving from Article 6(1).

2. THE RIGHT OF RESIDENCE

The Court of Justice has consistently held that the rights which Article 6(1) of Decision 1/80 confers on Turkish workers in regard to employment

> "necessarily imply the existence of a corresponding right of residence for the person concerned, since otherwise the right of access to the labour market and the right to work as an employed person would be deprived of all effect"[68]

Thus a worker qualifying under Article 6(1) for extensions of his employment in the Member State will have a corresponding right to remain in that Member State.

That right to residence exists where the worker concerned becomes a work seeker for a reasonable period.

Article 6(1) does not subject recognition of rights of residence or to continue working after specified time period to the condition that Turkish nationals must establish the legality of their employment by possession of any specific administrative document such as a work permit or residence permit. The Court of Justice has made it clear that

> "the fact that (the worker's) residence permit was issued to him only for a fixed period is not relevant, since it is settled case-law that the rights conferred on Turkish workers by Article 6(1) of Decision 1/80 are accorded irrespective of whether or not the authorities of the host Member State have issued a specific administrative document, such as a work permit or residence permit"[69]

In this context such administrative documents are only "declaratory" of the

---

[67] Ertanir v Land Hessen, C-98/96, [1997] ECR I-5179
[68] See most recently Birden, op. cit., para. 20, Gunaydin, op. cit., para.26 and Ertanir, op. cit., para.26.
[69] Gunaydin, op. cit., para. 26.

existence of the worker's rights and do not constitute a condition their existence. This is consistent with the position for workers in Community law in general.

In the United Kingdom there is no separate statutory provision giving effect to Article 6 of Decision 1/80. However Home Office instructions are that Turkish nationals who have rights under the Agreement are to be granted leave to remain in the United Kingdom, as appropriate.[70]

---

[70] Written Answer no. 230, 24 February 1999 from Minister Mike O'Brian.

V. The Standstill Clauses

1. WHAT IS A STANDSTILL CLAUSE?

A standstill clause is a provision in an agreement that forbids a party from changing conditions to the detriment of the applicant from how they stand at the time of entry into force of the agreement. In the context of the Ankara Agreement and the Council of Association Decision there are two such standstill: one relating to the conditions of access to employment and the other to the conditions of self employment in the Member States.

2. STANDSTILL CLAUSE: EMPLOYMENT

(a) *The Standstill clause in relation to workers*

Article 13 of Association Council Decision 1/80 provides the following:

> "The Member States of the Community and Turkey may not introduce new restrictions on the conditions of access to employment applicable to workers and members of their families legally resident and employed in their respective territories"

The provision in Decision 1/80 replaces that contained in Article 7 of Association Council Decision 2/76 which provided for a standstill in relation to workers and employment, but did not include family members.

In **Sevince**[71] the Court of Justice described the standstill clauses contained within Decisions 2/76 and 1/80 as "unequivocal" and to have direct effect in the Member States.

As the provision in Article 13 of Decision 1/80, as regards workers, reproduces the provision in Decision 2/76 and Decision 2/76 entered into force on 20 December 1976 and remained in force until the entry into force of Decision 1/80, Turkish workers may accordingly enjoy the conditions of access to employment which existed on 20 December 1976.

---

[71] Sevince v Staatssecretaris van Justitie, C-192/89, [1990] ECR I-3461, para.18

However, the standstill clause as it relates to the family members, was not incorporated in Decision 2/76 and therefore family members may only enjoy conditions of access to employment which existed on the date of entry into force of Decision 1/80.[72] The standstill clauses contained within Decisions 2/76 and 1/80 specifically related to persons "legally resident and employed" in the Member States. The Court of Justice has repeatedly stated in relation to Article 6(1) of Decision 1/80 that reference to persons already in legal employment means that Member States are able to control entry into their territory of Turkish nationals and conditions of initial employment. It would appear from the wording of the standstill clauses, that similar provisos exist. Member States are therefore able to apply whatever conditions of entry to the territory and first access to employment they wish.

However it is as well to underline that no new restrictions on access to continued employment can be imposed, than the restrictions in force in 1976 (with respect to workers) and in 1980 (with respect to family members) irrespective of the date on which the worker or his family member was allowed to first reside and work in the Member State.

(b) *Who benefits?*

The Turkish workers who principally benefit from the operation of the standstill clauses are those who are legally resident and employed within the Member States but who do not yet or no longer benefit from the provisions in Article 6 of Decision 1/80. Article 13 does not require that rights under Articles 6 or 7 of Decision 1/80 have been acquired. It is arguable for instance those who do not enjoy "*a stable and secure position in the labour force*" would benefit from the provisions of the standstill clause. In other words asylum seekers with work permission would benefit, as would a person married to a settled person whose marriage broke down within a year of legal employment in the United Kingdom.

Whether or not persons on temporary admission would be considered "legally resident" in the United Kingdom remains to be seen.

(c) *1976 Work Permit Scheme*

The 1976 work permit scheme is much more lenient than that in force at present. It is less strict in terms of advertising requirements and also in relation to the categories of persons who may be employed under a work permit.

The onus is on the employer to show that "he made adequate efforts to find a suitable worker among the resident labour force". Usually this will entail placing details in the local employment office or jobcentre and in appropriate journal or newspaper.

---

[72]   1 December 1980.

Work permits were available to those with professional qualifications, skills or experience and also to:

"…

(ii)   administrative and executive staff
(iii) skilled craftworkers and experienced technicians
(iv)   specialised clerical and secretarial staff
(v)   workers in commercial or retail distribution with special experience or qualifications relevant to the post offered
(vi)   exceptionally highly qualified senior staff in hotel and catering, for example, Departmental Head of appropriate establishments, and qualified cooks who have evidence of acceptable training in approved hotel schools abroad
(vii) resident domestic workers without children under the age of 16
(viii) certain workers in hospitals and similar institutions"

3. STANDSTILL CLAUSE: SELF EMPLOYMENT

(a) *Self Employment in the Ankara Agreement*

Articles 13 and 14 of the Ankara Agreement provide the foundation stone for freedom of establishment and the freedom to provide services, in much the same way as that foundation stone for the freedom of movement of workers is laid down by Article 12 of the Agreement. The provisions of Articles 13 and 14 are further developed in Article 41 of the Additional Protocol. However, the Council of Association has failed to provide for any specific measures in relation to a right of establishment in any of its decisions.

Article 13 of the Ankara Agreement provides

"The Contracting Parties agree to be guided by Articles 52 to 56 and Article 58 of the Treaty establishing the Community for the purpose of abolishing restrictions on the freedom of establishment between them"

Article 14 of the Agreement provides

"The Contracting Parties agree to be guided by Articles 55, 56 and 58 to 65 of the Treaty establishing the Community for the purpose of abolishing restrictions on freedom to provide services between them."

The similarities between Article 12, in relation to workers, and Articles 13 and 14 would suggest that the decision of the Court of Justice in **Demirel**[73] applies and that the two latter provisions do not have direct effect. They still provide guidance as to the general aims of the Contracting Parties and to interpretation of various concepts such as "establishment".

---

[73]   Demirel v Stadt Schwabisch Gmund, C-12/86, [1987] ECR 3719.

(b) *The Standstill Clause*

Article 41(1) of the Additional Protocol provides

> "The Contracting Parties shall refrain from introducing between them-
> selves any new restrictions on the freedom of establishment and the
> freedom to provide services."

The question of whether this provision has direct effect has not been the subject
of a decision of the Court of Justice to date.[74] However useful guidance can
be gained from Advocate General Darmon's opinion in **Demirel**[75] in which he
was examining Article 7 of the Ankara Agreement and making a comparison
with other provisions. Article 7 of the Ankara Agreement provides only that
Member States *"refrain from any measures liable to jeopardise the attainment
of the objectives"* of the Agreement. The Advocate General was of the view that
the provision was not capable of direct effect in the absence of any concrete
provisions to be read in conjunction with that provision and that the fact that
Article 36 of the Additional Protocol expressly envisaged the progressive implementation of rules by the Association Council.

The Advocate General compared the provisions on the free movement of
workers with those on the freedom of establishment and freedom to provide
services, in support of his view that Article 7 could not have direct effect.
Comparing Article 36 of the Additional Protocol, relating to workers, and
Article 41 relating to the establishment provisions, he stated

> "whereas Article 36 is drafted in the terms recited above, Article 41(1) of
> the same Protocol **expressly introduces a standstill clause**"

He does not examine that standstill clause any further. However, using the
criteria laid down by the Court of Justice in relation to direct effect, it is
certainly arguable that the provisions of Article 41(1) are clear, precise and
unconditional and pursue aims generally laid down in Articles 13 and 14 of
the Ankara Agreement. Whereas the remainder of Article 41 provides for the
progressive abolition of restrictions on freedom of establishment and on freedom to provide services under rules laid down by the Council of Association,
no such reference to implementing measures by the Council of Association in
relation to the standstill clause is made.

(c) *Conditions of establishment at time of entry into force*

The United Kingdom acceded to the Treaty of Rome on 1 January 1973. It is,
therefore, the law applicable to the establishment of persons on that date which
should be applied in respect of Turkish nationals wishing to establish themselves
in the United Kingdom today.

---

[74]   Although it is subject of a reference to the ECJ in the case of Adbul Nasir Savas, C-37/98.
[75]   op. cit.

The Immigration Rules HC80 came into force in January 1973 and are considerably more favourable to the Turkish national than the present rules.

The first advantage of the earlier rules is that there is no minimum amount of investment required although *"permission will depend a number of factors including evidence that the applicant will be devoting assets of his own to the business, proportional to his interest in it"*.

Secondly there was no requirement in the old rules that the investment had to create new paid employment for persons already settled here.

Thirdly persons wishing to establish themselves in business under the old rules were not required to obtain entry clearance for the purpose. There was no general rule to prevent persons admitted as visitors from setting up in business obtaining an appropriate extension of stay.

Fourthly there is a presumption in the old rules that if the conditions for initial stay on the basis of establishment are still satisfied that an extension of stay will be granted.

VI. Family Members

1. PROVISION FOR FAMILY MEMBERS IN THE ANKARA AGREEMENT AND THE DECISIONS OF THE COUNCIL OF ASSOCIATION

(a) *The Agreement*

Absent from the Ankara Agreement is any reference to rights in respect of family reunification. The question of whether freedom of movement in the Ankara Agreement included a right for the Turkish worker to bring with him his spouse and children was referred to the Court of Justice in **Demirel**. The Court declined to specifically answer the question, although it stated

> "There is at present no provision of Community law defining the conditions in which Member States must permit the family reunification of Turkish workers lawfully settled in the Community"[76]

Advocate General Darmon stated that

> "Although family reunification is certainly a necessary element in giving effect to the freedom of movement of workers, it does not become a right until the freedom which it presupposes has taken effect and a special provision on the matter has been adopted"[77]

By reference to Article 39 of the EC Treaty, however, it would impossible that family unity can not be at least an aim of the Agreement, as lack of family unity, must be one of the greatest bars to free movement of workers. It must be therefore envisaged that the Council of Association would decide rules in relation to this question.

---

[76] Demirel v Stadt Schwabisch Gmund, C-12/86, [1987] ECR 3719, para. 28.
[77] Demirel, loc. cit., p.3745.

(b) *Decisions of the Council of Association*

Article 7 of Decision 1/80 provides:

> The members of the family of a Turkish worker duly registered as belonging to the labour force of a Member State, who have been authorised to join him:
> –   shall be entitled - subject to the priority to be given to workers of Member States of the Community - to respond to any offer of employment after they have been legally resident for at least three years in that Member State;
> –   shall enjoy free access to any paid employment of their choice provided they have been legally resident there for at least five years.

Children of Turkish workers who have completed a course of vocational training in the host country may respond to any offer of employment there, irrespective of the length of time they have been resident in that Member State, provided one of their parents has been legally employed in the Member State concerned for at least three years.

Direct Effect

The Court of Justice has confirmed the direct effect of Article 7 on several occasions.[78] The Court has further emphasised that Article 7 contains social provision which constitute a further stage in securing freedom of movement for workers on the basis of Articles 39, 40 and 41 of the Treaty. In the context of Article 7 the Court has stated

> "it must be emphasised that the purpose of that provision is to favour employment and residence of Turkish workers duly registered as belonging to the labour force of a Member State by ensuring that their family links are maintained there ... .

> Accordingly, it provides, for the initial stage, that family members of a Turkish worker already duly registered as belonging to the labour force of a Member State may be authorised to join him and take up residence there so as to enable the family to be together"[79]

Clearly Article 7 does not place an obligation on the Member State to initially allow the entry of family members but suggests that it may, in line with a general *"objective of family unity"*.[80]

The Court then went on to state that the provisions of Article 7 existed to

---

[78] See Eroglu v Land Baden-Wurttemberg, C-355/93,[1994] I-5113 and Kadiman v State of Bavaria, C-351/97,[1997] ECR I-2133.
[79] Kadiman, loc. cit., paras. 34 and 35.
[80] Kadiman, loc. cit., para. 38.

consolidate the family member's position in the Member State and "deepen the integration" of the family unit in the Member State.

2. RIGHT OF RESIDENCE FOR FAMILY MEMBERS

Clearly there is no right of entry into the Member State for family members. However once they fulfil the conditions of Article 7 there is an implied recognition of a right of residence.[81] The Court of Justice has held, in line with its jurisprudence in relation to Article 39 of the EC Treaty and Article 6 of Decision 1/80, that in relation to the provisions on family members the right of residence is essential to access to and the pursuit of any paid employment.[82]

This right of residence will also include a period of grace when the person concerned is looking for employment in the Member State.[83] How long that period, is left to the Member State, although it should not be applied in a way that impairs the right.[84]

Children

As regards children it is clear from the Court of Justice's decision in **Eroglu**[85] that the fact that the child of a Turkish worker was originally granted a right to enter and stay for the purposes of vocational training only can not preclude that child from benefiting from his rights under the second paragraph of Article 7. Regardless of his conditions of entry and stay, if a Turkish national satisfies the conditions set out in the second paragraph of Article 7, he may respond to any offer of employment in the Member State concerned and by the same token, he may rely on that provision to obtain the extension of his residence permit.

Other family members

With regard family members who are authorised to join a Turkish worker in a Member State residence with the worker may be required, in order that they benefit from the provisions of Article 7 of Decision 1/80. In **Kadiman** the Court of Justice has stated that Member States are permitted to require that the family members of a Turkish worker live with that worker for the period of three years prescribed by the first indent of Article 7 in order to be entitled to

---

[81] There is a reference to the ECJ from the Austrian courts on this subject in the case of Safet Eyup, C-65/98.

[82] Akman v Oberkreisdirektor des Rheinisch-Bergischen-Kreises, C-210-97, Judgment of 19 November 1998.

[83] Eroglu v Land Baden-Wurttemberg, C-355/93, [1994] ECR I-5113, para. 21.

[84] Kus v Landehauptstadt Wiesbaden, C-237/91, [1992] ECR I-6781.

[85] op.cit.

reside in that Member State.[86] However there may be objective reasons to justify the family member concerned living apart from the Turkish worker. Furthermore once the three-year period has been completed it would appear that he or she will be entitled to enter the labour marker irrespective of whether he or she is still residing with the Turkish worker.[87]

3. Definition of "family members"

There is no definition of the family member in the Agreement or any of the Council of Association decisions. However having regard to Community law provisions in the context of free movement of workers, family members irrespectively include arguably include:

– Spouses, their descendants under the age of 21 years or their dependants
– Dependant relatives in the ascending line of the worker and his spouse.[88]

In contrast to its decision in **Diatta**[89] in relation to Article 39 of the EC Treaty, in the context of the Ankara Agreement, the Court of Justice has held that cohabitation is a necessary prerequisite to the operation of Article 7, except in certain circumstances. This is justified by the fact that the aim of Article 7, as stated above, is family unity and this should be evidenced by actual cohabitation. There may, however, be exceptional circumstances when there is justification for failure of the worker and his family to live together, particularly where the worker's occupation so required such separation.[90]

The reasoning may be a little strange bearing in mind the Court's earlier decision in **Eroglu** where it held that

> "The fact that the right was not given to [children of Turkish workers] with a view to reuniting the family but, for example, for the purpose of study does not, therefore, deprive the child of a Turkish worker who satisfies the conditions of the second paragraph of Article 7 of the enjoyment of the rights conferred thereunder.[91]

This may reflect the Court's strong view that the intentions of the Member State in admitting a person are unimportant once the individual has acquired rights in Community law. Thus the operation of Article 7 can not be hindered by a lack of motivation of the part of the Member States to encourage family unity.

---

[86]   Kadiman, op. cit., para.44.
[87]   Kadiman, op. cit., para. 37.
[88]   Article 10 of EC Regulation 1612/68 of 15 October 1968 on Freedom of Movement for Workers within the Community.
[89]   Diatta v Land Berlin, C-267/91, [1985] ECR 567.
[90]   See Kadiman, op. cit., para.40.
[91]   Eroglu, op.cit., para. 22.

4. ARTICLE 8 OF THE EUROPEAN CONVENTION ON HUMAN RIGHTS

The Court of Justice has declined to rule on whether or not Article 8 of the European Court applies in the context of family unity and the Ankara Agreement, by stating that where no Community law rule applies, it can not rule on possible breaches of the European Convention.[92] However, as Advocate General Darmon noted in **Demirel**,[93] that the jurisprudence of the European Court of Human Rights in relation to family unity does not greatly assist. In particular, the European Court of Human Rights' much repeated decision in **Abdulaziz, Cabales and Balkandali v United Kingdom**[94] that the Convention did not confer the right to choose country of residence adds little weight to the family unity argument.

5. REMAINING BEYOND THE WORKER

The Court of Justice has recently examined the possibility of family members remaining in the Member State beyond the worker in the context of the second paragraph of Article 7 of Decision 1/80 in the case of **Akman**.[95] It has stated unequivocally that in order to benefit from the provisions of the second paragraph of Article 7, it is not required that the parent of the child should still work or be resident in the Member State at the time when his child wishes to gain access to the employment market there.

The rational for this is that the second paragraph of Article 7 is intended to provide specific treatment for children with a view to facilitating their entry into the employment market following completion of a course of vocational training, the objective being the achievement by progressive stages of freedom of movement for workers. The Court of Justice is of the view that the second paragraph of Article 7 is not intended to provide the conditions for family unity and it would thus be unreasonable to require that the Turkish migrant worker should continue to reside in the host Member State even after his employment relationship there has ceased in order to secure his child's position, when that child has already completed training and wishes to respond to an offer of employment.

The German Government had tried to argue that the child should only be allowed to take up employment under the strict restrictions of Article 6(1) of Decision 1/80. The Court of Justice rejected this argument stating that such an interpretation of Article 7 would negate the effectiveness of Article 7.[96] Clearly Article 6(1) applies to a child who has been legally employed in the

---

[92] Although it has ruled that it applies in the context of Community nationals, see Commission v Germany.

[93] op.cit.

[94] Decision of the European Court of Human Rights, (1985) 7 EHRR 471.

[95] op. cit.

[96] Akman, op.cit., para. 49.

Member State for a year and wishes to extend his contract with that employer but the second paragraph of Article 7 goes beyond that and is a *"special provision specifically conferring on (children of Turkish workers) more favourable conditions as regards employment"* in Member States.

The Court of Justice was very careful, however, to distinguish the position under the second paragraph of Article 7 from that of the first paragraph of Article 7. It is clear that the Court of Justice's view of the first paragraph of Article 7 is that it is a provision for "family reunification" with the Turkish worker and is therefore only intended to benefit those family members authorised to join the Turkish worker whereas the second paragraph has the objective of the achievement by progressive stages the freedom of movement of workers.

6. Children and Education

In addition to the provisions relating to children in Article 7 of Decision 1/80, Article 9 of that Decision 1/80 provides that

> "Turkish children residing legally with their parents, who are or have been legally employed in a Member State of the Community, will be admitted to courses of general education, apprenticeship and vocational training under the same educational entry qualifications as the children of nationals of the Member States. They may in that Member State be eligible to benefit from the advantages provided for under the national legislation in this area"

The clear and unambiguous nature of this provision means that it would have direct effect. The Court of Justice has observed that it is clear that Article 9 does not require that the parents of the child are legally employed at the moment when they wish to exercise the rights thus conferred on them.[97]

The aim of Article 9 would appear to be the progressive integration of Turkish nationals into Member States and to pursue the effective realisation of the free movement of workers in line with Articles 39, 40 and 41 of the Treaty.

It is clear that a child who has benefited from the provisions of Article 9 may then benefit from the provisions of the second paragraph of Article 7 in that he may respond to any offer of employment having completed vocational training. In order to benefit from the provisions of Article 9 in terms of entry to the education system, the child will have to be resident with their parents in the Member State although the parents need not be employed any longer. Thereafter it would not appear necessary for the parents to even reside in the Member State.

It is not clear whether a Turkish child qualifying under the second paragraph of Article 7, having taken up a job, would be able to change occupation before he or she has fulfilled the temporal requirements of Article 6(1). Furthermore

---

[97]   ibid, para. 41.

it is not clear whether there is a time limit within which the Turkish child qualifying under the second paragraph of Article 7 has to take up employment. However, in view of the general aims of that provision of achieving the free movement of workers in progressive stages, it must not be restrictively interpreted.[98]

---

[98] Ibid, paras. 38 and 39.

VII. Benefits

1. WHICH BENEFITS

Article 39 of the Protocol provided that the Council of Association should adopt social security measures for Turkish workers and their families residing in the Community, implying that a number of social security benefits should be made available to Turkish workers and their families. Article 39 further provides that Turkish workers should be able to aggregate periods of insurance or employment completed in Member States in respect of old-age pensions, death benefits and invalidity pensions, and health services.

Decision 3/80 sets out to co-ordinate Member States' social security schemes with a view to enabling Turkish workers employed or formerly employed in the Community, members of their families and their survivors to qualify for benefits.

Title III of the Decision, in particular, refers to EC Regulation 1408/71 of 14 June 1971 on the application of social security schemes to employed persons and their families within the Community in relation to a wide range of benefits.

Article 3 of Decision 3/80 implements Article 39 of the Protocol by providing that Turkish workers and their families should be subject to "the same obligations" and "enjoy the same benefits" as nationals of that Member State in relation to certain social security benefits. Article 4 of Decision 3/80 states that the following branches of social security are covered by the Decision:

(a) sickness and maternity benefits
(b) invalidity benefits, including those intended for the maintenance or improvement of earning capacity
(c) old-age benefits
(d) survivors' benefits
(e) benefits in respect of accidents at work and occupational diseases
(f) death grants
(g) unemployment benefits
(h) family benefits.

Some Member States have sought to argue that since Decision 3/80 contains no provision on its entry into force, it can not have any binding effect. The

Court of Justice has, however, held that the Decision is deemed to have entered into force on the date on which it was adopted and has therefore been binding on Member States ever since.[99]

However that the explicit reference to EC Regulation 1408/71 in Decision 3/80 has troubled the Court of Justice. In **Taflan-Met** the Court held that as EC Regulation 1408/71 required an implementing measure to be adopted, namely Regulation 574/72 in order that it could be practically applied. Regulation 574/72 is extremely lengthly and detailed. The Court of Justice therefore felt that given Decision 3/80 does not provide any such detailed or precise provisions, it must be intended that it is intended to be supplemented by a subsequent act of the Association Council.[100]

The question of the direct effect of Decision 3/80 is under consideration in the case of **Surul**,[101] where in particular Article 3 of Decision 3/80 is to be applied in relation to family benefits. Advocate-General La Pergola has produced two opinions in the case. In the first he considers that Article 3 of the Decision does indeed have direct effect, although any judgment of the Court of Justice would not be retrospective in its effect. In the second he considers that Article 9 of the Ankara Agreement, prohibiting discrimination on grounds of nationality, remedies the fact that no Council act has been implemented. The Court of Justice decision in this case is now awaited.

2. Children and Educational Benefits

In addition to the provisions under Decision 3/80, Article 9 of Decision 1/80 refers to "advantages" in relation to some forms of education.

Article 9 of Decision 1/80 provides:

> "Turkish children residing legally with their parents, who are or have been legally employed in a Member State of the Community, will be admitted to courses of general education, apprenticeship and vocational training under the same educational entry qualifications as the children of nationals of the Member States. They may in that Member State be eligible to benefit from the advantages provided for under the national legislation in this area."

It is not entirely clear what constitute "courses of general education" and therefore whether non-vocational higher education falls within the provision. It is certainly clear that such children should not be charged oversees fees in relation to the applicable courses and should be treated like any other EC student.

---

[99]   See Taflan-Met v Bestuur van de Sociale Verzekeringsbank, C-277/94, 10. September 1996. Date of entry into force of Decision 3/80 is deemed to be 19 September 1980.

[100]   In fact a proposal was submitted by the Commission on 8 February 1983 but it was never adopted by the Council.

[101]   Surul v Bundesanstalt fur Arbeit, C-262/96.

It is also noteworthy that the parents of the Turkish child wishing to benefit from the provisions of Article 9 do not have to be working in the Member State in question. Article 9 is a provision that envisages the achievement of freedom of movement of workers in progressive stages and is clearly aimed at the eventual entry of the children of Turkish workers into the labour markets of Member States. It is anticipated therefore that it would not be restrictively interpreted.

3. The Right to Remain and Access to Employment

It is arguable that recourse to social security benefits outlined in Article 3 of Decision 3/80 should not affect a persons right to remain in the Member State in question nor should it prevent a Turkish worker exercising his or her rights under Article 6 of Decision 1/80 to continued employment.

Indeed the Court of Justice has held that a Turkish worker qualifying under Article 6(1) of Decision 1/80 for continued employment must be given a reasonable period in which to allow him to enter into a new employment.[102] There is nothing to suggest that the right to continued employment under Article 6(1) would be affected by recourse to public funds during that reasonable period of unemployment for instance.

---

[102]   Tetik v Land Berlin, C-171/95, [1997] ECR I-329.

VIII. Deportation

1. Public Policy, Public Security or Public Health

Article 14(1) of Decision 1/80 provides that:

> "The provisions of this section shall be applied subject to limitations justified on grounds of public policy, public security or public health"

This provision is identical to that in Article 39(3) of the EC Treaty. In **Kus**[103] the Court of Justice made reference to the fact that the provision in Article 14(1) of Decision 1/80 and that in Article 39(3) of the EC Treaty are identical although it did not consider the practical application of Article 14(1). However it did observe that the importance of a right of residence as a corollary to the right of access to the labour force is underlined by the fact that in certain circumstances a residence permit may be withdrawn, those circumstances being connected to public policy, public security and public health.

As the Court of Justice observed in **Kus** EC Directive 64/221 outlines the circumstances in relation to a Community worker in which the public policy proviso in Article 39(3) may be used. It has yet to be determined whether Directive 64/221 applies by analogy to Turkish workers.

The question of whether the expulsion of a Turkish worker who had obtained a residence permit by deceit is compatible with Article 14(1) of Decision 1/80, where that expulsion was justified solely with a view to deterring other aliens, was raised in **Kol**.[104] Unfortunately the question was phrased in the alternative to a question on whether periods of employment on the basis of a residence permit obtained by deceit are recognised under Article 6(1) and was never considered by the Court of Justice.

The question of whether the expulsion of a Turkish worker solely on preventative grounds, as a deterrent to other aliens, is compatible with Article 14 of Decision 1/80 is subject of a reference from the German Courts to the Court of Justice in the case of **Nazli**.[105] If the provision is to be interpreted uniformly

---

[103] Kus v Landeshauptstadt Wiesbaden, C-237/91, [1992] ECR I-6781.
[104] Kol v Land Berlin, C-285/95, [1997] ECR I-3069.
[105] C-340/97.

with Article 39(3) of the EC Treaty, then it would appear that criminal convictions in themselves are not enough to justify expulsion and will only be taken into account so far as there is a future threat to public policy.[106]

---

[106]   Bouchereau, C-30/77, [1997] ECR 1999.

Annex (A)

AGREEMENT

*Establishing an Association between the European Economic Community
and Turkey
(signed at Ankara, 12 September 1963)*

Article 4

1. During the transitional stage the Contracting Parties shall, on the basis of mutual and balanced obligation:
    –   establish progressively a customs union between Turkey and the Community;
    –   align the economic policies of Turkey and the Community more closely in order to ensure the proper functioning of the Association and the progress of the joint measures which this requires.
2. This stage shall last not more than twelve years, subject to such exceptions as may be made by mutual agreement. The exceptions must not impede the final establishment of the customs union within a reasonable period.

Article 5

The Final stage shall be based on the customs union and shall entail closer co-ordination of the economic policies of the Contracting Parties.

Article 6

To ensure the implementation and the progressive development of the Association, the Contracting Parties shall meet in a Council of Association, which shall act within the powers conferred upon it by this Agreement.

Article 7

The Contracting Parties shall take all appropriate measures, whether general or particular, to ensure the fulfilment of the obligations arising from this Agreement.

They shall refrain from any measures liable to jeopardise the attainment of the objectives of this Agreement.

Article 8

In order to attain the objectives set out in Article 4, the Council of Association shall, before the beginning of the transitional stage and in accordance with the procedure laid down in Article 1 of the Provisional Protocol, determine the conditions, rules and timetables for the implementation of the provisions relating to the fields covered by the Treaty establishing the Community which must be considered; this shall apply in particular to such of those fields as are mentioned under this Title and to any protective clause which may prove appropriate.

Article 9

The Contracting Parties recognise that within the scope of this Agreement and without prejudice to any special provisions which may be laid down pursuant to Article 8, any discrimination on grounds of nationality shall be prohibited in accordance with the principle laid down in Article 7 of the Treaty establishing the Community.

CHAPTER 3

Other economic provisions

Article 12

The Contracting Parties agree to be guided by Articles 48, 49 and 50[107] of the Treaty establishing the Community for the purpose of abolishing restrictions on freedom of establishment between them.

---

[107]   n.b. now Articles 39, 40 and 41, post the Amsterdam Treaty.

Article 14

The Contracting Parties agree to be guided by Articles 55, 56 and 58 to 65[108] of the Treaty establishing the Community for the purpose of abolishing restrictions on freedom to provide services between them.

ADDITIONAL PROTOCOL
FINANCIAL PROTOCOL
(SIGNED AT BRUSSELS, 23 NOVEMBER 1970)

TITLE II
MOVEMENT OF PERSONS AND SERVICES

CHAPTER I
WORKERS

Article 36

Freedom of movement for workers between Member States of the Community and Turkey shall be secured by progressive stages in accordance with the principles set out in Article 12 of the Agreement of Association between the end of the twelfth and the twenty-second year after the entry into force of that Agreement.

The Council of Association shall decide on the rules necessary to that end.

Article 37

As regards conditions of work and remuneration, the rules which each Member State applies to workers of Turkish nationality employed in the Community shall not discriminate on the grounds of nationality between such workers and workers who are nationals of other Member States of the Community.

Article 38

While freedom of movement for workers between Member States of the Community and Turkey is being brought about by progressive stages, the Council of Association may review all questions arising in connection with the geographical and occupational mobility of workers of Turkish nationality, in particular the extension of work and residence permits, in order to facilitate the employment of those workers in each Member State.

---

[108]   n.b. now Articles 45 and 46 and 48 to 54, post Amsterdam.

To that end, the Council of Association may make recommendations to Member States.

Article 39

1. Before the end of the first year after the entry into force of this Protocol the Council of Association shall adopt social security measures for workers of Turkish nationality moving within the Community and for their families residing in the Community.
2. These provisions must enable workers of Turkish nationality, in accordance with arrangements to be laid down, to aggregate periods of insurance or employment completed in individual Member States in respect of old-age pensions, death benefits and invalidity pensions, and also as regards the provisions of health services for workers and their families residing in the Community. These measures shall create no obligation on Member States to take into account periods completed in Turkey.
3. The abovementioned measures must ensure that family allowances are paid if a worker's family resides in the Community.
4. It must be possible to transfer to Turkey old-age pensions, death benefits and invalidity pensions obtained under the measures adopted pursuant to paragraph 2.
5. The measures provided for in this Article shall not affect the rights and obligations arising from bilateral agreements between Turkey and Member States of the Community, in so far as these agreements provide more favourable arrangements for Turkish nationals.

Article 40

The Council of Association may make recommendations to Member States and Turkey for encouraging the exchange of young workers; the Council of Association shall be guided in the matter by the measures adopted by Member States in implementation of Article 50[109] of the Treaty establishing the Community.

Chapter II
Rights of Establishment, Service and Transport

Article 41

1. The Contracting Parties shall refrain from introducing between themselves any new restrictions on the freedom of establishment and the freedom to provide services.

---

[109] Now Article 41, post Amsterdam.

2. The Council of Association shall, in accordance with the principles set out in Articles 13 and 14 of the Agreement of Association, determine the timetable and rules for the progressive abolition by the Contracting Parties, between themselves, of restrictions on freedom of establishment and on freedom to provide services.

The Council of Association shall, when determining such timetable and rules for the various classes of activity, take into account corresponding measures already adopted by the Community in these fields and also the special economic and social circumstances of Turkey. Priority shall be given to the activities making a particular contribution to the development of production and trade.

Article 42

1. The Council of Association shall extend to Turkey, in accordance with the rules which it shall determine, the transport provisions of the Treaty establishing the Community with due regard to the geographical situation of Turkey. In the same way it may extend to Turkey measures taken by the Community in applying those provisions in respect of transport by rail, road and inland waterway.
2. If provisions for sea and air transport are laid down by the Community, pursuant to Article 84(2)[110] of the Treaty establishing the Community, the Council of Association shall decide whether, to what extent and by what procedure provisions may be laid down for Turkish sea and air transport.

---

[110] Now Article 80(2), post Amsterdam.

Annex (B)

DECISION OF THE ASSOCIATION COUNCIL NO 2/76
On the Implementation of Article 12 of the Ankara Agreement
(adopted at the 23rd meeting of the Association Council, on 20 December
1976)

THE ASSOCIATION COUNCIL

Having regard to the Agreement establishing an Association between the European Economic Community and Turkey,

Having regard to the Additional Protocol referred to in Article 1(1) of the Provisional Protocol annexed to the said Agreement, and in particular Article 36 thereof,

Whereas the Contracting Parties agreed pursuant to Article 12 of the Ankara Agreement to be guided by Articles 48, 49 and 50[111] of the Treaty establishing the European Economic Community in gradually introducing freedom of movement for workers between their countries; whereas Article 36 of the Additional Protocol provides that this freedom of movement shall be secured by progressive stages between the end of the twelfth and of the twenty-second year after entry into force of the Association Agreement;

Whereas the Articles referred to above imply that the Member States of the Community and Turkey shall accord each other priority as regards access by their workers to their respective employment markets; whereas this principle must be given effect under conditions that exclude any serious danger to the standard of living and the level of employment in the various regions and branches of activity in the Member States of the Community and Turkey, and without prejudice to the application between Member States of the Community of Community provisions governing the freedom of movement of workers or to any international undertakings by either Party on the subject under consideration;

---

[111] Now Articles 39, 40 and 41, post Amsterdam.

Whereas the content of a first stage should be laid down, the Association Council having to decide on the content of the subsequent stages at a later date,

HAS DECIDED AS FOLLOWS:

Article 1

3.   This Decision establishes for a first stage the detailed rules for the implementation of Article 36 of the Additional Protocol.
4.   This first stage shall last four years, as from 1 December 1976.

Article 2

1.   (a)   After three years of legal employment in a Member State of the Community, a Turkish worker shall be entitled, subject to the priority to be given to workers of Member States of the Community, to respond to an offer of employment, made under normal conditions and registered with the employment services of that State, for the same occupation, branch of activity and region.
      (b)   After five years of legal employment in a Member State of the Community, a Turkish worker shall enjoy free access in that country to any paid employment of his choice.
      (c)   Annual holidays and short absences for reasons of sickness, maternity or an accident at work shall be treated as periods of legal employment. Periods of involuntary unemployment duly certified by the relevant authorities and long absences on account of sickness shall not be treated as periods of legal employment, but shall not affect rights acquired as the result of the preceding period of employment.
2.   The procedures for applying paragraph 1 shall be those established under national rules.

Article 3

Turkish children who are residing legally with their parents in a Member State of the Community shall be granted access in that country to courses of general education.

They may also be entitled to enjoy in that country the advantages provided for in this connection under national laws.

Article 4

Nationals of the Member States who are in paid employment in Turkey, and their children, shall enjoy in that country the rights and advantages referred to in Articles 2 and 3 if they meet the conditions laid down in these Articles.

Article 5

Should it not be possible in the Community to meet an offer of employment by calling on the labour available on the employment market of the Member States and should the Member States, within the framework of their provisions laid down by law, regulation or administrative action, decide to authorise a call on workers who are not nationals of a Member State of the Community in order to meet the offer of employment, they shall endeavour in so doing to accord priority to Turkish workers.

Article 6

Where a Member State of the Community or Turkey experiences or is threatened with disturbances on its employment market which might seriously jeopardise the standard of living or level of employment in a particular region, branch of activity or occupation, the State concerned may refrain from automatically applying Article 2(1)(a) and (b).

The State concerned shall inform the Association Council of any such temporary restriction.

Article 7

The Member States of the Community and Turkey may not introduce new restrictions on the conditions of access to employment applicable to workers legally resident and employed in their territory.

Article 8

This Decision shall not affect any rights or obligations arising from national laws or bilateral agreements existing between Turkey and the Member States of the Community where these provide for more favourable treatment for their nationals.

Article 9

The provisions of this Decision shall be applied subject to limitations justified on grounds of public policy, public security or public health.

Article 10

So as to be in a position to ensure the harmonious application of the provisions of this Decision and determine that they are applied in such a way as to exclude the danger of disturbance of the employment markets, the Association Council shall be informed of the employment situation in the Member States of the Community and in Turkey.

Article 11

One year before the end of the first stage and in the light of the results achieved during it, the Association Council shall commence discussions to determine the content of the subsequent stage and to ensure that the Decision on that stage is enforced as from the date of expiry of the first stage. The provisions of this Decision shall continue to apply until the beginning of the subsequent stage.

Article 12

The Contracting Parties shall each take the measures necessary to implement this Decision.

Article 13

This Decisions shall enter into force on 20 December 1976.

Annex (C)

DECISION No. 1/80 OF THE ASSOCIATION COUNCIL
OF 19 SEPTEMBER 1980
ON THE DEVELOPMENT OF THE ASSOCIATION

THE ASSOCIATION COUNCIL

Having regard to the Agreement establishing an Association between the European Economic Community and Turkey,

WHEREAS the revitalisation and development of the Association must, as agreed on 5 February 1980, cover the entire range of current association problems; whereas the search for solutions to these problems must take account of the specific nature of the Association links between the Community and Turkey;

WHEREAS in the agricultural sector, the elimination of customs duties applicable to Turkish products imported into the Community will make for the achievement of the desired result and for the alleviation of Turkey's concern as to the effects of the enlargement of the Community; whereas, moreover, Article 33 of the Additional Protocol should be implemented as a prior condition for the introduction of free movement of agricultural products; whereas the arrangements provided for must be implemented with due regard for the principles and mechanisms of the common agricultural policy;

WHEREAS, in the social field, and within the framework of the international commitments of each of the Parties, the above considerations make it necessary to improve the treatment accorded workers and members of their families in relation to the arrangements introduced by Decision No 2/76 of the Association Council; whereas, furthermore, the provisions relating to social security should be implemented as should those relating to the exchange of young workers;

WHEREAS development of the Association justifies the establishment of such economic, technical and financial co-operation as will help to attain the objectives of the Association Agreement, in particular by means of a Community contribution to the economic development of Turkey in various sectors,

HAS DECIDED AS FOLLOWS:

Article 1

The measures for the revitalisation and development of the Association between the Community and Turkey in each of the areas referred to by the Association Council on 5 February 1980 and specified on the following chapters.

CHAPTER II: Social provisions

SECTION 1: Questions relating to employment and the free movement of workers

Article 6

1. Subject to Article 7 on free access to employment for members of his family, a Turkish worker duly registered as belonging to the labour force of a Member State:
    –   shall be entitled in that Member State, after one year's legal employment, to the renewal of his permit to work for the same employer, if a job is available;
    –   shall be entitled in that Member State, after three years of legal employment and subject to the priority to be given to workers of Member States of the Community, to respond to another offer of employment, with an employer of his choice, made under normal conditions and registered with the employment service of that State, for the same occupation;
    –   shall enjoy free access in that Member State to any paid employment of his choice, after four years of legal employment.
2. Annual holidays and absences for reasons of maternity or an accident at work or short periods of sickness shall be treated as periods of legal employment. Periods of involuntary unemployment duly certified by the relevant authorities and long absences on account of sickness shall not be treated as periods of legal employment, but shall not affect rights acquired as the result of the preceding period of employment.
3. The procedures for applying paragraphs 1 and 2 shall be those established under national rules.

Article 7

The members of the family of a Turkish worker duly registered as belonging to the labour force of a Member State, who have been authorised to join him:
–   shall be entitled – subject to the priority to be given to workers of

Member States of the Community – to respond to any offer of employment after they have been legally resident for at least three years in that
Member State;
–   shall enjoy free access to any paid employment of their choice provided
     they have been legally resident there for at least five years.
Children of Turkish workers who have completed a course of vocational
training in the host country may respond to any offer of employment there,
irrespective of the length of time they have been resident in that Member State,
provided one of their parents has been legally employed in the Member State
concerned for at least three years.

Article 8

1.   Should it not be possible in the Community to meet an offer of employ-
     ment by calling on the labour available on the employment market of
     the Member State and should the Member States, within the framework
     of their provisions laid down by law, regulation or administrative action,
     decide to authorise a call on workers who are not nationals of a Member
     State of the Community in order to meet the offer of employment, they
     shall endeavour in so doing to accord priority to Turkish workers.
2.   The employment services of the Member State shall endeavour to fill
     vacant positions which they have registered and which the duly registered
     Community labour force has not been able to fill with Turkish workers
     who are registered as unemployed and legally resident in the territory of
     that Member State.

Article 9

Turkish children residing legally with their parents, who are or have been
legally employed in a Member State of the Community, will be admitted to
courses of general education, apprenticeship and vocational training under the
same educational entry qualifications as the children of nationals of the Member
States. They may in that Member State be eligible to benefit from the advantages provided for under the national legislation in this area.

Article 10

1.   The Member States of the Community shall as regards remuneration and
     other conditions of work grant Turkish workers duly registered as belong-
     ing to their labour forces treatment involving no discrimination on the
     basis of nationality between them and Community workers.
2.   Subject to the application of Articles 6 and 7, the Turkish workers referred

to in paragraph 1 and members of their families shall be entitled, on the same footing as Community workers, to assistance from the employment services in their search for employment.

Article 11

Nationals of the Member States duly registered as belonging to the labour force in Turkey, and members of their families living with them, shall enjoy in that country the rights and advantages referred to in Articles 6, 7, 9 and 10 if they meet the conditions laid down in those Articles.

Article 12

Where a Member State of the Community or Turkey experiences or is threatened with disturbances on its employment market which might seriously jeopardise the standard of living or level of employment in a particular region, branch of activity or occupation, the State concerned may refrain from automatically applying Articles 6 and 7. The State concerned shall inform the Association Council of any such temporary restriction.

Article 13

The Member States of the Community and Turkey may not introduce new restrictions on the conditions of access to employment applicable to workers and members of their families legally resident and employed in their respective territories.

Article 14

1.   The provisions of this section shall be applied subject to limitations justified on grounds of public policy, public security or public health.
2.   They shall not prejudice the rights and obligations arising from national legislation or bilateral agreements between Turkey and the Member States of the Community where such legislation or agreements provide for more favourable treatment for their nationals.

Article 15

1.   So as to be in a position to ensure the harmonious application of the provisions of this section and determine that they are applied in such a

way as to exclude the danger of disturbance of the employment markets, the Association Committee shall periodically exchange information in order to improve mutual knowledge of the economic and social situation, including the state of and outlook for the labour market in the Community and in Turkey.

It shall each year present a report on its activities to the Association Council.

2. The Association Committee shall be authorised to enlist the assistance of an ad hoc Working Party in order to implement paragraph 1.

Article 16

1. The provisions of this section shall apply from 1 December 1980.
2. From 1 June 1983, the Association Council shall, particularly in the light of the reports on activities referred to in Article 15, examine the results of application of the provisions of this section with a view to preparing solutions which might apply as from 1 December 1983.

SECTION 2: Social and cultural advancement and the exchange of young workers

Article 17

The Member States and Turkey shall co-operate, in accordance with their domestic situations and their legal systems, in appropriate schemes to promote the social and cultural advancement of Turkish workers and the members of their family, in particular literacy campaigns and courses in the language of the host country, activities to maintain links with Turkish culture and access to vocational training.

Article 18

The Association Committee shall prepare a recommendation to be forwarded by the Association Council to the Member States of the Community and Turkey with a view to the implementation of any action that may enable young workers who have received their basic training in their own country to complement their vocational training by participating in in-service training, under the conditions set out in Article 40 of the Additional Protocol.

It shall monitor the actual implementation of this provision.

Annex (D)

DECISION NO 3/80 OF THE ASSOCIATION COUNCIL
Of 19 September 1980 on the application of the social security schemes of
the Member States of the European Communities to Turkish workers and
members of their families

THE COUNCIL OF ASSOCIATION

Having regard to the Agreement establishing an Association between the
European Economic Community and Turkey,

Having regard to the Additional Protocol, and in particular Article 39 thereof,

HAS DECIDED AS FOLLOWS:

TITLE I
GENERAL PROVISIONS

Article 1

Definitions

For the purposes of this Decision:
(a)   the terms "frontier worker", "seasonal worker", "member of family",
      "survivor", "residence", "stay", "competent State", "insurance periods",
      "periods of employment", "periods of residence", "benefits", "pensions",
      "family benefits", "family allowances" and "death grants" have the mean-
      ings assigned to them in Article 1 of Counsel Regulation (EEC) No
      1408/71 of 14 June 1971 on the application of social security schemes to
      employed persons and their families moving within the Community,
      hereinafter referred to as "Regulation (EEC) No 1408/71";

(b)   "worker" means:
  (i)   subject to the restrictions set out in Annex V, A. BELGIUM (1),
        to Regulation (EEC) No 1408/71, any person who is insured, com-
        pulsorily or on an optional continued basis, against one or more of
        the contingencies covered by the branches of a social security scheme
        for employed persons,
  (ii) any person who is compulsorily insured against one or more of the
        contingencies covered by the branches of social security dealt with
        in this Decision, under a social security scheme for all residents or
        for the whole working population, if such a person:
          –   can be identified as an employed person by virtue of the
              manner in which that scheme is administered or financed, or
          –   failing such criteria, is insured against some other contingency
              specified in the Annex under a scheme for employed persons,
              either compulsorily or on an optional continued basis;
(c)   "legislation" means all the laws, regulations and other statutory provisions
      and all other implementing measures, present or future, of each Member
      State relating to the branches and schemes of social security covered by
      Article 4(1) and (2).
          This term excludes the provisions of existing or future industrial
      agreements, whether or not the public authorities have taken a decision
      rendering them compulsory or extending their scope;
(d)   "social security convention" means any bilateral of multilateral instrument
      which binds or will bind either two or more Member States exclusively,
      or one Member State and Turkey in the field of social security, for all or
      part of the branches and schemes set out in Article 4(1) and (2), together
      with agreement, of whatever kind, concluded pursuant to the said
      instruments;
(e)   "competent authority" means, in respect of each Member State and of
      Turkey, the Minister, Ministers or other equivalent authority responsible
      for social security schemes throughout, or in any part of, the territory of
      the State in question;
(f)   "institution" means, in respect of each Member State or of Turkey, the
      Minister, the body or authority responsible for administering all or part
      of the legislation;
(g)   "competent institution" means:
  (i)   the institution of the Member State with which the person concerned
        is insured at the time of the application for benefits, or
  (ii) the institution from which the person concerned is entitled or would
        be entitled to receive benefits if he or a member or members of his
        family were resident in the territory of the Member State in which
        the institution is situated, or
  (iii) the institution designated by the competent authority of the Member
        State concerned, or
  (iv) in the case of a scheme relating to an employer's liability in respect

of the benefits set out in Article 4(1), either the employer or the insurer involved or, failing these, a body or authority designated by the competent authority of the Member State concerned;

(h)   "institution of the place of residence" and "institution of the place of stay" mean respectively the institution which is competent to provide benefits in the place where the person concerned resides and the institution which is competent to provide benefits in the place where the person concerned is staying, under the legislation administered by that institution or, where no such institution exists, the institution designated by the competent authority of the State in question.

Article 2

Persons covered

This Decision shall apply:

—   to workers who are, or have been, subject to the legislation of one or more Member States and who are Turkish nationals.

—   to the members of the families of these workers, resident in the territory of one of the Member States,

—   to the survivors of the these workers.

Article 3

Equality of treatment

1.   Subject to the special provisions of this Decision, persons resident in the territory of one of the Member States to whom this Decision applies shall be subject to the same obligations and enjoy the same benefits under the legislation of any Member State as the nationals of that State.

2.   The provisions of paragraph 1 shall apply to the right to elect members of the organs of social security institutions or to participate in their nomination, but shall not affect the legislative provisions of any Member State relating to eligibility or methods of nomination of persons concerned to those organs.

Article 4

Matters covered

1.   This Decision shall apply to all legislation concerning the following branches of social security:

(a)   sickness and maternity benefits;
(b)   invalidity benefits, including those intended for the maintenance or improvement of earning capacity;
(c)   old-age benefits;
(d)   survivors' benefits;
(e)   benefits in respect of accidents at work and occupational diseases;
(f)   death grants;
(g)   unemployment benefits;
(h)   family benefits.

2.   This Decision shall apply to all general and special social security schemes, whether contributory or non-contributory, and to schemes concerning the liability of an employer or shipowner in respect of the benefits referred to in paragraph 1.

3.   The provisions of Title III shall not, however, affect the legislative provisions of any Member State concerning a shipowner's liability.

4.   This Decision shall not apply to social and medical assistance or to benefit schemes for victims of war and its consequences.

Article 5

Relationship between this Decision and social security conventions binding two or more Member States exclusively

This decision shall, as regards the persons and matters which it covers, replace the provisions of any social security convention, exclusively binding two or more Member States, save for such provisions of Part A of Annex II to Regulation (EEC) No 1408/71 as are not laid down in Part B of that Annex.

Article 6

Waiving of residence clause – Effect of compulsory insurance on reimbursement of contributions

1.   Save as otherwise provided in this Decision, invalidity, old-age or survivors' cash benefits and pensions for accidents at work or occupational diseases, acquired under the legislation of one or more Member States, shall not be subject to any reduction, modification, suspension, withdrawal or confiscation by reason of the fact that the recipient resides in Turkey or in the territory of a Member State other than that in which the institution responsible for payment is situated.

The provisions of the first subparagraph shall also apply to lump-sum benefits granted in the case of the remarriage of a surviving spouse who was entitled to a survivor's pension.

2. Where under the legislation of a Member State reimbursement of contributions is conditional upon the person concerned having ceased to be subject to compulsory insurance, this condition shall not be considered satisfied as long as the person concerned is subject as a worker to compulsory insurance under the legislation of another Member State.

Article 7

Rules for revalorisation provided by the legislation of a Member State shall apply to benefits due under that legislation subject to the provisions of this Decision.

Article 8

Prevention of overlapping of benefits

1. This decision can neither confer nor maintain the right to several benefits of the same kind for one and the same period of compulsory insurance. However, this provision shall not apply to benefits in respect of invalidity, old age, or death (pensions) which are awarded by the institutions of two or more Member States, in accordance with the provisions of Title III.
2. The provisions of the legislation of a Member State for reduction, suspension or withdrawal of benefit in cases of overlapping with other social security benefits or other income may be invoked against the beneficiary, even if the right to such benefits was acquired under the legislation of another Member State or of Turkey or the income was obtained in the territory of another Member State or of Turkey. However, this provision shall not apply when the person concerned receives benefits of the same kind in respect of invalidity, old age or death (pensions) which are awarded by the institutions of two or more Member States in accordance with Title III or by a Turkish institution pursuant to the provisions of a bilateral social security convention.
3. The provisions of the legislation of a Member State for reduction, suspension or withdrawal of benefits in the case of a person in receipt of invalidity benefits on anticipatory old-age benefits pursuing a professional or trade activity may be invoked against such person even though he is pursuing his activity in the territory of another Member State or of Turkey.
4. For the purposes of paragraphs 2 and 3, the institutions concerned shall, on request, exchange all appropriate information.

TITLE II
DETERMINATION OF THE LEGISLATION APPLICABLE

Article 9

The legislation applicable to Turkish workers employed in the Community shall be determined in accordance with the rules laid down by Article 13(1) and (2)(a) and (b), Articles 14, 15 and 17 of Regulation (EEC) No 1408/71.

TITLE III
SPECIAL PROVISIONS RELATING TO THE VARIOUS CATEGORIES OF BENEFITS

CHAPTER 1

Sickness and maternity

Article 10

For the purposes of acquisition, retention or recovery of the right to benefits, Article 18 of Regulation (EEC) No 1408/71 shall apply.

Article 11

For the purposes of the granting of benefits and reimbursements between institutions of the Member States, Articles 19 to 24, Article 25(3) and Articles 26 to 36 of Regulation (EEC) No 1408/71 shall apply.

Moreover, Article 19 of Regulation (EEC) No 1408/71 shall apply to wholly unemployed frontier works who satisfy the conditions specified by the legislation of the competent State for entitlement to sickness benefits.

CHAPTER 2

Invalidity

Article 12

The rights to benefits of a worker who has successively or alternately been subject to the legislation of two or more Member States shall be established in accordance with Article 37(1), first sentence, and (2), Articles 38 to 40, Article 41(1)(a), (b), (c) and (e) and (2), and Articles 42 and 43 of Regulation (EEC) No 1408/71.

However:

(a)   for the purpose of applying Article 39(4) of Regulation (EEC) No 1408/71, all the members of the family, including children, residing in the Community or in Turkey, shall be taken into account;

(b)   the reference in Article 40(1) of this Regulation to the provisions of Title III, Chapter 3, of Regulation (EEC) No 1408/71 shall be replaced by a reference to the provisions of Title III, Chapter 3 of this Decision.

CHAPTER 3

Old age and death (pensions)

Article 13

The rights to benefits of a worker who has been subject to the legislation of two or more Member States, or of his survivors, shall be established in accordance with Article 44(2), first sentence, Articles 45, 46(2), Articles 47, 48, 49 and 51 of Regulation (EEC) No 1408/71.

However:

(a)   Article 46(2) of Regulation (EEC) No 1408/71 shall apply even if the conditions for acquiring entitlement to benefits are satisfied without the need to have recourse to Article 45 of the said Regulation;

(b)   for the purposes of applying Article 47(3) of Regulation (EEC) No 1408/71, all the members of the family, including children , residing in the Community or in Turkey shall be taken into account;

(c)   for the purposes of applying Article 49(1)(a) and (2) and Article 51 of Regulation (EEC) No 1408/71, the reference to Article 46 shall be replaced by a reference to Article 46(2).

Article 14

1.   The benefit due under the legislation of a Member State, which is bound to Turkey by a bilateral social security convention, shall be awarded in accordance with the provisions of that convention.

Where a worker has been subject to the legislation of two or more Member States, a supplement shall be added, where appropriate, equal to the difference between the amount of the said benefit and the amount of the benefit obtained pursuant to Article 12 or Article 13 as the case may be.

2.   Where a supplement is due pursuant to the second subparagraph of paragraph 1, Article 51 of Regulation (EEC) 1408/71 shall apply to the whole amount of the benefit owed by the Member State concerned.

CHAPTER 4

Accidents at work and occupational diseases

Article 15

For the granting of benefits and for reimbursements between Member States' institutions, Articles 52 to 63 inclusive of Regulation (EEC) No 1408/71 shall apply.

CHAPTER 5

Death grants

Article 16

For the acquisition, retention or recovery of the right to benefits, the provisions of Article 64 of Regulation (EEC) No 1408/71 shall apply.

Article 17

Where the death occurs in the territory of a Member State other than the competent State, or the person entitled resides in such State, the death grants shall be awarded in accordance with Articles 65 and 66 of Regulation (EEC) No 1408/71.

CHAPTER 6

Family benefits and family allowances

Article 18

For the acquisition of the right to benefits, Article 72 of Regulation (EEC) No 1408/72 shall apply.

Article 19

1. Pensioners and their dependent children residing in the territory of a Member State shall be entitled to family allowances in accordance with Article 77(2) and Article 79(1)(a), (2) and (3) of Regulation (EEC) No 1408/71.
2. The natural or legal person responsible for an orphan and residing with him in the territory of a Member State shall be entitled to family allowances and, where appropriate, to supplementary or special allowances for orphans under the rules laid down in Article 78(2) and Article 79(1)(a), (2) and (3) of Regulation (EEC) No 1408/71.

TITLE IV
MISCELLANEOUS PROVISIONS

Article 20

1. The competent authorities of the Member States and of Turkey shall communicate to each other all information regarding measures taken to implement this Decision.
2. For the purposes of implementing this Decision, the authorities and institutions of the Member States and of Turkey shall lend their good offices and act as though implementing their own legalisation. The administrative assistance furnished by the said authorities and institutions shall, as a rule, be free of charge. However, the competent authorities of these States may agree to certain expenses being reimbursed.
3. The authorities and institutions of the Member States and of Turkey may for the purposes of implementing this Decision, communicate directly with one another and with the persons concerned or their representatives.
4. The authorities, institutions and courts or tribunals of a Member State may not reject claims or other documents submitted to them on the grounds that they are written in an official language of another Member State or in the Turkish language.

Article 21

1. Any exemption from or reduction of taxes, stamp duty, notarial or registration fees provided for in the legislation of a Member State or of Turkey in respect of certificates or documents required to be produced for the purposes of the legislation of that State shall be extended to similar documents required to be produced for the purposes of the legislation of another Member State or of Turkey, or of this Decision.

2.   All statements, documents and certificates of any kind whatsoever required to be produced for the purposes of this Decision shall be exempt from authentication by diplomatic and consular authorities.

Article 22

Any claim, declaration or appeal which, in order to comply with the legislation of a Member State, should have been submitted within a specified period to an authority, institution or court or tribunal of that State shall be admissible if it is submitted within that same period to a corresponding authority, institution or court or tribunal of another Member State or of Turkey. In such a case the authority, institution or court or tribunal receiving the claim, declaration or appeal shall forward it without delay to the competent authority, institution or court or tribunal of the former State either directly or through the competent authorities of the States concerned. The date on which such claims, declarations or appeals were submitted to the authority, institution or court or tribunal of another Member State or of Turkey shall be considered as the date of their submission to the competent authority, institution or court or tribunal.

Article 23

1.   Medical examinations provided for by the legislation of one Member State may be carried out, at the request of the competent institution, in the territory of another Member State or of Turkey, by the institution of the place of stay or residence of the person entitled to benefits, under conditions agreed between the competent authorities of the States concerned.
2.   Medical examinations carried out under the conditions laid down in paragraph 1 shall be considered as having been carried out in the territory of the competent State.

Article 24

1.   Money transfers effected in accordance with this Decision shall be made in accordance with the relevant agreements in force at the time of the transfer between the Member States concerned.

      In the cases where no such agreements are in force between two States, the competent authorities in those States or the authorities responsible for international payment shall, by common accord, adopt the measures required to make these transfers.
2.   Money transfers effected in accordance with this Decision shall be made

in accordance with the relevant agreements in force at the time of the transfer between the Member State concerned and Turkey. In the case where no such agreements are in force between Turkey and a Member State, the competent authorities in both States, or the authorities responsible for international payment shall, by common accord, adopt the measures required to make these transfers.

Article 25

1. For the purposes of implementing this Decision, Annexes I, III and IV to Regulation (EEC) NO 1408/71 shall be applicable.
2. For the purposes of implementing this Decision, Annex II to Regulation (EEC) No 1408/71 shall be applicable to the extent laid down in Article 5.
3. For the purposes of implementing this Decision, Annex V to Regulation (EEC) No 1408/71 shall be applicable to the extent laid down in Part I of the Annex hereto.

Other special procedures for applying the laws of certain Member States are laid down in Part II of the Annex hereto.

Article 26

1. The competent authorities may designate liaison bodies which may communicate directly with each other.
2. Any institution of a Member State or of Turkey, and any person residing or staying in the territory of a Member State or of Turkey, may make application to the institution of another Member State or of Turkey, either directly or through the liaison bodies.

Article 27

(a) Claims for invalidity, old-age and survivors benefits (including orphans' pensions) shall be submitted in accordance with Articles 35(1) and (2), 36(1), (2) and (4), first clause, 37(a), (b) and (c) and 38 of Council Regulation (EEC) No 574/72 of 21 March 1972 fixing the procedure for implementing Regulation (EEC) No 1408/71 on the application of social security schemes to employed persons and their families moving within the Community, hereinafter called "Regulation (EEC) NO 574/72".

(b) However:

   (i)   if the person concerned resides in Turkey, he shall submit his claim to the competent institution of that Member State to whose legislation the worker was subject, where appropriate through the institution of the place of residence,

(ii)   Article 38 of Regulation (EEC) No 574/72 shall apply to all members of the family of the claimant who reside in the territory of the Community or in Turkey.

Article 28

Administrative checks and medical examinations shall be effected in accordance with the provisions of Articles 51 and 52 of Regulation (EEC) No 574/72. These provisions shall apply if the recipient is resident in Turkey.

Article 29

1.   In order to draw a pension or supplementary allowance in respect of an accident at work or an occupational disease under the legislation of a Member State, a worker or his survivors residing in Turkey shall make a claim either to the competent institution, or to the institution of the place of residence, which shall forward such claim to the competent institution. The submission of the claim shall be subject to the following rules
    (a)   the claim must be accompanied by the required supporting documents and made out on the forms provided for by the legislation administered by the competent institution;
    (b)   the accuracy of the information given by the claimant must be established by official documents attached to the claim form, or confirmed by the competent bodies of Turkey.
2.   The competent institution shall notify the claimant of its decision directly or through the liaison body of the competent State; it shall send a copy of that decision to the liaison body of Turkey.
3.   Administrative checks and medical examinations provided for in the event of pensions being reviewed shall be carried out at the request of the competent institution by the Turkish institution in accordance with the procedure laid down by the legislation administered by the latter institution. The competent institution shall, however, retain the right to have the person entitled to benefits examined by a doctor of its own choice
4.   Any person drawing a pension for himself or for an orphan shall inform the institution responsible for payment of any change in his situation or in that of the orphan which is likely to modify the pension.
5.   Pensions due from the institution of a Member State to claimants resident in Turkey shall be made in accordance with the procedure laid down in Article 30.

Article 30

Benefits shall be paid in accordance with Articles 53 to 59 of Regulation (EEC) NO 574/72. Where the recipient is resident in Turkey, payment shall be direct save as otherwise provided in the convention binding the Member State concerned and Turkey.

TITLE V
FINAL PROVISIONS

Article 31

Two or more Member States, or Turkey and one or more Member States, or the competent authorities of those States may, where necessary, conclude agreements designed to supplement the administrative procedures for implementing this Decision.

Article 32

Turkey and the Community shall, each to the extent to which they are concerned, take the necessary steps to implement this Decision.
Done at Brussels 19 September 1980.

ANNEX

Special procedures for applying the laws of certain Member States referred to in Article 25(3) of this Decision

I. Special procedures for applying the laws of certain Member States provided for in Annex V to Regulation (EEC) No 1408/71 and applicable for the purposes of this Decision.
    Annex V to Regulation (EEC) No 1408/71 shall apply for the purposes of this Decision except for the following provisions:
    1. Point B DENMARK
        Paragraphs 1, 2, 3, 4, 5, 7, 8 and 11.
    2. Point C GERMANY
        Paragraphs 1, 4, 8 and 9.
    3. Point D FRANCE
        Paragraphs 1(a), (b) and paragraph 3.
    4. Point E IRELAND
        Paragraphs 1, 2, 3, 4, 6, 7 and 9.
    5. Point H NETHERLANDS
        Paragraph 1(a).
    6. Point I UNITED KINGDOM
        Paragraphs 1, 4, 6,7, 8 and 11.

II.   Other special procedures for applying the laws of certain Member States.

A.   BELGIUM

This Decision shall not apply to the guaranteed income for retired people, nor to the allowances paid to handicapped persons.

B.   DENMARK

1.   Any person who, by pursuing an activity as an employed person, is subject to legislation on accidents at work and occupational diseases shall be considered a worker within the meaning of Article 1(b)(ii) of the Decision.

2.   Workers and pensioners and members of their families referred to in Articles 19, 22(1) and (3), 25(3), 26(1) and Articles 28a, 29 and 31 of Regulation (EEC) No 1408/71, resident or staying in Denmark, shall be entitled to benefits in kind on the same terms as those laid down by Danish legislation for persons whose income does not exceed the level indicated in Article 3 of Law No 311 of 9 June 1971 concerning the Public Health Service, where the cost of the said benefits is payable by the institution of a Member State other than Denmark.

3.   Article 1(1), No 2, of the Law on old-age pensions, Article 1(1), No 2, of the Law on disability pensions and Article 2(1), No 2, of the Law on widows' pensions and allowances shall not be applicable to workers or their survivors whose residence is in the territory of a Member State other than Denmark or in Turkey.

4.   The terms of this Decision shall be without prejudice to the transitional rules under the Danish Laws of 7 June 1972 on the pension rights of Danish nationals having their effective residence in Denmark for a specified period immediately preceding the date of the application.

5.   The periods during which a frontier worker, residing within the territory of a Member State other than Denmark, has worked in Denmark are to be considered as periods of residence for the purposes of Danish legislation. The same shall apply to those periods during which such a worker is posted to the territory of a Member State other than Denmark.

6.   For the purposes of applying Article 8(2) of this Decision to Danish legislation, disability, old-age and widows' pensions shall be considered as benefits of the same kind.

7.   When a Turkish worker to whom this Decision applies has been subject to Danish legislation and to the legislation of one or more other Member States, and fulfils the requirements for a disability pension under Danish legislation, his entitlement to such pension shall be subject to the condition that he has been resident in Denmark for a period of at least one year

and during that period has been capable, physically and mentally, of carrying out a normal occupation.

8. The following provisions shall apply until the entry into force of a bilateral social security convention between Denmark and Turkey.

When a Turkish worker to whom this Decision applies has been subject to Danish legislation and not to the legislation of another Member State, his entitlement and that of his survivors to old-age, disability and death benefits (pensions) shall be determined in accordance with the following provisions:

(a) Turkish nationals resident in Denmark shall be entitled to an old- age pension granted in accordance with Danish legislation if, between the age of 18 and the minimum age for entitlement to an old-age pension, they have been resident in Denmark for at least 15 years, at least five of which immediately preceded the date of the application for a pension;

(b) Turkish nationals resident in Denmark shall be entitled to a disability pension granted in accordance with Danish legislation if they have been resident in Denmark for at least five years immediately preceding the date of the application for a pension and during that period have been capable, physically and mentally, of carrying out a normal occupation;

(c) Turkish nationals resident in Denmark shall be entitled to a widow's pension granted in accordance with Danish legislation:
  – if the deceased spouse had been resident in Denmark after the age of 18 for at least five years immediately preceding the date of death, or
  – if the widow had been resident in Denmark for at least five years immediately preceding the date of the application for a pension.

B. GERMANY

1. Article 6 of this Decision shall not affect the provisions under which accidents (and occupational diseases) occurring outside the territory of the Federal Republic of Germany, and periods completed outside that territory, do not give rise to payment of benefits, or only give rise to payment of benefits under certain conditions, when those entitled to them reside outside the territory of the Federal Republic of Germany.

2. Article 1233 of the insurance code (RVO) and Article 10 of the clerical staff insurance law (AVG), as amended by the

pension reform law of 16 October 1972, which govern voluntary insurance under German pension insurance schemes, shall apply to Turkish nationals who fulfil the general conditions:

(a) if the person concerned has his permanent address or residence in the territory of the Federal Republic of Germany;

(b) if the person concerned has his permanent address or residence in the territory of another Member State and at any time previously contributed compulsorily or voluntarily to a German pension insurance scheme.

D. FRANCE

The Decision shall not apply to the supplementary allowance of the National Mutual Aid Fund.

E. IRELAND

1. Any person who is compulsorily or voluntarily insured pursuant to the provisions of Section 4 of the Social Welfare Act 1952 shall be considered a worker within the meaning of Article 1(b)(ii) of this Decision.

2. Workers and pensioners, together with members of their families referred to in Articles 19, 22(1) and (3), 25(3), 26(1) and Articles 28a, 29 and 31 of Regulation (EEC) No 1408/71, resident or staying in Ireland, shall be entitled, free of charge, to any such form of medical treatment as it is provided for by Irish legislation, where the cost of this treatment is payable by the institution of a Member State other than Ireland.

3. For the purposes of applying Article 8(2) of this Decision to Irish legislation, invalidity, old age and widows pensions shall be considered as benefits of the same kind.

4. For the purpose of calculating earnings for the award of earnings related benefit payable with sickness and maternity benefit payable with sickness and maternity benefits under Irish legislation, a worker shall, in derogation from Article 23(1) of Regulation (EEC) No 1408/71 be credited for each week of employment completed under the legislation of another Member State during the relevant income tax year with an amount equivalent to the average weekly earnings in that year of male and female workers respectively.

F. ITALY

None.

G. LUXEMBOURG

The supplement to make up the minimum pension, as well as the children's supplement in Luxembourg pensions, shall be granted in the same proportion as the fixed part.

H. NETHERLANDS

A person receiving an old-age pension under Netherlands legislation and a pension under the legislation of another Member State shall, for the purposes of Article 27 and/or Article 28 of Regulation (EEC) No 1408/71, be considered to be entitled to benefits in kind if he satisfies the conditions required for entitlement to voluntary sickness insurance for elderly persons.

I.   UNITED KINGDOM

1. All persons who are "employed earners" within the meaning of the legislation of Great Britain or of the legislation of Northern Ireland, and all persons in respect of whom contributions are payable as "employed persons" in accordance with the legislation of Gibraltar, shall be regarded as "workers" for the purposes of Article 1(b)(ii) of this Decision.

2. This Decision shall not apply to those provisions of United Kingdom legislation implementing a social security agreement between the United Kingdom and a third State other than Turkey.

3. Wherever required by United Kingdom legislation for the purposes of determining entitlement to benefits, Turkish nationals born in a State other than a Member State or Turkey are to be treated as nationals of the United Kingdom born in such other State.

4. For the purposes of applying Article 8(2) of this Decision to the legislation of the United Kingdom, disability, old-age and widows' pensions shall be considered as benefits of the same kind.

Judgment of the Court of Justice of the European Communities

4 May 1999

SEMA SÜRÜL -v- BUNDESANSTALT FÜR ARBEIT

Case C-262/96,

REFERENCE to the Court under Article 234 EC (ex Article 177) by the Sozialgericht Aachen (Germany) for a preliminary ruling in the proceedings pending before that court on the interpretation of certain provisions of Decision No 3/80 of the Association Council of 19 September 1980 on the application of the social security schemes of the Member States of the European Communities to Turkish workers and members of their families (OJ 1983 C 110, p. 60),

THE COURT,

composed of: G.C. Rodríguez Iglesias, President, J.-P. Puissochet, G. Hirsch and P. Jann (Presidents of Chambers), J.C. Moitinho de Almeida, C. Gulmann, J.L. Murray, D.A.O. Edward, H. Ragnemalm, L. Sevón and R. Schintgen (Rapporteur), Judges,

Advocate General: A. La Pergola,

Registrar: H. von Holstein, Deputy Registrar,

after considering the written observations submitted on behalf of:
- Sema Sürül, by Rainer M. Hofmann, Rechtsanwälte, Aachen,
- the German Government, by Ernst Röder, Ministerialrat in the Federal Ministry of Economic Affairs, and Bernd Kloke, Oberregierungsrat in the same Ministry, acting as Agents,
- the French Government, by Catherine de Salins, Head of Subdirectorate in the Legal Affairs Directorate of the Ministry of Foreign Affairs, and Anne de Bourgoing, *chargé de mission* with the same Directorate, acting as Agents,
- the Austrian Government, by Wolf Okresek, Ministerialrat in the Federal Chancellor's Office, acting as Agent,
- the United Kingdom Government, by John E. Collins, Assistant Treasury Solicitor, acting as Agent, assisted by Eleanor Sharpston, Barrister,
- the Commission of the European Communities, by Peter Hillenkamp, Legal Adviser, and Pieter van Nuffel, of its Legal Service, acting as Agents,

having regard to the Report for the Hearing,

after hearing the oral observations of Mrs Sürül, represented by Rainer M. Hofmann; the German Government, represented by Claus-Dieter Quassowski, Regierungsdirektor in the Federal Ministry of Economic Affairs, acting as Agent; the French Government, represented by Kareen Rispal-Bellanger, Head of Subdirectorate in the Legal Affairs Directorate in the Ministry of Foreign Affairs, acting as Agent; the Netherlands Government, represented by Marc Fierstra, Assistant Legal Adviser in the Ministry of Foreign Affairs, acting as Agent; the United Kingdom Government, represented by Eleanor Sharpston; and the Commission, represented by Peter Hillenkamp, at the hearing on 25 November 1997,

after hearing the Opinion of the Advocate General at the sitting on 12 February 1998,

having regard to the order of 23 September 1998 re-opening the oral procedure,

having regard to the Report for the Hearing,

after hearing the oral observations of Mrs Sürül, represented by Rainer M. Hofmann; the German Government, represented by Claus-Dieter Quassowski; the French Government, represented by Anne de Bourgoing; the Netherlands Government, represented by Mark Fierstra; the United Kingdom Government, represented by John E. Collins, assisted by Mark Hoskins, Barrister; and the Commission, represented by Peter Hillenkamp, at the hearing on 11 November 1988,

after hearing the Opinion of the Advocate General at the sitting on 17 December 1998,

gives the following Judgment

1.   By order of 24 July 1996, received at the Court on 26 July 1996, the Sozialgericht (Social Court), Aachen, referred to the Court for a preliminary ruling under Article 234 EC (ex Article 177) three questions on the interpretation of certain provisions of Decision No 3/80 of the Association Council of 19 September 1980 on the application of the social security schemes of the Member States of the European Communities to Turkish workers and members of their families (OJ 1983 C 110, p. 60)

2.   Those questions were raised in proceedings brought by Sema Sürül, a Turkish national, against the Bundesanstalt für Arbeit (Federal Employment Office) concerning the latter's refusal to pay her family allowances as from 1 January 1994.

The association between the EEC and Turkey

3.   The Agreement establishing an association between the European Economic Community and Turkey (hereinafter "the Agreement") was signed at Ankara on 12 September 1963 by the Republic of Turkey of the one part and the Member States of the EEC and the Community of

the other part, and was concluded, approved and confirmed on behalf of the Community by Council Decision 64/732/EEC of 23 December 1963 (OJ 1977 L 361, p. 29).

4. Pursuant to Article 2(1) of the Agreement, its aim is to promote the continuous and balanced strengthening of trade and economic relations between the parties.

   To that end, the Agreement provides for a preparatory stage enabling the Republic of Turkey to strengthen its economy with aid from the Community (Article 3), a transitional stage in which a customs union will be progressively established and economic policies will be aligned (Article 4) and a final stage based on the customs union, entailing closer coordination of economic policies (Article 5).

5. Article 6 of the Agreement provides:

   "To ensure the implementation and the progressive development of the Association, the Contracting Parties shall meet in a Council of Association which shall act within the powers conferred on it by this Agreement."

6. According to Article 8 of the Agreement, in Title II, "Implementation of the transitional stage",

   "In order to attain the objectives set out in Article 4, the Council of Association shall, before the beginning of the transitional stage and in accordance with the procedure laid down in Article 1 of the provisional Protocol, determine the conditions, rules and timetables for the implementation of the provisions relating to the fields covered by the Treaty establishing the Community which must be considered; this shall apply in particular to such of those fields as are mentioned under this Title and to any protective clause which may prove appropriate."

7. Article 9, also in Title II, provides:

   "The Contracting Parties recognise that within the scope of this Agreement and without prejudice to any special provisions which may be laid down pursuant to Article 8, any discrimination on grounds of nationality shall be prohibited in accordance with the principle laid down in Article 7 of the Treaty establishing the Community."

8. According to Article 12 of the Agreement,

   "The Contracting Parties agree to be guided by Articles 48, 49 and 50 of the Treaty establishing the Community for the purpose of progressively securing freedom of movement for workers between them."

9.   Article 22(1) of the Agreement provides:

> "In order to attain the objectives of this Agreement the Council of Association shall have the power to take decisions in the cases provided for therein. Each of the parties shall take the measures necessary to implement the decisions taken. ..."

10.   Article 1 of the Additional Protocol signed in Brussels on 23 November 1970 and concluded, approved and confirmed on behalf of the Community by Council Regulation (EEC) No 2760/72 of 19 December 1972 (OJ 1977 L 361, p. 61,

> hereinafter "the Protocol") lays down the conditions, arrangements and timetables for implementing the transitional stage referred to in Article 4 of the Agreement. By virtue of Article 62 thereof, the Protocol forms an integral part of the Agreement.

11.   The Protocol includes a Title II, "Movement of persons and services", Chapter I of which concerns "Workers".

12.   Article 36 of Chapter I lays down the timetable for the progressive attainment of freedom of movement for workers between the Member States of the Community and Turkey in accordance with the principles set out in Article 12 of the Agreement and provides that the Council of Association is to decide on the rules necessary to that end.

13.   Article 39 of the Protocol provides:

> "1.   Before the end of the first year after the entry into force of this Protocol the Council of Association shall adopt social security measures for workers of Turkish nationality moving within the Community and for their families residing in the Community.
>
> 2.   These provisions must enable workers of Turkish nationality, in accordance with arrangements to be laid down, to aggregate periods of insurance or employment completed in individual Member States in respect of old-age pensions, death benefits and invalidity pensions, and also as regards the provision of health services for workers and their families residing in the Community. These measures shall create no obligation on Member States to take into account periods completed in Turkey.
>
> 3.   The abovementioned measures must ensure that family allowances are paid if a worker's family resides in the Community.
>   ..."

14.   It was on the basis of Article 39 of the Protocol that the Association Council established by the Agreement adopted Decision No 3/80 on 19 September 1980.

15.   The purpose of that decision is to coordinate the social security systems of the Member States so as to enable Turkish workers working or having worked in the Community, members of those workers' families and survivors of such workers to enjoy benefits in the traditional branches of social security.

16.   To that end, the provisions of Decision No 3/80 refer, for the most part, to a number of provisions of Council Regulation (EEC) No 1408/71 of 14 June 1971 on the application of social security schemes to employed persons, to self-employed persons and to members of their families moving within the Community (OJ, English Special Edition 1971 (II), p. 416) and, less frequently, to Council Regulation (EEC) No 574/72 of 21 March 1972 laying down the procedure for implementing Regulation (EEC) No 1408/71 (OJ, English Special Edition 1972 (I), p. 159).

17.   Articles 1 to 4 of Decision No 3/80 appear in Title I, "General provisions".

18.   Article 1, entitled "Definitions" provides,
      "For the purposes of this Decision:
      (a)   the terms ... "member of family", "survivor", "residence" ..."family benefits", "family allowances" ... have the meaning assigned to them in Article 1 of ... Regulation (EEC) No 1408/71 ...
      (b)   "worker" means:
            (i)   subject to the restriction set out in Annex V, A. BELGIUM (1), to Regulation (EEC) No 1408/71, any person who is insured, compulsorily or on an optional continued basis, against one or more of the contingencies covered by the branches of a social security scheme for employed persons,
            (ii)   any person who is compulsorily insured against one or more of the contingencies covered by the branches of social security dealt with in this Decision under a social security scheme for all residents or for the whole working population, if such a person:
                   –   can be identified as an employed person by virtue of the manner in which that scheme is administered or financed, or
                   –   failing such criteria, is insured against some other contingency specified in the Annex under a scheme for employed persons, either compulsorily or on an optional continued basis;
            ..."

19.   As far as Germany is concerned, the annex referred to in the second indent of Article 1(b)(ii) of Decision No 3/80 does not further define the concept of worker.

20.   Pursuant to Article 2 of Decision No 3/80, entitled "Persons covered":
      "This decision shall apply:
      –   to workers who are, or have been, subject to the legislation of one or more Member States and who are Turkish nationals,
      –   to the members of the families of these workers, resident in the territory of one of the Member States,
      –   to the survivors of these workers."

21.   Article 3(1) of Decision No 3/80, which is entitled "Equality of treatment" and adopts the wording of Article 3(1) of Regulation No 1408/71, provides:

> "Subject to the special provisions of this Decision, persons resident in the territory of one of the Member States to whom this Decision applies shall be subject to the same obligations and enjoy the same benefits under the legislation of any Member State as the nationals of that State."

22.   Article 4 of Decision No 3/80, entitled "Matters covered" provides, in paragraph 1:

> "This Decision shall apply to all legislation concerning the following branches of social security:
>
> (a)   sickness and maternity benefits;
> (b)   invalidity benefits, including those intended for the mainte-nance or improvement of earning capacity;
> (c)   old-age benefits;
> (d)   survivors' benefits;
> (e)   benefits in respect of accidents at work and occupational diseases;
> (f)   death grants;
> (g)   unemployment benefits;
> (h)   family benefits."

23.   Title III of Decision No 3/80, entitled "Special provisions relating to the various categories of benefits", includes coordinating provisions inspired by Regulation No 1408/71 concerning benefits for sickness and maternity, invalidity, old age and death (pensions), accidents at work and occupa-tional diseases, death grants, and family benefits and family allowances.

24.   Unlike the other two decisions adopted on the same date by the EEC-Turkey Association Council (Decision No 1/80 on the development of the Association and Decision No 2/80 determining the conditions for implementing the special aid to Turkey (not published)), Decision No 3/80 does not specify the date of its entry into force.

25.   Pursuant to Article 32 of Decision No 3/80:

> "Turkey and the Community shall, each to the extent to which they are concerned, take the necessary steps to implement this Decision".

26.   On 8 February 1983 the Commission submitted to the Council a proposal for a Council (EEC) Regulation implementing within the European Economic Community Decision No 3/80 (OJ 1983 C 110, p. 19) which provided that that decision was to be "applied within the Community" (Article 1) and laid down "detailed rules for implementing" that decision.

27.   The Council has not yet adopted that proposal for a regulation.

The national legislation

28. In Germany, family allowances are granted under the Bundeskindergeldgesetz (Federal Child Benefit Law, BGBl. I, p. 265; "the BKGG") of 14 April 1964.
29. The family allowances provided for by the BKGG, which form part of a set of family policy measures, alleviate the financial burden of bringing up children. Under Articles 10 and 11 of the BKGG, a family with one child receives DEM 70 per month, to which a supplement is added for persons with a low income.
30. Articles 1(1) and 2(5) of the BKGG provide that family allowances may be claimed by any person domiciled or habitually resident in the territory covered by that Law provided that his or her dependent child is domiciled or habitually resident in that territory.
31. However, following an amendment which was published on 31 January 1994 in BGBl. I at p. 167 and which entered into force on 1 January 1994, Paragraph 1(3) of the BKGG provides that foreign nationals living in Germany are entitled to family allowances only if they hold a residence entitlement (Aufenthaltsberechtigung) or a residence permit (Aufenthaltserlaubnis).
32. For that purpose, the BKGG assimilates to Germans only the nationals of other Member States of the European Community, refugees and stateless persons.
33. According to the Ausländergesetz (German Law on Aliens), the residence entitlement (Aufenthaltsberechtigung) and the residence permit (Aufenthaltserlaubnis) confer on the alien concerned an individual right of residence which is unlimited or else of specified duration but capable of extension. On the other hand, the accessory residence authorisation (Aufenthaltsbewilligung) is a residence document issued for a specific purpose and for a limited period, thereby precluding the holder from subsequently acquiring a permanent authorisation.

The dispute in the main proceedings

34. According to the order for reference, Mr and Mrs Sürül are Turkish nationals lawfully resident in Germany.
35. In 1987 Mr Sürül was authorised to enter Germany to study there.
36. In 1991 his wife was granted authorisation to join him in Germany in order to reunite the family.
37. Both Mr and Mrs Sürül hold an accessory residence authorisation (Aufenthaltsbewilligung) entitling them to live in Germany.
38. Mr Sürül was also authorised to work, whilst studying, in an auxiliary capacity for a specified employer for up to 16 hours a week, and he is so employed with the appropriate work permit. Mr Sürül pays no contributions to statutory sickness or old-age insurance schemes but is insured by his employer against accidents at work.

39.   Mrs Sürül, on the other hand, is not authorised to engage in any gainful employment.

40.   On 14 September 1992 Mrs Sürül gave birth within German territory to a child whom she cares for and brings up in the matrimonial home. In that regard, the Sozialgericht Aachen considers that under the German rules the compulsory insurance contributions to the statutory pension scheme are deemed to be paid for the benefit of the person who undertakes the bringing up of his or her child aged less than three years.

41.   The Bundesanstalt für Arbeit then paid family allowances to Mrs Sürül, who also received, for 1993, the supplementary allowance for persons with a low income.

42.   However, with effect from 1 January 1994, the Bundesanstalt für Arbeit terminated the payment of those family allowances on the ground that, as from that date, Mrs Sürül no longer fulfilled the qualifying criteria laid down by the BKGG because she did not possess a residence entitlement   (Aufenthaltsberechtigung)   or   a   residence   permit (Aufenthaltserlaubnis). In March 1994, the Bundesanstalt für Arbeit also refused, on the same grounds, to continue payment of the supplementary family allowance to Mrs Sürül.

43.   Following rejection of her administrative complaint against those decisions, Mrs Sürül brought proceedings before the Sozialgericht Aachen, claiming that she was entitled under the rules of the EEC-Turkey Association Agreement to be treated in the same way as German nationals, so that the type of residence document issued to her in the Member State concerned was irrelevant.

44.   That court considers that no provision of German law permits Mrs Sürül to continue to receive family allowances since the BKGG, in the version in force since 1 January 1994, assimilates to Germans only the nationals of other Member States of the European Community, refugees and stateless persons. However, it raises the question whether Mrs Sürül might be able to derive from the rules of the EEC-Turkey Association Agreement a right to be granted family allowances under the same conditions as German nationals.

The questions submitted

45.   On the view, therefore, that determination of the case called for an interpretation of Community law, the Sozialgericht Aachen has stayed proceedings pending a preliminary ruling from the Court on the following three questions:

   "1.   Does a Turkish national living in Germany who comes within the personal scope of Article 2 of Decision No 3/80 of 19 September 1980 of the Association Council set up pursuant to the Agreement establishing an Association between the European Economic Community and Turkey ("Decision No 3/80"), and who possesses merely an *Aufenthaltsbewilligung*, have a right, deriving directly from Article 3 in conjunction with Article 4(1)(h) of Decision No 3/80, to German child benefit, that right being one which is conditional solely on fulfilment of the conditions applying with regard to German nationals and not on fulfilment of the further conditions applying to aliens which are laid down in the first sentence of Article 1(3) of the Bundeskindergeldgesetz ("BKGG") in the version thereof published in the Official Notice of 31 January 1994 (BGBl. I, p. 168)?

Or, to phrase that question in more general terms:

Is a Member State prohibited from refusing a Turkish national who comes within the personal scope of Article 2 of Decision No 3/80 family benefits provided for under its law on the ground that that person does not possess an *Aufenthaltsberechtigung* or an *Aufenthaltserlaubnis*?

2.   Is a Turkish national residing in the territory of a Member State a worker within the meaning of Article 2 in conjunction with Article 1(b) of Decision No 3/80 during periods when, pursuant to the law of that State, compulsory contributions to the social security pension scheme are deemed, in favour of that person, to have been paid in respect of time spent in bringing up a child?

3.   Is a Turkish national residing in the territory of a Member State who, in addition to following a course of studies, is employed there on the basis of a corresponding work permit for up to 16 hours per week as an auxiliary worker to be regarded on that ground alone as a worker within the meaning of Article 2 in conjunction with Article 1(b) of Decision No 3/80, or in any event because that person is insured under a statutory accident insurance scheme against accidents at work?"

46.   The crux of those three questions, which it is appropriate to consider together, is whether, on a proper construction of Article 3(1) of Decision No 3/80, a Member State may require of a Turkish national covered by that decision whom it has authorised to reside in its territory, but who holds in that host State only a conditional residence authorisation issued for a specified purpose and for a limited duration, that, in order to receive family allowances for his child who resides with him in that Member State, he must be in possession of a residence entitlement or a residence permit whereas for that purpose nationals of that State are required only to be resident there.

47.   In order to provide a helpful answer to the questions so reformulated, it is necessary first to consider whether Article 3(1) of Decision No 3/80 is, by its nature, such as to confer directly on an individual rights which he may assert before a court of a Member State. If so, the question is then whether that decision covers the situation of a Turkish national such as

the plaintiff in the main proceedings who seeks, in the Member State in which he has been authorised to reside, the benefit of an allowance of the kind at issue in this case and, finally, whether the principle of non-discrimination in the field of social security embodied in that provision of Decision No 3/80 precludes the host Member State from making the grant of that benefit subject to more restrictive conditions for Turkish migrants than for nationals.

The direct effect of Article 3(1) of Decision No 3/80

48. The German, French, Netherlands, Austrian and United Kingdom Governments submit that although the Court had no occasion to rule as to the direct effect of Article 3(1) of Decision No 3/80 in Case C-277/94 *Taflan-Met and Others* v *Bestuur van de Sociale Verzekeringsbank* [1996] ECR I-4085, it is nevertheless clear from the reasoning of that judgment that it is of general scope.

49. In that judgment, the Court held that, by its nature, Decision No 3/80 is intended to be supplemented and implemented in the Community by a subsequent act of the Council (paragraph 33) and that, even though some of its provisions are clear and precise, that decision cannot be applied so long as supplementary implementing measures have not been adopted by the Council (paragraph 37).

50. It follows, those Governments maintain, that no provision of Decision No 3/80 can have direct effect in the territory of any Member State until the supplementary measures essential for the concrete implementation of that decision, such as those set out in the proposal for a regulation submitted by the Commission, have been adopted by the Council.

51. It should be observed that, in *Taflan-Met* the Court held, in paragraphs 21 and 22, that it follows from the binding character which the Agreement attaches to decisions of the EEC-Turkey Association Council that Decision No 3/80 entered into force on the date on which it was adopted, that is to say, 19 September 1980, and that, since then, the Contracting Parties have been bound by that decision.

52. In the same judgment, the Court ruled that, so long as the supplementary measures essential for implementing Decision No 3/80 have not been adopted by the Council, Articles 12 and 13 of that decision do not have direct effect in the territory of the Member States and are therefore not such as to entitle individuals to rely on them before the national courts.

53. In *Taflan-Met* the plaintiffs in the main proceedings claimed invalidity or survivors' pensions on the basis of the coordination rules laid down in Articles 12 and 13 of Decision No 3/80. That case thus concerned the right of Turkish migrant workers, employed successively in more than one Member State, or the right of survivors of those workers, to certain social security benefits on the basis of technical provisions for the coordination of the different national laws applicable thereto referred to in Chapter 2, entitled "Invalidity", and Chapter 3, entitled "Old age and death (pensions)", of Title III of that decision.

54. It was in that context that the Court observed, in paragraphs 29 and 30 of *Taflan-Met*, comparing Regulations No 1408/71 and its implementing regulation, No 574/72, with Decision No 3/80, that, even though the Decision refers specifically to certain provisions of the two regulations, the Decision does not contain a large number of precise, detailed provisions, deemed indispensable for the purpose of implementing Regulation No 1408/71 within the Community. It emphasised in paragraph 32 in particular that, whilst Decision No 3/80 sets out the fundamental principle of aggregation for the branches sickness and maternity, invalidity, old age, death grants and family benefits by reference to Regulation No 1408/71, supplementary implementing measures of the kind set out in Regulation No 574/72 must be adopted before that principle can be applied. The Court pointed out, at paragraphs 35 and 36, that such measures as well as detailed provisions relating, *inter alia*, to prevention of overlapping benefits and to determination of the applicable legislation, appear only in the proposal for a Council (EEC) Regulation implementing within the European Economic Community Decision No 3/80 submitted by the Commission on 8 February 1983, which has not yet been adopted by the Council. It concluded that, until adoption of those implementing measures, the coordinating rules in Decision No 3/80 on which the plaintiffs had based their claims could not be relied on by them directly before the national courts of a Member State.

55. In contrast, this case is not concerned with those coordinating provisions in Title III of Decision No 3/80. Mrs Sürül relies solely on the principle of non-discrimination on grounds of nationality laid down in Article 3(1) of that decision, with a view to obtaining, in the Member State of her residence and solely under the legislation of that State, entitlement to a social security benefit under the same conditions as those laid down for the nationals of the host Member State.

56. Moreover, the proposal for a regulation submitted by the Commission for the implementation of Decision No 3/80 in the Community contains no provision concerning the application of Article 3(1), which is taken word for word from Regulation No 1408/71, whose implementing regulation, No 574/72, likewise contains no measures for giving effect to that provision.

57. The reasoning which led the Court to hold that, as Community law stands, Articles 12 and 13 of Decision No 3/80 do not have direct effect, must apply by analogy to all the other provisions of that decision which require additional measures for their application in practice. That reasoning cannot, however, be transposed to the principle of equal treatment in the field of social security, embodied in Article 3(1) of that decision.

58. Circumstances such as those in the main proceedings are not such as to give rise to problems of a technical nature relating in particular to the aggregation of periods completed in different Member States, to non-overlapping of benefits paid by different competent institutions or to

determination of the applicable national legislation, since the plaintiff in the main proceedings merely invokes for the combined application of the legislation of the host Member State and of the principle of non-discrimination on grounds of nationality embodied in Article 3(1) of Decision No 3/80. That claim can be examined without any need for recourse to coordinating measures which the Council has not yet adopted.

59. In those circumstances, the submission of the German, French, Netherlands, Austrian and United Kingdom Governments cannot be accepted and it is therefore necessary to verify whether Article 3(1) of Decision No 3/80 fulfils the requirements for it to have direct effect in the territory of the Member States.

60. It is settled case-law that a provision in an agreement concluded by the Community with non-member countries must be regarded as being directly applicable when, regard being had to its wording and to the purpose and nature of the agreement itself, the provision contains a clear and precise obligation which is not subject, in its implementation or effects, to the adoption of any subsequent measure (see, in particular, Case 12/86 *Demirel* [1987] ECR 3719, paragraph 14; Case C-18/90 *Kziber* [1991] ECR I-199, paragraph 15, and Case C-162/96 *Racke* [1998] ECR I-3655, paragraph 31). In Case C-192/89 *Sevince* v *Staatssecretaris van Justitie* [1990] ECR I-3461, paragraphs 14 and 15, the Court made it clear that the same conditions apply in determining whether the provisions of a decision of the EEC-Turkey Association Council may have direct effect.

61. In deciding whether Article 3(1) of Decision No 3/80 meets those criteria, it is necessary first to examine its terms.

62. That provision lays down in clear, precise and unconditional terms a prohibition of discrimination, based on nationality, against persons residing in the territory of any Member State to whom the provisions of Decision No 3/80 are applicable.

63. As the Commission rightly pointed out, that rule of equal treatment lays down a precise obligation of result and, by its nature, can be relied on by an individual before a national court as a basis for requesting it to disapply the discriminatory provisions of the legislation of a Member State under which the grant of a right is subject to a condition not imposed on nationals. No further implementing measures are required (see paragraphs 56 and 58 of this judgment).

64. That finding is supported by the fact that Article 3(1) of Decision No 3/80 constitutes merely the implementation and the concrete expression, in the particular field of social security, of the general principle of non-discrimination on grounds of nationality laid down in Article 9 of the Agreement, which refers to Article 7 of the EEC Treaty (subsequently, Article 6 of the EC Treaty and now, after amendment, Article 12 EC).

65. That interpretation is also confirmed by settled case-law of the Court (see *Kziber*, cited above, paragraphs 15 to 23, confirmed by Case C-58/93

Yousfi [1994] ECR I- 1353, paragraphs 16 to 19; Case C-103/94 *Krid* [1995] ECR I-719, paragraphs 21 to 24; Case C-126/95 *Hallouzi-Choho* v *Bestuur van de Sociale Verzekeringsbank* [1996] ECR I-4807, paragraphs 19 and 20; and Case C-113/97 *Babahenini* [1998] ECR I-183, paragraphs 17 and 18) relating to the principle of equal treatment contained in Article 39(1) of the Cooperation Agreement between the European Economic Community and the People's Democratic Republic of Algeria, signed in Algiers on 26 April 1976 and concluded on behalf of the Community by Council Regulation (EEC) No 2210/78 of 26 September 1978 (OJ 1978 L 263, p. 1) and to Article 41(1) of the Cooperation Agreement between the European Economic Community and the Kingdom of Morocco, signed in Rabat on 26 April 1976 and concluded on behalf of the Community by Council Regulation (EEC) No 2211/78 (OJ 1978 L 264, p. 1).

66. According to that case-law, those provisions, which provide for the prohibition of all discrimination based on nationality in the field of social security against Algerian and Moroccan nationals as compared with the nationals of the host Member State, are directly effective notwithstanding the fact that the Cooperation Council has not adopted measures implementing Article 40(1) of the EEC-Algeria Agreement or Article 42(1) of the EEC-Morocco Agreement relating to the implementation of the principles stated in Articles 39 and 41 respectively.

67. The foregoing interpretation is not invalidated by the fact that Article 3(1) of Decision No 3/80 states that the prohibition of discrimination on grounds of nationality which it contains is to take effect "[s]ubject to the special provisions of this Decision".

68. It is sufficient to note that, with respect to the family allowances at issue in this case, Decision No 3/80 neither makes any exception to nor imposes any restriction on the principle of equal treatment laid down in Article 3(1). In view of the fundamental nature of that principle, the existence of that reservation, taken word for word from Article 3(1) of Regulation No 1408/71 and appearing also in Article 9 of the Agreement and in Article 12 EC, is not in itself such as to affect the direct effect of the provision from which it allows derogations (see, to that effect, *Sevince*, cited above, paragraph 25) by depriving the rule on national treatment of its unconditional nature.

69. Consideration of the purpose and the nature of the Agreement of which that provision forms part does not contradict the finding that the principle of non-discrimination embodied in Article 3(1) of Decision No 3/80 is capable of directly governing the situation of individuals.

70. The purpose of the Agreement is to establish an association to promote the development of trade and economic relations between the parties, including in the field of employment, through the progressive achievement of freedom of movement for workers, with a view to improving the standard of living of the Turkish people and facilitating the accession of

the Turkish Republic to the Community at a later date (see the fourth recital in the preamble to the Agreement).

71. The Protocol, which, in accordance with Article 62 thereof, forms an integral part of the Agreement, provides in Article 36 for the timetable for the progressive achievement of such freedom of movement for workers and provides, in Article 39, for the Association Council to adopt social security measures for workers of Turkish nationality moving within the Community and for their families residing in the Member States. It was on that basis that the Association Council adopted Decision No 3/80, the aim of which is to guarantee the payment of social security benefits to migrant workers in the Community.

72. Moreover, the fact that the Agreement is intended essentially to promote the economic development of Turkey and therefore involves an imbalance in the obligations assumed by the Community towards the non-member country concerned is not such as to prevent recognition by the Community of the direct effect of certain of its provisions (see, by analogy, Case 87/75 *Bresciani* v *Amministrazione delle Finanze* [1976] ECR 129, paragraph 23; *Kziber*, cited above, paragraph 21; and Case C-469/93 *Amministrazione delle Finanze dello Stato* v *Chiquita Italia* [1995] ECR I-4533, paragraph 34).

73. Finally, it follows from paragraphs 55, 56 and 58 of this judgment that the rule in question assimilates persons who are covered by Decision No 3/80 and reside in the host Member State to nationals of the host State, by prohibiting any discrimination based on nationality and resulting from the legislation of that Member State. That rule is set out in Article 3(1) of the Decision and is not affected by its other provisions.

74. It follows from the foregoing considerations that Article 3(1) of Decision No 3/80 establishes, in the area in which that decision applies, a precise and unconditional principle such as is capable of being applied by a national court and, therefore, of governing the legal situation of individuals. The direct effect which must therefore be accorded to that provision means that the persons to whom it applies are entitled to rely on it before the courts of the Member States.

The scope of Article 3(1) of Decision No 3/80

75. Although it is common ground that the family allowances at issue in the main proceedings constitute family benefits within the meaning of Article 4(1)(h) of Decision No 3/80 and therefore fall within its scope, the German Government nevertheless denies that Mrs Sürül is one of the persons to whom that decision applies.

76. Thus, the plaintiff in the main proceedings cannot, in its submission, be regarded as a worker within the meaning of Article 1(b) and Article 2, first indent, of Decision No 3/80.

77. The German Government submits, in its written observations, that affiliation to a branch of social security is not sufficient to confer the status

of worker as regards the other branches of social security since the definitions contained in Article 1(b)(i) and (ii) of Decision No 3/80 should be construed not as alternatives but, on the contrary, as being specifically applicable to clearly identified and distinct schemes. Accordingly, even if it were assumed that Mrs Sürül were covered by statutory pension insurance for the first three years following the birth of her child (see paragraph 40 of this judgment), that fact alone is not such as to bring her within the cover of the other branches of social security, particularly as regards entitlement to family allowances.

78. The German Government adds that in Germany entitlement to family allowances does not depend on compulsory or optional affiliation to a social insurance scheme but accrues to all residents, irrespective of their occupational or professional status. Even though the annex to Decision No 3/80, referred to in the second indent of Article 1(b)(ii), does not lay down special implementing rules for Germany, it is necessary in this case, in accordance with Article 25(1) of that decision, to apply by analogy Annex I, point I, C ("Germany"), of Regulation No 1408/71.

79. According to the German Government, it follows that, in the field of family benefits which extends to the allowance at issue in the main proceedings, only a person who is compulsorily insured against the risk of unemployment or who, as a result of such insurance, obtains cash benefits under sickness insurance or comparable benefits can be classified as a worker. Mrs Sürül fulfils none of those conditions.

80. Nor, according to the German Government, can the plaintiff in the main proceedings be regarded as a member of a worker's family within the meaning of Article 1(a) and Article 2, second indent, of Decision No 3/80.

81. Mrs Sürül's spouse was, admittedly, engaged in gainful employment as well as his studies but, under German legislation, he was not required to insure himself against the risks of unemployment, sickness or old age. Only contributions to the statutory insurance scheme against accidents at work were compulsory, and these were paid in their entirety by Mr Sürül's employer. For the same reasons as those set out in paragraph 77 of this judgment, Mr Sürül is therefore covered only by the provisions of Decision No 3/80 which relate to accident insurance but not by those governing other branches of social security, in particular family allowances. In those circumstances, Mr Sürül cannot be regarded as a worker or his spouse as a member of a worker's family, within the meaning of that decision, for the purposes of receiving family allowances.

82. In order to determine the merits of that argument, it must first be noted that the definition which, for the purpose of the application of Decision No 3/80, Article 1(b) thereof gives to "workers" corresponds very broadly to that of the concept of "worker" in Article 1(a) of Regulation No 1408/71.

83. Pursuant to Article 1(a) of Decision No 3/80, the term "member of family" has the meaning given to it by Article 1(f) of Regulation No 1408/71.

84. The definition of the persons to whom Decision No 3/80 applies contained in Article 2 thereof is inspired by the same definition set out in Article 2(1) of Regulation No 1408/71.

85. Second, it must be borne in mind that according to settled case-law the definition of "worker" in Article 1(a) of Regulation No 1408/71 "for the purpose of this regulation" is of general scope and in the light of that consideration covers any person who has the status of a person insured under the social security legislation of one or more Member States, whether or not he pursues a professional or trade activity (see Case 182/78 *Algemeen Ziekenfonds Drenthe-Plattenland* v *Pierik* [1979] ECR 1977, paragraph 4). That expression means any person who is insured under one of the social security schemes mentioned in Article 1(a) of Regulation No 1408/71 for the contingencies and under the conditions mentioned in that provision (see Case C-2/89 *Kits van Heijningen* [1990] ECR I-1755, paragraph 9).

86. It follows that, as the Court has also stated in relation to Regulation No 1408/71 in Case C-85/96 *Martínez Sala* [1998] ECR I-2691, paragraph 36, and Case C-275/96 *Kuusijärvi* [1998] ECR I-3419, paragraph 21, a person has the status of worker where he is covered, even if only in respect of a single risk, on a compulsory or optional basis, by a general or special social security scheme, irrespective of the existence of an employment relationship.

87. As regards the German Government's objection based on an application by analogy of point I, C ("Germany"), of Annex I to Regulation No 1408/71, it must be borne in mind that Article 25(1) of Decision No 3/80 provides that "[f]or the purposes of implementing this Decision, Annexes I, III and IV to Regulation (EEC) No 1408/71 shall be applicable", so that that annex is applicable in relation to Decision No 3/80.

88. According to Annex I, point I, – "Employed persons and/or self-employed persons (Article 1(a)(ii) and (ii) of the Regulation)" – C ("Germany") of Regulation No 1408/71:

"If the competent institution for granting family benefits in accordance with Chapter 7 of Title III of the Regulation is a German institution, then within the meaning of Article 1(a)(ii) of the Regulation:

(a) "employed person" means any person compulsorily insured against unemployment or any person who, as a result of such insurance, obtains cash benefits under sickness insurance or comparable benefits;
..."

89. As is clear from the wording of that provision, Annex I, Point I, C, of Regulation No 1408/71 clarified or narrowed the definition of employed person within the meaning of Article 1(a)(ii) of that regulation solely for the purpose of the grant of family benefits pursuant to Title III, Chapter 7 (*Martínez Sala*, cited above, paragraph 43).

90. As the Advocate General pointed out in points 57 and 58 of his Opinion of 12 February 1998, the situation of a person such as the plaintiff in the main proceedings is not covered by any of the provisions of Chapter 7 of Title III. In this case, all the relevant aspects are internal to the host Member State in which Mr and Mrs Sürül reside with their child and in which the plaintiff in the main proceedings claims family allowances under the legislation of that State (see paragraphs 55 and 58 of this judgment).

91. In those circumstances, the restriction provided for in Annex I to Regulation No 1408/71, point I, C, cannot be applied to the plaintiff in the main proceedings, so that the question whether she has the status of worker for the purposes of Decision No 3/80 must be determined solely with respect to Article 1(b) thereof.

92. It is clear, furthermore, from the documents in the main proceedings that the competent German authorities initially paid family allowances to Mrs Sürül despite the fact that she did not fulfil the conditions laid down in that annex to Regulation No 1408/71 and that they did not terminate that payment until after the entry into force on 1 January 1994 of the new national legislation making the availability of that kind of benefit for aliens residing in Germany conditional upon the possession of a certain type of residence document.

93. In the light of the foregoing considerations, a Turkish national such as the plaintiff in the main proceedings will thus be able to benefit from the rights attaching to the status of worker within the meaning of Decision No 3/80 provided that it is established that she is insured, even if against only one risk, by virtue of compulsory or optional insurance with a general or special social security scheme mentioned in Article 1(b) of that decision. That would be the case for the period for which she was covered by statutory pension insurance, as indicated by the national court in its second question.

94. Similarly, with regard to the period for which Mrs Sürül was not affiliated to a social security scheme she will be able to benefit from the rights attaching to the status of member of the family of a worker within the meaning of Decision No 3/80 provided that it is established that her husband is insured, even if against only one risk, by virtue of compulsory or optional insurance under a general or special social security scheme mentioned in Article 1(b) of that decision. That condition would be satisfied if, as the national court observes in its third question, he is covered by statutory insurance against accidents at work.

95. It is for the national court, which alone has jurisdiction to find and assess the facts in the case before it and to interpret and apply national law, to decide whether, during the period at issue, Mrs Sürül is herself to be regarded as a worker. Should that not be so for all or part of that period, it is again for that court to determine whether, for the period concerned, Mrs Sürül's husband fulfilled the condition mentioned in paragraph 94

of this judgment as having to be satisfied for him to be regarded as a worker, so that Mrs Sürül, in her capacity as the spouse of a Turkish worker whom she has been authorised to join in the host Member State in order to reunite the family, would be a member of a worker's family within the meaning of Decision No 3/80.

The scope of the principle of non-discrimination laid down in Article 3(1) of Decision No 3/80

96. In the event of a person such as the plaintiff in the main proceedings coming within the scope *ratione personae* of Decision No 3/80, it is necessary, finally, to determine whether Article 3(1) of that decision must be interpreted as precluding the application of legislation of a Member State which requires that a Turkish national, who has been authorised to reside in its territory and is lawfully resident there, hold a certain type of residence document in order to receive family allowances.

97. In that connection, it is important to emphasise first that the principle laid down in Article 3(1) of Decision No 3/80, prohibiting all discrimination based on nationality in the field covered by that decision, means that a Turkish national to whom that decision applies must be treated in the same way as nationals of the host Member State, so that the legislation of that Member State cannot impose upon such a Turkish national more or stricter conditions than those applicable to its own nationals (see, by analogy, Case 186/87 *Cowan* v *Trésor Public* [1989] ECR 195, paragraph 10, *Kziber*, paragraph 28, and *Hallouzi-Choho*, paragraphs 35 and 36, both cited above).

98. It follows that a Turkish national who has been authorised to enter the territory of a Member State in order to reunite the family of a Turkish migrant worker and who lawfully resides there with that worker must be able to obtain in the host Member State a social security benefit provided for by the legislation of that State under the same conditions as the nationals of the Member State concerned.

99. Next, under legislation such as the BKGG, family allowances may be claimed by any person who is domiciled or habitually resident in the territory covered by that legislation provided that his or her dependent children are domiciled or habitually resident in the same territory.

100. However, since 1 January 1994, the BKGG has provided that aliens residing in Germany who cannot be assimilated to Germans are entitled to family allowances only if they hold a particular type of residence document.

101. Thus, a Turkish national such as the plaintiff in the main proceedings who has been authorised to reside in the territory of the host Member State, actually resides there with her child and therefore fulfils all the conditions imposed on nationals of that State by the relevant legislation is refused family allowances for her child solely because she does not

meet the requirement of possession of a residence entitlement or a residence permit.

102. That requirement, not being applicable to a national of the Member State concerned, even in the event of his staying there temporarily, by its nature covers only aliens and its application therefore leads to unequal treatment on grounds of nationality.

103. In those circumstances, it must be held that the fact that a Member State requires a Turkish national covered by Decision No 3/80 to possess a certain type of residence document in order to receive a benefit such as the allowance at issue in the main proceedings, no such document being required of nationals of that State, constitutes discrimination within the meaning of Article 3(1) of that decision.

104. Since no argument such as to provide objective justification for that difference of treatment has been raised before the Court, such discrimination is incompatible with that provision of Decision No 3/80.

105. In the light of all the foregoing considerations, the answer to the questions submitted must be that, on a proper construction of Article 3(1) of Decision No 3/80, a Member State may not require of a Turkish national covered by that decision whom it has authorised to reside in its territory, but who holds in that host State only a conditional residence authorisation issued for a specified purpose and for a limited duration, that, in order to receive family allowances for his child who resides with him in that Member State, he must be in possession of a residence entitlement or a residence permit, whereas for that purpose nationals of that State are required only to be resident there.

The temporal effects of this judgment

106. When presenting oral argument, the German, French and United Kingdom Governments asked the Court to limit the temporal effects of this judgment in the event of its ruling that the principle of non-discrimination on grounds of nationality contained in Article 3(1) of Decision No 3/80 must be construed as enabling a Turkish national such as the plaintiff in the main proceedings to claim family allowances in the host Member State under the same conditions as the nationals of that State. Those Governments state that a judgment to that effect would be such as to undermine a large number of legal relationships established on the basis of national legislation which has been in force for some time and to have serious financial repercussions for the social security systems of the Member States.

107. In that connection, regard must be had to the case-law of the Court to the effect that the interpretation which, in the exercise of the jurisdiction conferred on it by Article 234 EC (ex Article 177), the Court gives to a rule of Community law clarifies and defines where necessary the meaning and scope of that rule as it must be or ought to have been understood

and applied from the time of its entry into force. It follows that the rule as thus interpreted may, and must, be applied by the courts even to legal relationships which arose and were established before the judgment ruling on the request for interpretation, provided that in other respects the conditions for bringing a dispute relating to the application of that rule before the competent courts are satisfied (see, in particular, Case 24/86 *Blaizot* v *University of Li'ge* [1988] ECR 379, paragraph 27).

108. It is only exceptionally that, in application of a general principle of legal certainty which is inherent in the Community legal order, the Court may decide to restrict the right to rely upon a provision it has interpreted with a view to calling in question legal relations established in good faith. As the Court has consistently held, such a restriction may be allowed only in the actual judgment ruling upon the interpretation sought (see in particular Case C-35/97 *Commission* v *France* [1998] ECR I-5325, paragraph 49).

109. In this case it must be observed, first, that this is the first time that the Court has been called on to interpret Article 3(1) of Decision No 3/80.

110. Next, the judgment in *Taflan-Met*, cited above, may well have created a situation of uncertainty as to the right of individuals to rely before a national court on Article 3(1) of Decision No 3/80.

111. In those circumstances, pressing considerations of legal certainty preclude any reopening of the question of legal relationships which have been definitively determined before the delivery of this judgment, where that would retroactively throw the financing of the social security systems of the Member States into confusion.

112. However, in order not to affect unduly the judicial protection of the rights which individuals derive from Community law, it is appropriate to make an exception to that limitation of the effects of this judgment for the benefit of those persons who, before the date of delivery hereof, initiated proceedings or made an equivalent claim.

113. It must therefore be held that the direct effect of Article 3(1) of Decision No 3/80 may not be relied on in support of claims relating to benefits in respect of periods prior to the date of this judgment except as regards those persons who, before that date, initiated proceedings or made an equivalent claim.

Costs

114. The costs incurred by the German, French, Netherlands, Austrian and United Kingdom Governments and by the Commission, which have submitted observations to the Court, are not recoverable. Since these proceedings are, for the parties to the main proceedings, a step in the action pending before the national court, the decision on costs is a matter for that court.

On those grounds, THE COURT, in answer to the questions referred to it by the Sozialgericht Aachen by order of 24 July 1996, hereby rules:

1. On a proper construction of Article 3(1) of Decision No 3/80 of the Association Council of 19 September 1980 on the application of the social security schemes of the Member States of the European Communities to Turkish workers and members of their families, a Member State may not require of a Turkish national covered by that decision whom it has authorised to reside in its territory, but who holds in that host State only a conditional residence authorisation issued for a specified purpose and for a limited duration, that, in order to receive family allowances for his child who resides with him in that Member State, he must be in possession of a residence entitlement or a residence permit, whereas for that purpose nationals of that State are required only to be resident there.

2. The direct effect of Article 3(1) of Decision No 3/80 may not be relied on in support of claims relating to benefits in respect of periods prior to the date of this judgment except as regards those persons who, before that date, initiated proceedings or made an equivalent claim.

Rodríguez	Puissochet	Hirsch		
			Jann	
Mointinho de Almeida		Gulmann		Murray
				Edward
Ragnemalm				
	Sevón			
				Schintgen

Delivered in open court in Luxembourg on 4 May 1999.

R. Grass   G.C. Rodríguez Iglesias
Registrar   President

Judgment of the Court of Justice of the European Communities
(Sixth Chamber)
26 November 1998

MEHMET BIRDEN V STADTGEMEINDE BREMEN

Case C-1/97,

REFERENCE to the Court under Article 177 of the EC Treaty by the Verwaltungsgericht der Freien Hansestadt Bremen (Germany) for a preliminary ruling in the proceedings pending before that court between the interpretation of Article 6(1) of Decision No 1/80 of 19 September 1980 on the development of the Association, adopted by the Association Council established by the Association Agreement between the European Economic Community and Turkey,

THE COURT (Sixth Chamber),

composed of: P.J.G. Kapteyn, President of the Chamber, G.F. Mancini, J.L. Murray, H. Ragnemalm and R. Schintgen (Rapporteur), Judges,

Advocate General: N. Fennelly,
Registrar: L. Hewlett, Administrator,

after considering the written observations submitted on behalf of:
- Mr Birden, by J. Kempas, Rechtsanwalt, Bremen,
- the German Government, by E. Röder and B. Kloke, Ministerialrat and Oberregierungsrat respectively, in the Federal Ministry of Economic Affairs, acting as Agents,
  the Greek Government, by A. Samoni-Rantou, special assistant legal adviser in the Community Legal Affairs Department of the Ministry of Foreign Affairs, and by L. Pnevmatikou, specialist technical adviser in that department, acting as Agents,
- the French Government, by K. Rispal-Bellanger, Head of Subdirectorate in the Legal Affairs Directorate of the Ministry of Foreign Affairs, and C. Chavance, Foreign Affairs Secretary in the same Directorate, acting as Agents,
- the Commission of the European Communities, by P.J. Kuijper, Legal Adviser, acting as Agent, and by P. Gilsdorf, Rechtsanwalt, Hamburg and Brussels,

having regard to the Report for the Hearing,

after hearing the oral observations of Mr Birden, represented by J. Kempas, of the German Government, represented by C.-D. Quassowski, Regierungsdirektor in the Federal Ministry of Economic Affairs, acting as Agent, of the Greek Government, represented by A. Samoni-Rantou and L. Pnevmatikou, and of the Commission, represented by P. Gilsdorf, at the hearing on 2 April 1998,

after hearing the Opinion of the Advocate General at the sitting on 28 May 1998, gives the following Judgment

1.   By order of 9 December 1996, received at the Court on 6 January 1997, the Verwaltungsgericht der Freien Hansestadt Bremen (Administrative Court of the Free Hanseatic City of Bremen) referred to the Court for a preliminary ruling under Article 177 of the EC Treaty a question on the interpretation of Article 6(1) of Decision No 1/80 of the Association Council of 19 September 1980 on the development of the Association (hereinafter "Decision No 1/80"). The Association Council was set up by the Agreement establishing an Association between the European Economic Community and Turkey, signed at Ankara on 12 September 1963 by the Republic of Turkey and by the Member States of the EEC and the Community, and concluded, approved and confirmed on behalf of the Community by Council Decision 64/732/EEC of 23 December 1963 (OJ 1973 C 113, p. 2).

2.   The question referred to the Court was raised in proceedings between Mr Birden, a Turkish national, and the Stadtgemeinde Bremen (City of Bremen) concerning the latter's refusal to extend Mr Birden's permit to reside in Germany.

Background to the dispute and legal framework.

3.   According to the file on the case in the main proceedings, Mr Birden was permitted to enter Germany in 1990, where he married a German national in 1992.

4.   As a result of that marriage, he was granted a residence permit by that State, valid until June 1995, and an unconditional work permit of unlimited duration.

5.   Having failed to find work in Germany, however, Mr Birden initially received social assistance pursuant to the Bundessozialhilfegesetz) (Federal Law on Social Assistance, hereinafter "the BSHG").

6.   Paragraph 1 of the BSHG provides:

(a)   Social assistance comprises the grant of maintenance assistance and the assistance given to persons in particular circumstances.

(b)   The function of social assistance is to permit the beneficiary to live a life compatible with human dignity. To that effect, wherever possible, the assistance should place the beneficiary in a position to maintain himself; in that respect, the beneficiary of the assistance must cooperate to the best of his ability.

7.   According to paragraph 19 of the BSHG,

    (a)   Work opportunities shall be created for people seeking assistance, in particular young people who are unable to find work. In order to create and maintain work opportunities, costs may also be assumed. The work opportunities shall normally be of temporary duration and apt to improve the integration into working life of the person seeking assistance.

    (b)   If an opportunity of performing ancillary, public utility work is created for the person seeking assistance, he may be granted either the usual remuneration or maintenance assistance plus appropriate expenses. Work offered will be ancillary only if it would not otherwise be done, or not on that scale or at that time. The requirement for the work offered to be ancillary may be disregarded in individual cases if this helps to promote integration into working life or if it is made necessary by the entitled person's and his family's particular circumstances.

    (c)   If maintenance assistance is granted under subparagraph (2) above, no contract of employment for the purpose of employment law and no employment relationship for the purpose of statutory health and pension insurance will arise. However, the provisions on protection at work shall apply.

8.   On 3 January 1994, Mr Birden entered into a contract of employment as a semi- skilled odd-job man with the Kulturzentrum (Cultural Centre) Lagerhaus Bremen-Ostertor eV from 1 January 1994 to 31 December 1994. His net pay was DM 2 155.70 per month, after deduction of income tax, the solidarity surcharge, and contributions for health, care, pension and unemployment insurance; he was required to work 38.5 hours per week.

9.   That employment relationship was subsequently extended under the same conditions until 31 December 1995.

10.   For the duration of those contracts, Mr Birden did not receive any social assistance in the form of maintenance payments.

11.   Those employment contracts were wholly funded by the Werkstatt Bremen (Workshop Bremen), an office of the Senator für Gesundheit, Jugend und Soziales (Senator for Health, Youth and Social Affairs) of the Freien Hansestadt Bremen, under a programme adopted by the Senate of that city and intended, in accordance with paragraph 19(2) of the BSHG, to provide paid employment, on a temporary basis, to recipients of social assistance in order to enable, in particular, unemployed persons with no entitlement to unemployment benefits to enter or re-enter the general labour market. That period of one or two years' work, which is subject to payment of compulsory social insurance contributions, thus affords participants in the programme the right to draw social security benefits or the possibility of placement on a work creation scheme.

12.   On 10 June 1995, Mr Birden's marriage was dissolved.

13. On 15 August 1995 the competent authorities then refused to extend Mr Birden's permit to reside in Germany, on the grounds that, under national law, such an extension was no longer possible following his divorce and that he was not duly registered as belonging to the labour force of a Member State, for the purposes of Article 6(1) of Decision No 1/80, because the contracts of employment entered into on the basis of the BSHG were only temporary, their sole purpose was to enable a limited group of persons, in this case recipients of social assistance, to integrate into working life, they were funded by the public authorities and related to public utility work for a public employer not in competition with undertakings in the general labour market.

14. Mr Birden considered that he was entitled to an extension of his residence permit pursuant to the first indent of Article 6(1) of Decision No 1/80, on the ground that he had been in paid employment for more than one year with the same employer, and brought proceedings before the Verwaltungsgericht der Freien Hansestadt Bremen. Mr Birden stated in that respect that a new contract of employment, entered into with the same Kulturzentrum Lagerhaus Bremen-Ostertor eV for an indefinite period from 1 January 1996 and relating to a caretaker's post had not come into effect solely because he had been unable to provide his employer with a valid residence permit.

15. The national court considered that the contested decision complied with German law. None the less, it raised the question whether a solution more favourable to Mr Birden might not be derived from Article 6(1) of Decision No 1/80.

16. That provision, which appears in Chapter II (Social provisions), Section 1 (Questions relating to employment and the free movement of workers), is worded as follows:

     "1. Subject to Article 7 on free access to employment for members of his family, a Turkish worker duly registered as belonging to the labour force of a Member State:

     – shall be entitled, in that Member State, after one year's legal employment, to the renewal of his permit to work for the same employer, if a job is available;

     – shall be entitled in that Member State, after three years of legal employment and subject to the priority to be given to workers of Member States of the Community, to respond to another offer of employment, with an employer of his choice, made under normal conditions and registered with the employment services of that State, for the same occupation;

     – shall enjoy free access in that Member State to any paid employment of his choice, after four years of legal employment."

17. Although it pointed out that, at the time his residence permit expired, Mr Birden was in legal employment, held a valid work permit, had been

in paid employment for more than one year with the same employer and had a job available, the Verwaltungsgericht der Freien Hansestadt Bremen none the less expressed doubts as to whether he was duly registered as belonging to the labour force of a Member State within the meaning of Article 6(1) of Decision No 1/80, since the activity performed by him in 1994 and 1995 had been supported by the public authorities within the framework of paragraph 19(2) of the BSHG.

The question submitted for a preliminary ruling

18. The Verwaltungsgericht der Freien Hansestadt Bremen therefore considered that the resolution of the dispute required an interpretation of that provision of Decision No 1/80 and stayed proceedings in order to refer the following question to the Court for a preliminary ruling:

> "Is a Turkish worker a duly registered member of the labour force of a Member State, within the meaning of Article 6(1) of Decision No 1/80 of the EEC-Turkey Association Council on the development of the Association, if he has a job sponsored by that Member State with public funds and requiring payment of social security contributions which is meant to enable him to enter or re-enter working life and which, on account of the purpose of the State sponsorship, may only be offered (pursuant to Paragraph 19(2) of the Bundessozialhilfegesetz) to a limited group of persons?

19. The first point to be noted is that since the judgment in Case C-192/89 *Sevince* v *Staatssecretaris van Justitie* [1990] ECR I-3461, paragraph 26, the Court has consistently held that Article 6(1) of Decision No 1/80 has direct effect in the Member States and that Turkish nationals who satisfy its conditions may therefore rely directly on the rights which the three indents of that provision confer on them progressively, according to the duration of their employment in the host Member State (see, most recently, Case C-36/96 *Günaydin* v *Freistaat Bayern* [1997] ECR I-5143, paragraph 24, and Case C-98/96 *Ertanir* v *Land Hessen* [1997] ECR I-5179, paragraph 24).

20. Second, it should be borne in mind that the Court has consistently held that the rights which that provision confers on Turkish workers in regard to employment necessarily imply the existence of a corresponding right of residence for the person concerned, since otherwise the right of access to the labour market and the right to work as an employed person would be deprived of all effect (see, most recently, *Günaydin*, paragraph 26, and *Ertanir*, paragraph 26).

21. Third, it should be noted that, as is apparent from the actual wording of Article 6(1) of Decision No 1/80, that provision requires the person concerned to be a Turkish worker in a Member State, to be duly registered

as belonging to the labour force of the host Member State and to have been in legal employment there for a certain period.

22.   In order to give a useful reply to the national court to enable it to assess the relevance of the arguments relied on by the defendant in order to deny Mr Birden the benefit of the rights conferred by Decision No 1/80, those three concepts should be examined in turn.

The concept of worker

23.   As regards the first of those concepts, it should be recalled at the outset that the Court has consistently concluded from the wording of Article 12 of the EEC-Turkey Association Agreement and Article 36 of the additional protocol, signed on 23 November 1970, annexed to that Agreement and concluded by Council Regulation (EEC) No 2760/72 of 19 December 1972 (OJ 1973 C 113, p. 18), as well as from the objective of Decision No 1/80, that the principles enshrined in Articles 48, 49 and 50 of the EC Treaty must be extended, so far as possible, to Turkish workers who enjoy the rights conferred by Decision No 1/80 (see, to that effect, Case C-434/93 *Bozkurt* v *Staatssecretaris van Justitie* [1995] ECR I-1475, paragraphs 14, 19 and 20; Case C-171/95 *Tetik* v *Land Berlin* [1997] ECR I-329, paragraphs 20 and 28, and the judgments in *Günaydin*, paragraph 21, and *Ertanir*, paragraph 21).

24.   Reference should consequently be made to the interpretation of the concept of worker under Community law for the purposes of determining the scope of the same concept employed in Article 6(1) of Decision No 1/80.

25.   In that respect, the Court has consistently held that the concept of worker has a specific Community meaning and must not be interpreted narrowly. It must be defined in accordance with objective criteria which distinguish the employment relationship by reference to the rights and duties of the persons concerned. In order to be treated as a worker, a person must pursue an activity which is effective and genuine, to the exclusion of activities on such a small scale as to be regarded as purely marginal and ancillary. The essential feature of an employment relationship is that for a certain period of time a person performs services for and under the direction of another person in return for which he receives remuneration. By contrast, the nature of the legal relationship between the worker and the employer is not decisive for the purposes of determining whether a person is a worker within the meaning of Community law (see, as regards Article 48 of the Treaty, in particular, Case 66/85 *Lawrie-Blum* v *Land Baden-Württemberg* [1986] ECR 2121, paragraphs 16 and 17; Case 197/86 *Brown* v *Secretary of State for Scotland* [1988] ECR 3205, paragraph 21; Case C-357/89 *Raulin* [1992] ECR I-1027, paragraph 10; and, as regards Article 6(1) of Decision No 1/80, *Günaydin*, paragraph 31, and *Ertanir*, paragraph 43).

26. A Turkish national such as Mr Birden, who is employed on the basis of a law such as the BSHG, performs, as a subordinate, services for his employer in return for which he receives remuneration, thus satisfying the essential criteria of the employment relationship.

27. Since Mr Birden worked 38.5 hours per week and received net pay of DM 2 155.70 per month, in keeping, moreover, with the collective agreement applicable to workers in the Member State concerned, it cannot be argued that he pursued an activity which was purely marginal and ancillary.

28. That interpretation is not altered by the fact that the remuneration of the person concerned is provided using public funds since, by analogy with the case-law relating to Article 48 of the Treaty, neither the origin of the funds from which the remuneration is paid, nor the "sui generis" nature of the employment relationship under national law and the level of productivity of the person concerned can have any consequence in regard to whether or not the person is to be regarded as a worker (see, for example, Case 344/87 *Bettray* [1989] ECR 1621, paragraphs 15 and 16).

29. Contrary to the assertions of the German Government, that conclusion is also not affected by the fact that, in *Bettray*, the Court held that work which constitutes merely a means of rehabilitation or reintegration for the persons concerned cannot be regarded as a genuine and effective activity and concluded that such persons cannot be regarded as workers for the purposes of Community law (paragraphs 17 to 20).

30. As the Commission pointed out in its observations and the Advocate General stated at paragraphs 25 and 45 of his Opinion, the situation of a person such as the applicant in the main proceedings differs considerably from that at issue in *Bettray*. It is thus apparent from the reasoning of that judgment that that case concerned a person who, by reason of his addiction to drugs, had been recruited on the basis of a national law intended to provide work for persons who, for an indefinite period, are unable, by reason of circumstances related to their situation, to work under normal conditions; furthermore, the person concerned had not been selected on the basis of his ability to perform a certain activity but, to the contrary, had performed activities adapted to his physical and mental possibilities, in the framework of undertakings or work associations created specifically in order to achieve a social objective.

31. Under those circumstances, the conclusion reached by the Court in *Bettray*, according to which a person employed under a scheme such as that at issue in that case could not, on that basis alone, be regarded as a worker and the fact that that conclusion does not follow the general trend of the case-law concerning the interpretation of that concept in Community law (see paragraph 25 above) can be explained only by the particular characteristics of that case and it cannot therefore be applied

to a situation such as that of the applicant in the main proceedings, the features of which are not comparable.

32.   A person such as Mr Birden must consequently be regarded as a worker within the meaning of Article 6(1) of Decision No 1/80.

The concept of being duly registered as belonging to the labour force

33.   Next, in order to ascertain whether such a worker, recruited under an employment contract relating to the pursuit of a genuine and effective economic activity, is duly registered as belonging to the labour force of a Member State for the purposes of Article 6(1) of Decision No 1/80, it must be determined, in accordance with settled case-law (*Bozkurt*, paragraphs 22 and 23, *Günaydin*, paragraph 29, and *Ertanir*, paragraph 39), whether the legal relationship of employment of the person concerned can be located within the territory of a Member State or retains a sufficiently close link with that territory, taking account in particular of the place where the Turkish national was hired, the territory on or from which the paid activity is pursued and the applicable national legislation in the field of employment and social security law.

34.   In a situation such as that of the applicant in the main proceedings, that condition is undoubtedly satisfied, since the person concerned pursued a paid activity on the territory of the Member State whose authorities had offered him employment subject to the legislation of that State, *inter alia* its employment and social security law.

35.   However, the German Government contended that the employment contracts entered into with Mr Birden on the basis of Paragraph 19 of the BSHG had been limited to the temporary pursuit of a paid activity with a named employer.

36.   It should none the less be pointed out in that respect that, from January 1992, the Turkish worker concerned held a permit to work in Germany that was of unlimited duration.

37.   Furthermore, the Court has held that, although, as the law stands at present, Decision No 1/80 does not encroach upon the competence of the Member States to refuse Turkish nationals the right of entry into their territories and to take up first employment there and does not preclude those Member States, in principle, from regulating the conditions under which Turkish nationals work for up to one year as provided for in the first indent of Article 6(1) of that decision, none the less that provision cannot be construed as permitting a Member State to modify unilaterally the scope of the system of gradual integration of Turkish workers in the host State's labour force, by denying a worker who has been permitted to enter its territory and who has lawfully pursued a genuine and effective economic activity for a continuous period of more than one year with the same employer the rights which the three indents of that provision confer on him progressively according to the duration of his employment.

The effect of such an interpretation would be to render Decision No 1/80 meaningless and deprive it of any practical effect (see, to that effect, the judgment in *Günaydin*, paragraphs 36 to 38).

38. Accordingly the Member States have no power to make conditional or restrict the application of the precise and unconditional rights which that decision grants to Turkish nationals who satisfy its conditions, particularly since the general and unconditional wording of Article 6(1) does not permit the Member States to restrict the rights which that provision confers directly on Turkish workers (see, to that effect, *Günaydin*, paragraphs 39 and 40).

39. In those circumstances, the fact that the employment contracts offered to the person concerned by the public authorities were only temporary has no relevance for the purposes of interpreting Article 6(1) of Decision No 1/80, in so far as the activity pursued by him in the host Member State satisfies the conditions laid down by that provision.

40. The German Government also submitted that, even though Mr Birden received the usual remuneration, subject to income tax and the payment of compulsory social security contributions, for the work he performed and did not simultaneously receive social assistance and although, in accordance with the BSHG, he was thus in an employment relationship with his employer for the purposes of German employment law, the employment in question was none the less of an essentially social nature. That employment consisted of public utility work which, in other circumstances would not be carried out; it was financed by public funds and intended to improve the integration into working life of a limited group of persons unable to compete with most other job seekers. Those persons can therefore be distinguished from workers as a whole and consequently do not belong to the general labour force of the Member State concerned.

41. Likewise, the Commission submitted that a Turkish worker such as Mr Birden cannot be regarded as being duly registered as belonging to the labour force of a Member State within the meaning of Article 6(1) of Decision No 1/80, on the ground that that provision lays down two separate conditions, namely that the worker be duly registered as belonging to the labour force and that he be in legal employment. The first of those requirements should not be interpreted as referring to the lawful pursuit of a paid activity, since to do so would duplicate the second; it can therefore be regarded only as referring to the pursuit of a normal economic activity on the labour market, as opposed to employment created artificially and financed by the public authorities such as that undertaken by Mr Birden.

42. In that respect, it should be recalled, first, that a migrant Turkish worker – the applicant in the main proceedings – was recruited legally, within the terms of the requisite national permits and for a continuous period of two years, under an employment contract which involved the pursuit of a genuine and effective economic activity for the same employer in

return for the usual remuneration. In that respect, the legal position of a person such as Mr Birden is therefore no different from that of migrant Turkish workers in general working on the territory of the host Member State.

43. Second, in accordance with the case-law of the Court, the specific purpose which the paid employment in question sought to achieve is not capable of depriving a worker who satisfies the conditions laid down in Article 6(1) of the progressive rights which that provision confers upon him (*Günaydin*, paragraph 53).

44. It follows that a worker in Mr Birden's position, to whom a new contract of employment had been offered by his employer from 1 January 1996, was therefore entitled, in accordance with the first indent of Article 6(1) of Decision No 1/80, to continue working for that employer until, after three years, he had the possibility of changing employer within the same occupation pursuant to the second indent of that provision.

45. Furthermore, as regards a job offered under circumstances such as those in the present case, any other interpretation would be contradictory, in so far as it would amount to a refusal to maintain as a member of the labour force of the host Member State a Turkish national to whom that State had applied national legislation specifically intended to integrate the persons concerned into the labour force.

46. Furthermore, that national legislation itself provides that, in a situation such as that of the applicant in the main proceedings, who no longer received social assistance during the period in which he was pursuing an activity under the BSHG, the person concerned is in an employment relationship with his employer for the purposes of national law.

47. Third, it is apparent from a comparison of the language versions in which Decision No 1/80 was drawn up that the Dutch ("die tot de legale arbeidsmarkt van een Lid-Staat behoort" and "legale arbeid"), Danish ("med tilknytning til det lovlige arbejdsmarked i en bestemt medlemsstat" and "lovlig beskæftigelse") and Turkish ("… bir üye ülkenin yasal isgücü piyasasina nizamlara uygun bir surette …" and "yasal calismadan") versions use the same adjective ("legal") to describe both the labour force of a Member State and the employment pursued in that State. Although it does not use the same word in both respects, the English version ("duly registered as belonging to the labour force of a Member State" and "legal employment") undeniably has the same meaning.

48. It follows from those versions that entitlement to the rights enshrined in the three indents of Article 6(1) is subject to the condition that the worker complied with the legislation of the host Member State governing entry to its territory and pursuit of employment.

49. There is no doubt that a migrant Turkish worker such as Mr Birden satisfies that requirement, since it is not disputed that he legally entered the territory of the Member State concerned and occupied a post organised and financed by the public authorities of that State.

50. Both the French ("appartenant au marché régulier de l'emploi d'un … tat membre" and "emploi régulier") and Italian ("inserito nel regolare mercato del lavoro di uno Stato membro" and "regolare impiego") versions use the word "regular" twice. Finally, the German version ("der dem regulären Arbeitsmarkt eines Mitgliedstaats angehört" and "ordnungsgemässer Beschäftigung") is less clear, in so far as it uses two different expressions, the first of which corresponds to "regular" and the second more closely to "legal". However, those versions are clearly open to an interpretation consistent with that resulting from the other language versions, since the term "regular" can undoubtedly be understood, for the purposes of the uniform application of Community law, as a synonym for "legal"

51. Consequently, the concept of "being duly registered as belonging to the labour force" must be regarded as applying to all workers who have complied with the requirements laid down by law and regulation in the Member State concerned and are thus entitled to pursue an occupation in its territory. By contrast, contrary to the assertions of the German Government and the Commission, it cannot be interpreted as applying to the labour market in general as opposed to a specific market with a social objective supported by the public authorities.

52. That interpretation is, furthermore, confirmed by the objective of Decision No 1/80 which, according to the third recital in its preamble, seeks to improve, in the social field, the treatment accorded to workers and members of their families in relation to the arrangements introduced by Decision No 2/76 which the Council of Association set up by the Agreement establishing an Association between the European Economic Community and Turkey adopted on 20 December 1976. The provisions of Section 1 of Chapter II of Decision No 1/80, of which Article 6 forms part, thus constitute a further stage in securing freedom of movement for workers on the basis of Articles 48, 49 and 50 of the Treaty (see *Bozkurt*, paragraphs 14, 19 and 20, *Tetik*, paragraph 20, *Günaydin*, paragraphs 20 and 21, and *Ertanir*, paragraphs 20 and 21).

53. In view of that objective and the fact that Decision No 2/76 refers only to legal employment, the concept of being duly registered as belonging to the labour force of a Member State, used in Decision No 1/80 alongside that of legal employment, cannot be interpreted as further restricting the rights derived by workers from Article 6(1) of Decision No 1/80 on the ground that it sets out an additional condition, different from the condition that the person concerned be in legal employment for a certain period. To the contrary, that newly-introduced concept merely clarifies the requirement of the same nature already used in Decision No 2/76.

54. A Turkish worker such as Mr Birden must consequently be regarded as being duly registered as belonging to the labour force of a Member State for the purposes of Article 6(1) of Decision No 1/80.

The concept of legal employment

55. Finally as regards the question whether such a worker was in legal employment in the host Member State for the purposes of Article 6(1) of Decision No 1/80, it should be recalled that, according to settled case-law (judgments in Sevince, paragraph 30, *Bozkurt*, paragraph 26, and Case C-237/91 *Kus* v *Landeshauptstadt Wiesbaden* [1992] ECR I-6781, paragraphs 12 and 22), the legality of the employment presupposes a stable and secure situation as a member of the labour force of a Member State and, by virtue of this, implies the existence of an undisputed right of residence.

56. In *Sevince*, paragraph 31, the Court held that a Turkish worker was not in a stable and secure situation as a member of the labour force of a Member State during a period in which a decision refusing him the right of residence was suspended as a consequence of his appeal against that decision and he obtained authorisation, on a provisional basis pending the outcome of the dispute, to reside and be employed in the Member State in question.

57. Likewise, in *Kus*, paragraph 13, the Court held that a worker who has a right of residence only as a result of the effect of national legislation allowing a person to reside in the host country during the procedure for granting a residence permit does not satisfy that condition of stability, on the ground that the person concerned had obtained the rights to reside and work in that country on a provisional basis only pending a final decision on his right of residence.

58. The Court considered that periods during which the person concerned was employed could not be regarded as legal employment for the purposes of Article 6(1) of Decision No 1/80 so long as it was not definitely established that, during those periods, the worker had a legal right of residence. Otherwise, a judicial decision finally refusing him that right would be rendered nugatory and he would thus have been enabled to acquire the rights provided for in Article 6(1) during a period when he did not fulfil the conditions laid down in that provision (judgment in *Kus*, paragraph 16).

59. Finally, in Case C-285/95 *Kol* v *Land Berlin* [1997] ECR I-3069, paragraph 27, the Court held that periods in which a Turkish national was employed under a residence permit obtained only by means of fraudulent conduct on his part, which led to a conviction, were not based on a stable situation and such employment could not be regarded as having been secure in view of the fact that, during the periods in question, the person concerned was not legally entitled to a residence permit.

60. By contrast, in a case such as this, it must be pointed out that the Turkish worker's right of residence in the host Member State was never challenged and the person concerned was not in a precarious situation that could be called into question at any time: in January 1992, he had obtained a

permit to reside in Germany until 29 June 1995 together with an uncondi-tional work permit of unlimited duration and for an uninterrupted period from 1 January 1994 to 31 December 1995 he had lawfully pursued a genuine and effective activity for the same employer, so that his legal position was guaranteed for that whole period.

61. Such a worker must consequently be regarded as having been in legal employment in the Member State concerned for the purposes of Article 6(1) of Decision No 1/80, so that, in so far as he satisfies all the conditions of that provision, he may rely on the rights conferred by it.

62. In that respect, it should be pointed out that it is not disputed that when his employment contract expired on 31 December 1995, Mr Birden had entered into a new contract of employment, with the same employer, for an indefinite period from 1 January 1996. He therefore had a job available with the same employer within the meaning of the first indent of Article 6(1) of Decision No 1/80; the only reason that contract could not be put into effect was that he had not obtained an extension of his residence permit in the host Member State.

63. The foregoing interpretation cannot be affected by the fact that the two employment contracts awarded to Mr Birden in 1994 and in 1995 were for a limited period pursuant to the national legislation.

64. If the temporary nature of the employment contract was sufficient to raise doubts as to whether the employment of the person concerned was in fact legal, Member States would be able wrongly to deprive Turkish migrant workers whom they permitted to enter their territory and who have lawfully pursued an economic activity there for an uninterrupted period of at least one year of rights on which they are entitled to rely directly under Article 6(1) of Decision No 1/80 (see paragraphs 37 to 39) above.

65. Likewise, the fact that Mr Birden's residence permit was issued to him only for a fixed period is not relevant, since it is settled case-law that the rights conferred on Turkish workers by Article 6(1) of Decision No 1/80 are accorded irrespective of whether or not the authorities of the host Member State have issued a specific administrative document, such as a work permit or residence permit (see, to that effect, the judgments in *Bozkurt*, paragraphs 29 and 30, *Günaydin*, paragraph 49, and *Ertanir*, paragraph 55).

66. Furthermore, the fact that, in a case such as the present, work and residence permits were granted to the worker only after his marriage to a German national does not affect that interpretation, even though the marriage was subsequently dissolved.

67. According to settled case-law, Article 6(1) of Decision No 1/80 does not make the recognition of the rights it confers on Turkish workers subject to any condition connected with the reason the right to enter, work or reside was initially granted (*Kus*, paragraphs 21 to 23, *Günaydin*, para-graph 52, and, by analogy, Case C-355/93 *Eroglu v Land Baden-Württemberg* [1994] ECR I-5113, paragraph 22).

68.   A Turkish worker such as Mr Birden must consequently be regarded as having been in legal employment in the host Member State for the purposes of Article 6(1) of Decision No 1/80.

69.   In view of all the foregoing considerations, the answer to the question referred by the Verwaltungsgericht der Freien Hansestadt Bremen must be that Article 6(1) of Decision No 1/80 is to be interpreted as follows:

> A Turkish national who has lawfully pursued a genuine and effective economic activity in a Member State under an unconditional work permit for an uninterrupted period of more than one year for the same employer, in return for which he received the usual remuneration, is a worker duly registered as belonging to the labour force of that Member State and in legal employment there within the meaning of that provision.
>
> In so far as he has available a job with the same employer, a Turkish national in that situation is thus entitled to demand the renewal of his residence permit in the host Member State, even if, pursuant to the legislation of that Member State, the activity pursued by him was restricted to a limited group of persons, was intended to facilitate their integration into working life and was financed by public funds.

Costs

70.   The costs incurred by the German, Greek and French Governments, and by the Commission, which have submitted observations to the Court, are not recoverable. Since these proceedings are, for the parties to the main proceedings, a step in the proceedings pending before the national court, the decision on costs is a matter for that court.

On those grounds, THE COURT in answer to the question referred to it by the Verwaltungsgericht der Freien Hansestadt Bremen, by order of 9 December 1996, hereby rules:

Article 6(1) of Decision No 1/80 of 19 September 1980 on the development of the Association, adopted by the Association Council established by the Association Agreement between the European Economic Community and Turkey is to be interpreted as follows:

> A Turkish national who has lawfully pursued a genuine and effective economic activity in a Member State under an unconditional work permit for an uninterrupted period of more than one year for the same employer, in return for which he received the usual remuneration, is a worker duly registered as belonging to the labour force of that Member State and in legal employment there within the meaning of that provision.
>
> In so far as he has available a job with the same employer, a Turkish national in that situation is thus entitled to demand the renewal of his

residence permit in the host Member State, even if, pursuant to the legislation of that Member State, the activity pursued by him was restricted to a limited group of persons, was intended to facilitate their integration into working life and was financed by public funds.

Mancini   Murray   Kapteyn
              Ragnemalm   Schintgen

Delivered in open court in Luxembourg on 26 November 1998.

R. Grass   P.J.G. Kapteyn
Registrar   President of the Sixth Chamber

Judgment of the Court of Justice of the European Communities

(Sixth Chamber)
19 November 1998

<small>Haydar Akman v Oberkreisdirektor des Rheinisch-Bergischen-Kreises</small>

Case C-210/97,

REFERENCE to the Court under Article 177 of the EC Treaty by the Verwaltungsgericht Köln (Germany) for a preliminary ruling in the proceedings pending before that court between joined party: **Vertreter des öffentlichen Interesses beim Verwaltungsgericht Köln**, on the interpretation of the second paragraph of Article 7 of Decision No 1/80 of 19 September 1980 on the development of the Association, adopted by the Association Council established by the Association Agreement between the European Economic Community and Turkey,

THE COURT (Sixth Chamber),

composed of: P.J.G. Kapteyn, President of the Chamber, G.F. Mancini, H. Ragnemalm, R. Schintgen (Rapporteur) and K.M. Ioannou, Judges,

Advocate General: P. Léger,
Registrar: H.A. Rühl, Principal Administrator,

after considering the written observations submitted on behalf of:
- Mr Akman, by R. Gutmann, Rechtsanwalt, Stuttgart,
- the German Government, by E. Röder, Ministerialrat at the Federal Ministry of the Economy, and C.-D. Quassowski, Regierungsdirektor at the same Ministry, acting as Agents,
- the Greek Government, by A. Samoni-Rantou, Special Assistant Legal Adviser in the Community Legal Affairs Department of the Ministry of Foreign Affairs, and L. Pnevmatikou, specialist technical adviser in that department, acting as Agents, and
- the Commission of the European Communities, by P.J. Kuijper and P. Hillenkamp, Legal Advisers, acting as Agents,

having regard to the Report for the Hearing,

after hearing the oral observations of Mr Akman, represented by R. Gutmann; of the German Government, represented by C.-D. Quassowski; of the Austrian Government, represented by G. Hesse, Magister in the Federal Ministry of Foreign Affairs, acting as Agent; and of the Commission, represented by P. Hillenkamp, at the hearing on 14 May 1998, after hearing the Opinion of the Advocate General at the sitting on 9 July 1998, gives the following Judgment

1. By order of 6 May 1997, received at the Court on 2 June 1997, the Verwaltungsgericht Köln (Administrative Court, Cologne) referred to the Court for a preliminary ruling under Article 177 of the EC Treaty a question on the interpretation of the second paragraph of Article 7 of Decision No 1/80 of the Association Council of 19 September 1980 on the development of the Association (hereinafter "Decision No 1/80"). The Association Council was established by the Agreement creating an Association between the European Economic Community and Turkey, signed on 12 September 1963 in Ankara by the Republic of Turkey by the Member States of the EEC and by the Community, and concluded, approved and confirmed on behalf of the Community by Council Decision 64/732/EEC of 23 December 1963 (OJ 1973 C 113, p. 1).

2. That question arose in proceedings brought by Mr Akman, a Turkish national, against the Oberkreisdirektor des Rheinisch-Bergischen-Kreises (Chief Administrative Officer of the Rheinisch-Bergischer-Kreis administrative district), concerning the refusal to grant him a residence permit of indefinite duration in Germany.

3. It appears from the papers in the main proceedings that Mr Akman was given leave to enter Germany in 1979 and there obtained a residence permit of limited duration for the purpose of training as an engineer.

4. Initially, he resided at Gross Gerau with his father, who was legally employed in Germany from 21 May 1971 to 31 December 1985. On 1 February 1986, his contract of employment in Germany having come to an end, Mr Akman's father returned to Turkey.

5. In 1981, Mr Akman moved to Remscheid, still in Germany, as Gross Gerau was too far from the establishment at which he was following his course of training.

6. His residence permit was renewed on a number of occasions in order to enable him to continue his training in Germany.

7. On 16 January 1991 Mr Akman was granted a residence permit unfettered by any restrictions as to duration or otherwise.

8. He was then employed part-time in various capacities by two employers successively, but it is common ground that he does not meet the requirements for entitlement to the rights provided for in Article 6(1) of Decision No 1/80.

9. That provision, which forms part of Chapter II ("Social Provisions"), Section 1 ("Questions relating to employment and the free movement of workers"), provides as follows:

"(1) Subject to Article 7 on free access to employment for members of his family, a Turkish worker duly registered as belonging to the labour force of a Member State:

– shall be entitled in that Member State, after one year's legal employment, to the renewal of his permit to work for the same employer, if a job is available;

-    shall be entitled in that Member State, after three years of legal employment and subject to the priority to be given to workers of Member States of the Community, to respond to another offer of employment, with an employer of his choice, made under normal conditions and registered with the employment services of that State, for the same occupation;
-    shall enjoy free access in that Member State to any paid employment of his choice, after four years of legal employment."

10. On 6 April 1993, Mr Akman successfully completed his engineering course in Germany.

11. On 24 June 1993, he applied for a residence permit of unlimited duration.

12. However, by decision of 25 August 1993, the German authorities granted him only a limited residence permit, valid until 25 August 1994, for the purpose of completing a further course of study.

13. Mr Akman appealed against that decision to the Verwaltungsgericht Köln, relying on the second paragraph of Article 7 of Decision No 1/80.

14. Article 7, which also forms part of Chapter II, Section 1, of Decision No 1/80, provides:

"The members of the family of a Turkish worker duly registered as belonging to the labour force of a Member State, who have been authorised to join him:
-    subject to the priority to be given to workers of Member States of the Community; to respond to any offer of employment after they have been legally resident for at least three years in that Member State;
-    shall enjoy free access to any paid employment of their choice provided they have been legally resident there for at least five years.

Children of Turkish workers who have completed a course of vocational training in the host country may respond to any offer of employment there, irrespective of the length of time they have been resident in that Member State, provided one of their parents has been legally employed in the Member State concerned for at least three years".

15. In Mr Akman's view, the second paragraph of that article entitles him, in the Member State in which he has completed his training and in which his father was legally employed for more than three years, to respond to offers of employment made to him and to claim a residence permit for the purpose of actually taking up employment.

16. The defendant authority, however, argues that the conditions laid down by that provision are not met in Mr Akman's case because his father,

whilst having been legally employed in the Member State concerned for over 14 years, was no longer working there at the time when his son wished to gain access to the employment market.

17. The Verwaltungsgericht found that Mr Akman had no entitlement to be issued with an unlimited residence permit under German law. It wondered, however, whether he might not be in a more favorable position under the second paragraph of Article 7 of Decision No 1/80.

18. It raised, in that context, the question whether that provision implies that, at the time when the child has completed vocational training and wishes to respond to an offer of employment, the parent employed as a worker must still be present; and indeed perhaps in salaried employment; in the host Member State, or whether on the contrary it is sufficient that he should have been legally employed there, at some earlier stage, for at least three years. In the Verwaltungsgericht's view, the wording of the provision ("has been ... employed") tends to favor the latter interpretation.

19. Considering, however, that an interpretation of that provision of Decision No 1/80 was necessary in order to settle the dispute before it, the Verwaltungsgericht Köln stayed proceedings and requested a preliminary ruling by the Court on the following question:

> "For a child of a Turkish worker to have the right to extension of his residence permit, which, according to the judgment of the Court of Justice in Case C-355/93 *Eroglu* v *Land Baden-Württemberg*, arises from the second paragraph of Article 7 of Decision No 1/80 of the EEC-Turkey Association Council on the development of the Association, must the employed parent still be resident in Germany, or even still be in an employment relationship, at the time when the child has completed his course of vocational training and wishes to take up an offer of employment, or is that provision sufficiently complied with if the Turkish parent was legally employed *at an earlier time* for at least three years?"

20. When the question is considered, it must be noted that, according to the third recital in its preamble, Decision No 1/80 is intended to improve, in the social field, the treatment accorded to workers and members of their families in relation to the arrangements introduced by Decision No 2/76, which was adopted on 20 December 1976 by the Association Council established by the Association Agreement between the European Economic Community and Turkey. The provisions of Chapter II, Section 1, of Decision No 1/80 thus constitute a further stage in securing freedom of movement for workers on the basis of Articles 48, 49 and 50 of the EC Treaty (see, in particular, Case C-434/93 *Bozkurt* v *Staatssecretaris van Justitie* [1995] ECR I-1475, paragraphs 14 and 19, and Case C-171/95 *Tetik* v *Land Berlin* [1997] ECR I-329, paragraph 20).

21. Within the structure of Decision No 1/80, that section regulates in particular the rights of Turkish nationals as regards employment in the host

Member State. It draws a distinction between the situation of Turkish workers who have been legally employed in the Member State concerned for a specified period (Article 6) and that of members of the families of such workers in the territory of the host Member State (Article 7). Within the latter category it distinguishes further between members of a worker's family who have been authorised to join him in the host Member State and who have been legally resident there for a specified period (Article 7, first paragraph) and the children of such workers who have completed a course of vocational training in the Member State concerned (Article 7, second paragraph).

22. The question raised by the Verwaltungsgericht concerns the situation of a Turkish national who, as the child of a migrant Turkish worker having himself been legally in salaried employment in a Member State for some 14 years, has been authorised to enter that State for the purpose of pursuing a course of study and who, on completion of that training, applies for a residence permit in accordance with the second paragraph of Article 7 of Decision No 1/80 in order to be able to take up an offer of employment made to him in the host Member State. The national court has noted that the individual concerned, although he has himself been legally employed for a certain period in the Member State in question, cannot claim the rights conferred by Article 6 of the same decision on a Turkish worker who is already part of the labour force in a Member State, because he does not meet the conditions laid down in that provision.

23. With regard to the second paragraph of Article 7, with which the national court's question is concerned, it must first be borne in mind that the Court has held that, like Article 6(1) (see, primarily, Case C-192/89 *Sevince* v *Staatssecretaris van Justitie* [1990] ECR I-3461, paragraph 26) and the first paragraph of Article 7 (Case C-351/95 *Kadiman* v *Freistaat Bayern* [1997] ECR I-2133, paragraph 28), the second paragraph of Article 7 of Decision No 1/80 has direct effect in the Member States, so that Turkish nationals fulfilling the conditions which it lays down may directly rely on the rights conferred on them by that provision (Case C-355/93 *Eroglu* v *Land Baden-Württemberg* [1994] ECR I-5113, paragraph 17).

24. Secondly, it must be noted that the rights conferred by the second paragraph of Article 7 on the child of a Turkish worker with regard to employment in the Member State concerned necessarily imply the existence of a concomitant right of residence for that child, without which the right to have access to the employment market and to actually take up salaried employment would be rendered totally ineffective (*Eroglu*, cited above, paragraphs 20 and 23).

25. Thirdly, the wording of the second paragraph of Article 7 makes it clear that the right conferred on the child of a Turkish worker to respond to any offer of employment in the host Member State is dependent on two

conditions: the child in question must have completed a course of vocational training in the Member State concerned and one of his or her parents must have been legally employed there for at least three years.

26.   The German and Greek Governments have raised the preliminary objection that a Turkish national in the position of Mr Akman does not have the status of a child of a Turkish worker for the purposes of the second paragraph of Article 7 of Decision No 1/80 because, in substance, his father had definitively ceased to be part of the labour force of the host Member State at the time when his son wished to claim rights as the child of a Turkish worker.

27.   In that regard, it need merely be pointed out that it is not disputed that Mr Akman's father was legally in salaried employment in the host Member State for over 14 years, and he must therefore be regarded as a worker within the meaning of the provision in question. The argument put forward by the German and Greek Governments thus cannot be accepted.

28.   Turning next to the two conditions referred to in paragraph 25 above, it must be noted that in a case such as that of Mr Akman the first of those conditions is undoubtedly met, since he has completed a course of study in engineering in the host Member State.

29.   With regard to the second condition, it must be determined whether the right of access to the employment market and the concomitant right of residence under the second paragraph of Article 7 of Decision No 1/80 are dependent on the presence; and indeed perhaps the employment; of the parent in the host Member State at the time when, on completion of a course of vocational training, the child wishes to respond to an offer of employment, or whether, on the contrary, it is sufficient that the parent has in the past been legally in salaried employment in that Member State for at least three years, without its being necessary for the parent still to be there when the child wishes to gain access to the employment market there.

30.   The first point to be noted here is that, as the national court has itself observed, the verb used in the condition in question is in a past tense in most of the language versions in which Decision No 1/80 was drafted ("beschäftigt war" in German, "ait ... exercé" in French, "abbia ... esercitato" in Italian and "heeft gewerkt" in Dutch), whereas the first paragraph of Article 7 uses a present tense in those languages ("ihren ... Wohnsitz haben", "résident", "risiedono", "wonen"). That use of different tenses thus suggests that the relevant requirement under the second paragraph of Article 7 must have been fulfilled at some earlier stage than that at which the child has completed a course of vocational training.

31.   However, some doubt is still raised by the preposition used in certain language versions; whilst the word "gedurende" in Dutch does not necessarily suggest a continuing condition, terms such as "depuis" in French and "seit" in German could on the contrary be interpreted as requiring

the parent's employment, having commenced in the past, to be still continuing at the time when the child meets the further condition relating to the completion of a course of vocational training.

32. Since an unequivocal answer to the question raised cannot be gleaned by interpreting the letter of the text in question, it is necessary to view the second paragraph of Article 7 in its context and to interpret it in terms of its spirit and purpose.

33. Here, it must be borne in mind that, as already stated in paragraph 21 above, the second paragraph of Article 7 of Decision No 1/80 specifically regulates the right of children of a Turkish worker to gain access to the employment market.

34. As members of the family of a Turkish worker, such children may also claim rights in the field of employment under the first paragraph of Article 7.

35. It is, however, clear that the conditions laid down by the first paragraph for all family members are stricter than those laid down in the second paragraph, which apply to children alone.

36. Thus, the rights of family members in matters of employment depend on the period of residence in the host Member State and, initially, workers of Member States of the Community enjoy preferential access to the employment market. No such condition is imposed, however, on children by the second paragraph of Article 7. That latter provision even expressly provides that the rights which it confers on children of workers are not to depend on the length of time they have been resident in the Member State concerned. It is further clear from the first phrase of Article 6(1) of Decision No 1/80 that Article 7 grants family members; and thus, in particular, children; "free access to employment" in the Turkish worker's host Member State.

37. Nor, furthermore, does the second paragraph of Article 7 require; unlike the first paragraph; that the children should have been authorised to join the parent in the host Member State (see also, to the same effect, *Eroglu*, cited above, paragraph 22).

38. Consequently, the second paragraph of Article 7 is a more favorable provision than the first and is intended to provide specific treatment for children, as opposed to other members of the family of a Turkish worker, with a view to facilitating their entry into the employment market following completion of a course of vocational training, the objective being the achievement by progressive stages of freedom of movement for workers, in accordance with the aims of Decision No 1/80 (see paragraph 20 above).

39. In those circumstances, the provision must not be interpreted strictly and cannot, failing any clear indication to that effect, be construed as requiring the Turkish migrant worker still to be employed in the host Member State at the time when his child wishes to gain access to the employment market there.

40.   As the Advocate General has observed at point 56 of his Opinion, that finding is borne out by Article 9 of Decision No 1/80, which provides: "Turkish children residing legally in a Member State of the Community with their parents who are or have been legally employed in that Member State, shall be admitted to courses of general education, apprenticeship and vocational training under the same educational entry qualifications as the children of nationals of that Member State.

They may in that Member State be eligible to benefit from the advantages provided for under the national legislation in this area."

41.   That provision, which confers on Turkish children a right of access without discrimination to education and training in the host Member State, prior to the right of access to employment under the second paragraph of Article 7, does not require that one of their parents be legally employed at the moment when they wish to exercise the rights thus conferred on them; on the contrary, it specifically states that the fact that the parents no longer work in the State in question is not such as to deprive the children of the rights they derive thereunder.

42.   *A fortiori*, the requirement of present employment on the part of the parent cannot be imposed on completion of the child's vocational training without seriously undermining the coherence of the system established by Chapter II, Section 1, of Decision No 1/80.

43.   It follows, moreover, from what is stated in paragraph 37 above that, unlike the first paragraph (see *Kadiman*, cited above, in particular at paragraph 36), the second paragraph of Article 7 is not designed to create conditions conducive to family unity in the host Member State.

44.   The provision with which the national court's question is concerned consequently cannot be interpreted as making the child's right to respond to any offer of employment conditional upon the parent's residing in the Member State in question at the time when the child wishes to take up employment there following completion of vocational training.

45.   As the Commission has cogently argued, the child of a Turkish migrant worker legally employed for at least three years in a Member State, who is himself legally resident in that Member State, has completed training there and is then offered an opportunity to work there, is no longer at that stage to be regarded as depending on the presence of one of his parents since, on gaining access to the employment market, he is no longer materially dependent on them but is able to provide for his own needs.

46.   Since the second paragraph of Article 7 is in no way intended to provide the conditions for family unity, it would be unreasonable to require, in a situation such as that of the case in the main proceedings, that the Turkish migrant worker should continue to reside in the host Member State even after his employment relationship there has ceased, the consequence of his not doing so being to jeopardise the right to employment of his child

who has completed training and who, by responding to an offer of employment, has an opportunity to become independent.

47. Having regard to the spirit and purpose of the provision in question and to the context of which it forms part, the second condition laid down in the second paragraph of Article 7 of Decision No 1/80 can thus only be construed as requiring merely that the parent should have been legally in salaried employment for at least three years in the host Member State at some stage prior to the date on which his child completes a course of vocational training there.

48. It must be added that the argument put forward at the hearing by the German Government, to the effect that where a Turkish worker has already returned to his home country at the time when his child has the opportunity of gaining access to the employment market, that child may take up salaried employment in the host Member State only under the strict conditions laid down in Article 6(1) of Decision No 1/80, disregards the fact that Article 6(1) applies subject to the provisions of Article 7 on free access to employment for members of the worker's family.

49. Such an interpretation would, moreover, wholly negate the effectiveness of the second paragraph of Article 7 by wrongly preventing Turkish children who have completed a course of vocational training in a Member State from enjoying the rights to which they are directly entitled pursuant to a special provision specifically conferring on them more favorable conditions as regards employment in that State.

50. As the law stands at present, Article 6(1) of Decision No 1/80 does not detract from the power which the Member States have to refuse a Turkish national the right to take up employment in their territory for the first time, nor does it in principle preclude them from regulating the conditions for such employment during the period of one year specified in its first indent. The three indents of Article 6(1) thus make entitlement to the rights which they confer in progressive stages on a Turkish migrant worker, depending on the length of time he has been in salaried employment, subject to the condition that the individual concerned should already be duly registered as belonging to the labour force of the Member State concerned. Article 7, on the other hand, as already pointed out at paragraph 36 above, provides for a right of free access to employment for Turkish nationals legally resident in the host Member State: either for family members in general after a specified period of legal residence on the basis of family unification with a Turkish worker (first paragraph); or for the children of such a worker irrespective of the length of time they have been resident but following completion of training in the State in which one of the parents has been employed for a certain period (second paragraph).

51. In the light of all the foregoing considerations, the answer to the question raised by the Verwaltungsgericht Köln must be that the second paragraph of Article 7 of Decision No 1/80 must be interpreted as follows:

a Turkish national such as the plaintiff in the main proceedings is entitled to respond to any offer of employment in the host Member State after having completed a course of vocational training there, and consequently to be issued with a residence permit, when one of his parents has in the past been legally employed in that State for at least three years; however, it is not required that the parent in question should still work or be resident in the Member State in question at the time when his child wishes to gain access to the employment market there.

Costs

52.   The costs incurred by the German, Greek and Austrian Governments and by the Commission, which have submitted observations to the Court, are not recoverable. Since these proceedings are, for the parties to the main proceedings, a step in the action pending before the national court, the decision on costs is a matter for that court.

On those grounds, THE COURT in answer to the question referred to it by the Verwaltungsgericht Köln by order of 6 May 1997, hereby rules:

The second paragraph of Article 7 of Decision No 1/80 of 19 September 1980, on the development of the Association, adopted by the Association Council established by the Agreement creating an Association between the European Economic Community and Turkey must be interpreted as follows:

a Turkish national such as the plaintiff in the main proceedings is entitled to respond to any offer of employment in the host Member State after having completed a course of vocational training there, and consequently to be issued with a residence permit, when one of his parents has in the past been legally employed in that State for at least three years;

however, it is not required that the parent in question should still work or be resident in the Member State in question at the time when his child wishes to gain access to the employment market there.

Mancini	Ragnemalm	Kapteyn
Schintgen		Ioannou

Delivered in open court in Luxembourg on 19 November 1998.

R. Grass   P.J.G. Kapteyn
Registrar   President of the Sixth Chamber

Judgment of the Court of Justice of the European Communities

(Sixth Chamber)
30 September 1997

KASIM ERTANIR -V- LAND HESSEN

Case C-98/96,

REFERENCE to the Court under Article 177 of the EC Treaty by the Verwaltungsgericht Darmstadt (Germany) for a preliminary ruling in the proceedings pending before that court on the interpretation of Article 6 of Decision No 1/80 of 19 September 1980 on the development of the Association, adopted by the Association Council established by the Association Agreement between the European Economic Community and Turkey,

THE COURT (Sixth Chamber),

composed of: G.F. Mancini, President of the Chamber, J.L. Murray, P.J.G. Kapteyn, H. Ragnemalm and R. Schintgen (Rapporteur), Judges,

Advocate General: M.B. Elmer,
Registrar: H.A. Rühl, Principal Administrator,

after considering the written observations submitted on behalf of:
- the German Government, by E. Röder, Ministerialrat in the Federal Ministry of Economic Affairs, and S. Maass, Regierungsrätin zur Anstellung in the same ministry, acting as Agents,
- the Commission of the European Communities, by J. Sack, Legal Adviser, and B. Brandtner, of its Lcoal Service, acting as Agents,

having regard to the Report for the Hearing,

after hearing the oral observations of Mr Ertanir, represented by B. Münch, of the Heidelberg Bar, the German Government, represented by E. Röder, and the Commission, represented by J. Sack and B. Brandtner, at the hearing on 6 March 1997,

after hearing the Opinion of the Advocate General at the sitting on 29 April 1997, gives the following Judgment

1. By order of 29 February 1996, received at the Court on 26 March 1996, the Verwaltungsgericht (Administrative Court), Darmstadt, referred to the Court for a preliminary ruling under Article 177 of the EC Treaty three questions on the interpretation of Article 6 of Decision No 1/80 of the Council of Association of 19 September 1980 on the development

of the Association (hereinafter "Decision No 1/80"). The Council of Association was set up by the Agreement establishing an Association between the European Economic Community and Turkey, signed at Ankara on 12 September 1963 by the Republic of Turkey and by the Member States of the EEC and the Community, and concluded, approved and confirmed on behalf of the Community by Council Decision 64/732/EEC of 23 December 1963 (OJ 1973 C 113, p. 1).

2.   The questions were raised in the course of a dispute between Mr Ertanir, a Turkish national, and Land Hessen, concerning the refusal to extend his permit to reside in Germany.

3.   According to the file on the case in the main proceedings, Mr Ertanir was permitted in April 1991 to enter Germany, where he obtained a temporary residence permit valid until 1 August 1991 allowing him to work as a chef specializing in Turkish cuisine in the Ratskeller Restaurant in Weinheim.

4.   Despite the fact that he had obtained a work permit which did not expire until April 1992, the competent authorities refused to extend his residence permit on the around that, Under Paragraph 4(4) of the Arbeitsaufenthalteverordnung (Regulation on residence for the purpose of employment) of 18 December 1990 (Bundesgesetzblatt I, p. 2994), specialist chefs permitted to work in Germany must be nationals of the country in the cuisine of which the restaurant specializes, whereas the restaurant in question specialized essentially in Greek cuisine.

5.   Subsequently, however, they agreed to allow him to resume employment as a specialist chef in the same restaurant. Mr Ertanir, who had meantime returned to his country of origin, therefore returned to Germany on 14 April 1992. It is common ground that his attention was drawn on several occasions to the fact that under German law specialist chefs were permitted to reside in Germany for no more than a total of three years.

6.   Mr Ertanir remained in Germany under an entry visa valid for three months and subsequently a residence permit which expired on 13 April 1993 but was extended to 13 April 1994. However, it was not until 19 April 1994 that he applied for a further extension of his residence permit.

7.   Despite that delay of six days., the competent authorities extended the residence permit to 14 April 1995, pointing out again, however, that the total duration of his residence could not exceed three years, as provided for by the German legislation on specialist chefs.

8.   Every residence permit issued to Mr Ertanir bore a remark to the effect that the permit to reside in Germany would expire at the end of his employment as specialist chef in the restaurant which had engaged him.

9.   Mr Ertanir was employed at the Ratskeller Restaurant, Weinhelm, under a work permit which was valid initially until 23 April 1993. On 13 May 1993, that permit was extended for the period from 24 April 1993 to

23 April 1994. On 6 May 1994, it was renewed for the period 24 April 1994 to 23 April 1996.

10. On 13 April 1995 he applied for his residence permit to be extended for two years.

11. His application was rejected on 17 July 1995 on the ground that under German law residence permits for specialist chefs could be granted only for a maximum period of three years and that under a decree of 3 February 1995 issued by the Ministry of the Interior for Hessen Decision No 1/80 did not apply to specialist chefs.

12. The dispute was referred to the Verwaltungsgericht Dannstadt, which considers that Mr Ertanir has exhausted the maximum of three years' residence to which specialist chefs are entitled Under Paragraph 4(4) of the Arbeitsaufenthalteverordnung of 18 December 1990 and that an extension of his residence permit is not possible under any other provision of German law. However, it is uncertain whether Mr Ertanir may not claim a right of residence under Article 6(1) of Decision No 1/80.

13. Article 6(1), which appears in Chapter 11 (Social provisions), Section 1 (Questions relating to employment and the free movement of workers), of Decision No 1/80 is worded as follows:

"1. Subject to Article 7 on free access to employment for members of his family, a Turkish worker duly registered as belonging to the labour force of a Member State:
    – shall be entitled in that Member State, after one year's legal employment, to the renewal of his permit to work for the same employer, if a job is available;
    – shall be entitled in that Member State, after three years of legal employment and subject to the priority to be given to workers of Member States of the Community, to respond to another offer of employment, with an employer of his choice, made under normal conditions and registered with the employment services of that State, for the same occupation;
    – shall enjoy free access in that Member State to any paid employment of his choice, after four years of legal employment.

2. Annual holidays and absences for reasons of maternity or an accident at work or short periods of sickness shall be treated as periods of legal employment. Periods of involuntary unemployment duly certified by the relevant authorities and long absences on account of sickness shall not be treated as periods of legal employment, but shall not affect rights acquired as the result of the preceding period of employment.

3. The procedures for applying paragraphs 1 and 2 shall be those established under national rules."

14. The Verwaltungsgericht Darmstadt is uncertain first of all whether periods of unauthorized residence or periods without a residence permit, occurring after the first stage provided for in the first indent of Article 6(1) of

Decision No 1/80, but which are not treated as periods of legal employment under Article 6(2) of that decision, result in the qualifying period under Article 6(1) continuing, to run on the date on which authorized residence is resumed or the work permit extended, without rights that have already arisen being affected thereby, or whether, on the contrary, such periods cause rights that have hitherto arisen to be extinguished. Mr Ertanir's work permit was extended twice with retroactive effect after expiry and it appears that in April 1994 he failed to apply for the extension of his residence permit within the requisite time-limit. The national court points out that in Germany the employer is in a position to ensure that an application for extension is submitted to the employment authorities in good time and that it is normal practice, even in cases where an application for extension has been submitted in good time, not to extend the work permit until after expiry of the authorized period. However, responsibility for ensuring that a residence permit is extended in due time lies exclusively with the holder.

15.   The Verwaltungsgericht Darmstadt seeks to ascertain, next, whether a Turkish national who holds work and residence permits granted to him for the purpose of employment as a specialist chef is duly registered as belonging to the labour force of a Member State within the meaning of Article 6(1) of Decision No 1/80 even where he was aware from the beginning of his residence in that Member State that the residence permit was granted only in respect of employment with a specific employer, and where the competent authorities pointed out to him that the residence permit could not be extended beyond a maximum of three years.

16.   Finally, the court seeks to ascertain whether, in the light of paragraph 25 of Case C-237/91 *Kus* v *Landeshauptstadt Wiesbaden* [1992] ECR 1-6781, according to which Decision No 1/80 does not encroach upon the competence retained by the Member States to regulate both the entry into their territories of Turkish nationals and the conditions under which they may take up their first employment, Article 6(3) of that decision allows the Member States to create rights of residence that do not from the outset include the benefit of Article 6(1) of Decision No 1/80.

17.   Taking the view that a decision on the case accordingly required an interpretation of that article, the Verwaltungsgericht Darmstadt stayed proceedings and referred the following three questions to the Court of Justice for a preliminary ruling:

"1.   What are the consequences, for the maintenance of work and residence permits, of interruptions in lawful residence or periods of work without a work permit with regard to rights that have already arisen under Article 6(1) of Decision No 1/80 of the EEC No 1/80 of the EEC-Turkey Association Council on the development of the Association in so far as such periods are not treated as periods of legal employment under Article 6(2) of Decision No 1/80?

2.   Is a Turkish employee who holds work and residence permits

entitling him to work as a specialist chef duly registered as belonging to the labour force of a Member State within the meaning of Article 6(1) of Decision No 1/80 even if he was aware from the beginning of his residence in that Member State that he would be granted a residence permit only for a total period of three years and only to do specific work for a named employer?

3.   If the Court of Justice should take the view that a person as described in Question 2 is duly registered as belonging to the labour force of a Member State, does the power conferred by Article 6(3) of Decision No 1/80 entitle Member States to create rights of residence that do not from the outset confer the benefit of Article 6(1) of Decision No 1/80?

18.   It should be observed at the Outset that the first question presupposes that a Turkish migrant worker such as the applicant in the main proceedings falls within the scope of Article 6 of Decision No 1/80. The second and third questions should therefore be answered first, since that problem forms their subject-matter. Furthermore, in view of the link between the second and third questions, they should be considered together.

The second and third questions

19.   By its second and third questions, the national court seeks first of all to ascertain whether Article 6(3) of Decision No 1/80 is to be interpreted as permitting Member States to adopt national legislation which excludes at the outset whole categories of Turkish migrant workers. such as specialist chefs, from the rights conferred by the three indents of Article 6(1). It then asks whether a Turkish national is duly registered as belonging to the labour force of a Member State and is leally employed. within the meaning of Article 6(1) of Decision No 1/80, so that he may seek the renewal of his permit to reside in the host Member State, even though he was advised when the work and residence permits were granted that they were granted for a maximum of three years and only for specific work, in this case as a specialist chef, for a specific employer.

20.   It should be observed, *in limine*, that according to the third recital in its preamble, Decision No 1/80 seeks to improve, in the social field, the treatment accorded to workers and members of their families in relation to the arrangements introduced by Decision No 2/76 which the Council of Association set up by the Agreement establishing an Association between the European Economic Community and Turkey adopted on 20 December 1976.

21.   The provisions of Section 1 of Chapter II of Decision No 1/80, of which Article 6 forms part, thus constitute a further stage in securing freedom of movement for workers on the basis of Articles 48, 49 and 50 of the Treaty. The Court has accordingly considered it essential to extend, so far as possible, the principles enshrined in those Treaty articles to Turkish

workers who enjoy the rights conferred by Decision No 1/80 (see the Judgments in Case C-434/93 *Bozkurt* v *Staatssecretaris van Justitie* [1995] ECR I-1475, paragraphs 14, 19 and 20, and Case C-171/95 *Tetik* v *Land Berlin* [1997] ECR I-329, paragraph 20).

22. As the law now stands, however, Turkish nationals are not entitled to move freely within the Community but merely enjoy certain rights in the host Member State whose territory they have lawfully entered and where they have been in legal employment for a specified period (*Tetik*, cited above, paragraph 29).

23. Likewise, the Court has consistently held (see, in particular, the judgment in *Kus*, cited above, paragraph 25) that Decision No 1/80 does not encroach upon the competence retained by the Member States to regulate both the entry into their territories of Turkish nationals and the conditions under which they may take up their first employment, but merely regulates, in Article 6, the situation of Turkish workers already integrated into the labour force of the host Member State.

24. The first point to be noted in that regard is that since the judgment in Case C-1 92/89 *Sevince* v *Staatssecretaris van Justitie* [1990] ECR I-3461 the Court has consistently held that Article 6(1) of Decision No 1/80 has direct effect in the Member States and that Turkish nationals who satisfy its conditions may therefore rely directly on the rights given them by the various indents of that provision (Case C-355/93) *Eroglu* v *Land Baden-Wurttemberg* [1994] ECR I-5113, paragraph 11).

25. As is clear from the three indents of Article 6(1), those rights themselves vary and are subject to conditions which differ according to the duration of the legal employment in the relevant Member State (*Eroglu*, paragraph 12).

26. Second, it should be borne in mind that the Court has consistently held that the rights which the three indents of Article 6(1) confer on Turkish workers in regard to employment necessarily imply the existence of a right of residence for the person concerned, since otherwise the right of access to the labour market and the right to work as an employed person would be deprived of all effect (*Sevince*, paragraph 29, *Kus*, paragraphs 29 and 30, and *Bozkurt*, paragraph 28).

27. The second and third questions raised by the Verwaltungsgericht Darmstadt must be considered in the light of those principles.

28. The first of those questions, as rephrased in paragraph 19 of this judgment, concerns the scope of Article 6(3) of Decision No 1/80, according to which the procedures for applying Article 6(1) are to be those established under national rules. It is settled case-law (*Sevince*, paragraph 22, and *Kus*, paragraph 31, cited above) that that provision merely clarifies the obligation incumbent on the Member States to take such administrative measures as may be necessary for the implementation of Article 6, without empowering them to make conditional or restrict the application of the precise and unconditional right which the provision grants to Turkish workers.

29. Moreover, in *Kus*, paragraph 25, the Court pointed out that Article 6 of Decision No 1/80 merely regulates the situation of Turkish workers already integrated into the labour force of a Member State and the decision cannot, therefore, constitute justification for depriving Turkish workers already in possession of a work permit and, if necessary, a right of residence in accordance with the legislation of a Member State of the rights provided for in Article 6(1) thereof.

30. It follows that even though, as the law now stands, Decision No 1/80 does not in any way affect the competence of the Member States to refuse the entry into their territories of Turkish nationals and to take up their first employment, and does not, in principle, preclude those Member States from determining the conditions under which they work for up to one year as provided for in the first indent of Article 6(1) of that decision, Article 6(3) merely provides that the competent authorities of the Member States may adopt such national legislation as may be required for the application of the rights conferred on Turkish workers by paragraphs (1) and (2) of that provision.

31. However, that provision cannot be construed as reserving to the Member States the power to adapt as they please the rules governing Turkish workers already integrated in their labour force, permitting them to adopt unilaterally measures preventing certain categories of workers who already satisfy the conditions of Article 6(1) from benefiting from the progressively more extensive rights enshrined in the three indents of that paragraph.

32. The effect of such an interpretation would be to render Decision No 1/80 meaningless and deprive it of any practical effect. Likewise, its purpose would not be achieved if restrictions imposed by a Member State could result in denying Turkish workers the rights which the three indents of Article 6(1) confer on them progressively once they have been in gainful employment in the host Member State for a certain time.

33. Moreover, the wording of Article 6(1) is general and unconditional: it does not permit the Member States to deprive certain categories of Turkish workers of the rights which that provision confers directly on them or to restrict or attach conditions to such rights.

34. Accordingly, national legislation which provides that the work and residence of certain Turkish nationals in the host Member State concerned are limited to a specific activity with a given employer and may on no account exceed three years must be considered to be incompatible with the scheme and purpose of that decision and cannot therefore be adopted under Article 6(3) thereof.

35. Such legislation would undermine the gradual integration of Turkish workers in the host Member State's labour force provided for in the three indents of Article 6(1), by depriving some of those workers – such as the applicant in the main proceedings – who entered that State lawfully and

were permitted to take up paid employment there not only of the possibility of continuing to work for the same employer beyond the time-limit unilaterally imposed by the Member State concerned, but also of the right to respond, after three years of legal employment, to an offer of employment made by another employer in the same occupation (second indent) and of free access, after four years of legal employment, to any paid employment of their choice (third indent).

36.   That is all the more evident in a case such as that at issue in the main proceedings, where the relevant national legislation not only imposes restrictions capable of depriving Turkish workers of the rights accorded them by Article 6(1) but also provides that Decision No 1/80 does not apply to an entire occupation, in this case that of specialist chef.

37.   It follows that the answer to the first of those questions, as rephrased, must be that Article 6(3) of Decision No 1/80 is to be interpreted as meaning that it does not permit Member States to adopt national legislation which excludes at the outset whole categories of Turkish migrant workers, such as specialist chefs, from the rights conferred by the three indents of Article 6(1).

38.   As regards the second of those questions, which concerns the interpretation of "duly registered as belonging to the labour force of a Member State" and "legal employment" for the purposes of Article 6(1) of Decision No 1/80 as regards a Turkish worker who has been authorised to work as a specialist chef in a given restaurant for a maximum of three years and who has had his attention expressly drawn to such restrictions, it should be observed from the outset that he was permitted to enter the territory of the Member State concerned and was there lawfully employed, within the terms of the requisite national permits and without interruption for over one year, by the same employer.

39.   In order to ascertain whether such a worker is duly registered as belonging to the labour force of a Member State it must be determined first of all, in accordance with settled case-law (*Bozkurt*, cited above, paragraphs 22 and 23), whether the legal relationship of employment of the person concerned can be located within the territory of a Member State or retains a sufficiently close link with that territory, taking account in particular of the place where the Turkish national was hired, the territory on or from which the paid employment is pursued and the applicable national legislation in the field of employment and social security law.

40.   In a situation such as that of the applicant in the main proceedings, that condition is undeniably satisfied.

41.   Next, contrary to the German Government's assertion, it cannot be claimed that specialist chefs permitted to work in its territory are not duly registered as belonging to the labour force of a Member State because such persons may be distinguished from the other workers in general by the fact that they must be nationals of the country whose cuisine is the speciality of the restaurant which employs them.

42. The Commission has argued cogently that the occupation of specialist chef does not present, by comparison with other professions and trades in other sectors of the economy, such objective characteristics as to make it possible to exclude Turkish workers legally employed in that occupation in the host Member State from being regarded as duly registered as belonging to the labour force of that Member State, as referred to in Article 6(1), on the sole ground that their occupation is that of specialist chef.

43. A specialist chef performing services for and under the direction of another person for remuneration is bound by an employment relationship covering a genuine and effective economic activity.

44. Accordingly, the legal situation of a specialist chef such as Mr Ertanir is in no way different to that of Turkish migrant workers as a whole employed in the host Member State.

45. The fact that, as in the main proceedings, a Member State imposes on all Turkish nationals whose occupation is that of specialist chef a restriction as to the duration of their residence in the Member State concerned and prohibits them from changing employers cannot affect that interpretation.

46. It follows from paragraphs 31 to 35 of this judgment that such restrictions on the rights deriving from Decision No 1/80 must be considered to be incompatible therewith and are therefore not relevant for the purposes of interpretation.

47. As regards the meaning of "legal employment" for the purposes of Article 6(1) of Decision No 1/80, it is settled case-law (*Sevince*, paragraph 30, *Kus*, paragraphs 12 and 22 and *Bozkurt*, paragraph 26, cited above) that legal employment presupposes a stable and secure situation as a member of the labour force of a Member State and, by virtue of this, implies the existence of an undisputed right of residence.

48. Thus, in paragraph 31 of the *Sevince* Judgment, cited above, the Court stated that a Turkish worker was not in a stable and secure situation as a member of the labour force of a Member State during the period in which he benefitted from the Suspensory effect of an appeal he had lodged against a decision refusing him a residence permit and had obtained provisional authorisation, pending the outcome of the dispute, to reside and be employed in the Member State in question.

49. Similarly, in *Kus*, cited above, the Court held that a worker did not fulfil that requirement where a right of residence was conferred on him only by the operation of national legislation permitting residence in the host country pending completion of the procedure for the grant of a residence permit, on the ground that he had been given the right to remain and work in that country only on a provisional basis pending a final decision on his right of residence (paragraph 13).

50. The Court considered that it was not possible to regard as legal, within the meaning of Article 6(1) of Decision No 1/80, periods in which the

worker was employed so long as it was not definitively established that during that period the worker had a legal right of residence, since otherwise a judicial decision finally refusing him that right would be rendered negatory, and he would thus have been enabled to acquire the rights provided for in Article 6(1) during a period in which he did not fulfil the conditions laid down in that provision (*Kus*, cited above, paragraph 16).

51. Finally, in Case C-285/95 *Kol* v *Land Berlin* [1997] ECR I-0000, paragraph 27, the Court held that the periods in which a Turkish national was employed under a residence permit which was issued to him only as a result of fraudulent conduct which led to his conviction were not based on a stable situation, and that such employment could not be regarded as having been secure in view of the fact that, during the periods in question, the person concerned was not legally entitled to a residence permit.

52. By contrast, as regards the case at issue in the main proceedings, the Turkish worker's right to reside in the host Member State was not disputed and his situation was not insecure and thus likely to be called in question at any time, since he had been authorised in April 1992 to pursue genuine and effective paid employment in that State for three years without interruption and therefore his legal situation was secure throughout that period.

53. A worker employed in such circumstances in a Member State must accordingly be considered to have been legally employed there within the meaning of Article 6(1) of Decision No 1/80 and, provided he satisfies its conditions, may therefore rely directly on the rights conferred by the various indents of that provision.

54. In that regard, it cannot be argued that under the relevant national legislation the worker's residence and/or work permits in the host Member State were merely provisional and conditional.

55. It is settled case-law that the rights conferred on Turkish workers by Article 6(1) are accorded irrespective of whether or not the authorities of the host Member State have issued a specific administrative document, such as a work permit or residence permit (see, to this effect, the judgment in *Bozkurt*, cited above, paragraphs 29 and 30).

56. Furthermore, if conditions or restrictions applied by a Member State to residence and/or work permits for Turkish nationals could result in their lawful employment there being regarded as not legal, Member States would be able wrongly to deprive Turkish migrant workers whom they permitted to enter their territory and who have been legally employed there for an uninterrupted period of at least one year of rights on which they are entitled to rely directly under Article 6(1) (see paragraphs 31 to 35 of this judgment).

57. It follows from the wording, the scheme and the purpose of that provision that Member States may not make conditional or restrict the application of the precise and unconditional rights which Turkish nationals who

satisfy its conditions derive from Decision No 1/80 (see paragraphs 28, 32, 33 and 35 of this judgment).

58.   Moreover, the fact that the worker was notified upon being issued with his permit to enter the host Member State that his residence and his employment were subject to the observance of certain conditions regarding duration and substance does not affect that interpretation.

59.   The term "legal employment" used by Article 6(1) is a concept of Community law which must be defined objectively and uniformly in the light of the spirit and the purpose of the provision.

60.   The progressively more extensive rights which the three indents of Article 6(1) confer on Turkish workers derive directly from Decision No 1/80; therefore those rights may not be denied to those entitled to them on the grounds which have been put forward, and no objection can be raised to reliance thereon in circumstances such as those in point in the main proceedings.

61.   Accordingly, the interpretation of the concept in question does not depend on subjective circumstances, such as the awareness on the part of the person concerned of the existence of restrictions, of such a kind as to deprive him of rights acquired under Decision No 1/80, to which the national authorities have made subject his residence and/or his work in the host Member State.

62.   In view of all the foregoing considerations, the answer to the second of those questions as rephrased in paragraph 19 of this judgment must be that a Turkish national who has been lawfully employed in a Member State for an uninterrupted period of more than one year as a specialist chef by the same employer is duly registered as belonging to the labour force of that Member State and is legally employed within the meaning of Article 6(1) of Decision No 1/80. A Turkish national in that situation may accordingly seek the renewal of his permit to reside in the host Member State notwithstanding the fact that he was advised when the work and the residence permits were granted that they were for a maximum of three years and restricted to specific work, in this case as a specialist chef, for a specific employer.

The first question

63.   By this question, the national court is asking essentially whether Article 6(1) of Decision No 1/80 is to be interpreted as meaning that it requires account to be taken, for the purpose of Calculating periods of legal employment as referred to in that provision, of short periods during which the Turkish worker did not hold a valid residence or work permit in the host Member State and which are not covered by Article 6(2) of that decision.

64.   In order to answer that question, it must first be pointed out that Decision No 1/80 does not make clear whether periods of employment which a

Turkish worker completes in the host Member State without being covered by a valid work or residence permit affect the calculation of the periods of legal employment provided for in the three indents of Article 6(1).

65.   The decision merely regulates, in Article 6(2), the effect on the calculation of the periods of legal employment referred to in the three indents of Article 6(1) of certain periods of inactivity which are treated as periods of legal employment within the meaning of paragraph (1) or which do not cause the worker to lose entitlement to the rights acquired by virtue of earlier periods of legal employment (see, in particular, the judgment in *Tetik* cited above, paragraphs 36 to 39).

66.   Next, it should be recalled that, although Decision No 1/80 does not encroach upon the Competence retained by the Member States to regulate both the entry into their territories of Turkish nationals and the conditions under which they may take up their first employment (paragraphs 23 and 30 of this judgment), it is settled case-law that the rights referred to in Article 6(1) are accorded irrespective of whether or not the authorities of the host Member State have issued a specific administrative document, such as a work permit or residence permit (paragraph 55 of this judgment).

67.   Finally, it should be observed that, in a situation such as that at issue in the main proceedings, first, the periods during which the Turkish worker did not hold in the host Member State a valid residence or work permit were of no more than a few days and, second, he received a new permit each time, the validity of which was moreover extended on two occasions with retroactive effect to the expiry date of the (previous) permit, without the competent authorities challenging on that ground the legality of the residence of the worker in the country.

68.   Accordingly, the fact that the person concerned was briefly without a valid residence or work permit does not affect the periods of legal employment referred to in Article 6(1) of Decision No 1/80.

69.   The answer to the first question must therefore be that Article 6(1) of Decision No 1/80 is to be interpreted as requiring account to be taken, for the purpose of calculating the periods of legal employment referred to in that provision, of short periods during which the Turkish worker did not hold a valid residence or work permit in the host Member State and which are not covered by Article 6(2) of that decision, where the competent authorities of the host Member State have not called in question on that ground the legality of the residence of the worker in the country but have, on the contrary, issued him with a new residence or work permit.

Costs

70.   The costs Incurred by the German Government and by the Commission of the European Communities, which have submitted observations to the Court, are not recoverable. Since these proceedings are, for the parties to

the main proceedings, a step in the proceedings pending before the national court, the decision on costs is a matter for that court.

On those grounds, THE COURT in answer to the questions referred to it by the Verwaltungsgericht Darmstadt by order of 29 February 1996, hereby rules:

1. Article 6(3) of Decision No 1/80 of 19 September 1980 on the development of the Association, adopted by the Association Council established by the Association Agreement between the European Economic Community and Turkey, is to be interpreted as meaning that it does not permit Member States to adopt national legislation which excludes at the outset whole categories of Turkish migrant workers, such as specialist chefs, from the rights conferred by the three indents of Article 6(1).

2. A Turkish national who has been lawfully employed in a Member State for an uninterrupted period of more than one year as a specialist chef by the same employer is duly registered as belonging to the labour force of that Member State and is legally employed within the meaning of Article 6(1) of Decision No 1/80. A Turkish national in that situation may accordingly seek the renewal of his permit to reside in the host Member State notwithstanding the fact that he was advised when the work and residence permits were granted that they were for a maximum of three years and restricted to specific work, in this case as a specialist chef, for a specific employer.

3. Article 6(1) of Decision No 1/80 is to be interpreted as requiring account to be taken, for the purpose of calculating the periods of real employment referred to in that provision, of short periods during which the Turkish worker did not hold a valid residence or work permit in the host Member State and which are not covered by Article 6(2) of that decision, where the competent authorities of the host Member State have not called in question on that ground the reality of the residence of the worker in the country but have, on the contrary, issued him with a new residence or work permit.

Mancini   Murray   Ragnemalm   Schintgen

Delivered in open Court in Luxembourg on 30 September 1997.

R. Grass   G.F. Mancini
Registrar   President of the Sixth Chamber

Judgment of the Court of Justice of the European Communities

(Sixth Chamber)
30 September 1997

Faik Günaydin, Hatice Günaydin, Günes Günaydin and
Seda Günaydin -v- Freistaat Bayern

Case C-36/96,

REFERENCE to the Court under Article 177 of the EC Treaty by the Bundesverwaltungsgericht (Germany) for a preliminary ruling in the proceedings pending before that court on the interpretation of Article 6(1) of Decision No 1/80 of 19 September 1980 on the development of the Association, adopted by the Association Council established by the Association Agreement between the European Economic Community and Turkey,

THE COURT (Sixth Chamber),

composed of : G.F. Mancini, President of the Chamber, J.L. Murray, P.J.G Kapteyn, H.G. Ragnemalm and R. Schintgen (Rapporteur), Judges,

Advocate General: M.B. Elmer,
Registrar: H.A. Rühl, Principal Administrator,

after considering the written observations submitted on behalf of :
- Mr and Mrs Günaydin, by F. Auer, of the Regensburg Bar,
- Freistaat Bayern, by W. Rzepka, Generallandesanwalt at the Landesanwaltschaft Bayern, acting as Agent,
- The Germany Government, by E. Röder, Ministerialrat in the Federal Ministry of Economic Affairs, acting as Agent,
- the Greek Government, by A. Samoni-Rantou, special assistant legal adviser in the Community Legal Affairs Department of the Ministry of Foreign Affairs, acting as Agent, assisted by L. Pnevmatikou, specialist technical adviser in that department,
- the French Government, by C. de Salins and A. de Bourgoing, Deputy Director and Special Adviser respectively in the Legal Affairs Directorate at the Ministry of Foreign Affairs, acting as Agents,
- the Commission of the European Communities, by J. Sack, Legal Adviser, acting as Agent,

having regard to the Report for the Hearing,

after hearing the oral observations of Mr and Mrs Günaydin, the German, Greek and French Governments and the Commission at the hearing on 6 March 1997, after hearing the Opinion of the Advocate General at the sitting on 29 April 1997, gives the following Judgment

1.   By order of 24 November 1995, received at the Court on 12 February 1996, the Bundesverwaltungsgericht (Federal Administrative Court) referred to the Court for a preliminary ruling under Article 177 of the EC Treaty two questions on the interpretation of Article 6(1) of Decision No 1/80 of the Council of Association of 19 September 1980 on the development of the Association (hereinafter "Decision No 1/80"). The Council of Association was set up by the Agreement establishing an Association between the European Economic Community and Turkey, signed at Ankara on 12 September 1963 by the Republic of Turkey and by the Member States of the EEC and the Community, and concluded, approved and confirmed on behalf of the Community by Council Decision of 23 December 1963 (OJ 1973 C 113.p.1).

2.   The questions were raised in the course of a dispute between Mr Günaydin, together with his wife and their two minor children, all Turkish nationals, and Freistaat Bayern concerning the refusal to extend Mr Günaydin's permit to reside in Germany.

3.   According to the file on the case in the main proceedings, Mr Günaydin was permitted to enter Germany in April 1976.

4.   In that Member State he first successfully completed German language courses and then undertook a course of study at the end of which in 1986 he received a diploma in engineering.

5.   During his studies he was granted residence permits with restrictions as to time and place, paid employment not being permitted.

6.   In 1982, Mr Günaydin married a Turkish national. The couple had two children, born in 1984 and 1988 respectively.

7.   In November 1986, Mr Günaydin was taken on by Siemens with a view to pursuing at the factory in Amberg (Germany) a training course of several years' duration at the end of which he was to be transferred to Turkey in order to manage there a subsidiary of that company. That purpose is apparent from the correspondence between Siemens and the German authorities and from the two statements made by Mr Günaydin. Thus, on 17 February 1987, the latter took note of the fact that the employment and residence permits for Germany were granted to him solely for the purpose of preparing there to take up a post in Siemens subsidiary in Turkey. Moreover, Mr Günaydin pointed out on 9 August 1989 that he intended to return with his family to that country in the latter half of 1990.

8.   On 12 January 1987, the German authorities granted Mr Günaydin a temporary residence permit which was extended several times, on the last occasion to 5 July 1990. The permit bore the remark that it would lapse upon his ceasing to be employed by Siemens in Amberg and that it had been granted exclusively for the purpose of introducing its holder to the commercial and working methods of the company in question.

9.   At the same time, several temporary work permits, restricted to employment at the Siemens factory in Amberg were issued in turn to Mr Günaydin. The last of those permits lapsed on 30 June 1990.

10. On 15 February 1990, Mr Günaydin applied for a permanent residence permit on the ground that as a result of his career development in Germany that country had become his home, that he would now feel like a stranger in Turkey and that his two minor children, born in Germany and attending German schools, would experience the greatest difficulty in integrating into his country of origin.

11. Despite the efforts deployed by Siemens to be permitted to extend the employment of Mr Günaydin who, according to Siemens, was a particularly valued member of staff whom it would be impossible to replace by an equally qualified person and who was very important for the Amberg factory's contacts with its Turkish subsidiary, the application for an extension of the residence permit was refused, so that Mr Günaydin had to cease work with Siemens on 30 June 1990. That decision was not varied subsequently, despite the fact that Siemens' Turkish subsidiary had informed its parent company in January 1991 that the situation in Turkey did not make it possible for the time being to employ Mr Günaydin and that the German employment authorities had already agreed to extend Mr Günaydin's work permit.

12. The refusal to extend the residence permit was based on the fact that he could not rely on either an entitlement to an unrestricted residence permit or the principle of the protection of legitimate expectations; moreover, it was claimed that to extend his residence would be contrary to German development aid policy which was intended to encourage foreigners trained in that Member State to work in their country of origin.

13. The action which Mr Günaydin, his spouse and their two minor children brought against that decision was dismissed both at first instance and on appeal on the ground that, because his work was limited to participation in a training programme in a particular undertaking with a view to taking up a post in one of its subsidiaries in Turkey, Mr Günaydin had not been available on the general labour market in Germany and that, consequently, he had not been duly registered as belonging to the labour force of a Member State, within the meaning of Article 6(1) of Decision No 1/80. The court hearing the appeal added that, in view of those facts, Mr Günaydin's situation as a member of the German labour force was not secure.

14. Hearing an appeal on a point of law, the Bundesverwaltungsgericht found that the contested decision complied with German law. None the less, it raised the question of whether solution more favourable to Mr Günaydin might not be derived from Article 6(1) of Decision No 1/80.

15. Article 6(1), which appears in Chapter II (Social provisions), Section 1 (Questions relating to employment and a free movement of workers), is worded as follows:

"1.   Subject to Article 7 on free access of employment for members of his family, a Turkish worker duly registered as belonging to the labour force of a Member State:

— shall be entitled, in that Member State, after one year's legal employment, to the renewal of his permit to work for the same employer, if a job is available;

— shall be entitled in that Member State, after three years of legal employment subject to the priority to be given to workers of Member States of the Community, to respond to another offer of employment, with an employer of his choice, made under normal conditions and registered with the employment services of that State, for the same occupation;

— shall enjoy free access in that Member State to any paid employment of his choice, after four years of legal employment".

16. The Bundesverwaltungsgericht pointed out that Mr Günaydin had been legally employed in Germany for over three and a half years, but expressed doubt as to whether he was duly registered as belonging to the labour force of a Member State, within the meaning of that provision, because he had been permitted to pursue gainful employment in the Member State only temporarily.

17. The court was also in doubt as to whether he had abused his rights because he had accepted the restrictions on his residence in Germany and had made clear his intention to return to Turkey in the autumn of 1990.

18. Taking the view that a decision on the case accordingly required an interpretation of the abovementioned provisions, the Bunmdesverwaltungsgericht stayed proceedings and referred the following two questions to the Court of Justice for a preliminary ruling:

1. Is a Turkish worker duly registered as belonging to the labour force of a Member State within the meaning of Article 6(1) of Decision No 1/80 of the EEC-Turkey Association Council on the development of the Association ("Decision No 1/80") and is he legally employed there if he has been authorized to pursue paid employment with an employer in the Member State only temporarily and only for the purpose of preparing for work with a subsidiary company of his employer in Turkey?

2. If the answer to Question 1 is yes:
Can a claim under Article 6(1) of Decision No 1/80 be opposed as an abuse of law if the Turkish worker has expressly declared his intention of returning to Turkey after preparation for the work there and the competent authority has authorized him to reside in the country temporarily only in view of that declaration?"

The first question

19. By its first question, the national court seeks essentially to ascertain whether Article 6(1) of Decision No 1/80 is to be interpreted as meaning

that a Turkish national is duly registered as belonging to the labour force of a Member State and is legally employed, within the meaning of that provision, and may therefore seek to renew his permit to reside in the host Member State, even though he was permitted to pursue gainful employment there only temporarily for a specific employer for the purpose of becoming acquainted with and preparing for work in one of its subsidiaries in Turkey, and had obtained work and residence permits for that purpose only.

20. It should be observed, *in limine*, that according to the third recital in its preamble, Decision No 1/80 seeks to improve, in the social field, the treatment accorded to workers and members of their families in relation to the arrangements introduced by Decision No 2/76 which the Council of Association set up by the Agreement established in Association with the European Economic Community and Turkey adopted on 20 December 1976.

21. The provision of Section 1 of Chapter II of Decision No 1/80, of which Article 6 forms part, thus constitute a further stage in securing freedom of movement for workers on the basis of Articles 48, 49 and 50 of the Treaty. The Court has accordingly considered it essential to extend, so far as possible, the principles enshrined in those Treaty articles to Turkish workers who enjoy the rights conferred by Decision No 1/80 (see the judgments in Case C-434/93 *Bozkurt* v *Staatssecretaris van Justitie* [1995] ECR 1-475, paragraphs 14, 19 and 20, the Case C-171/95 *Tetik* v *Land Berlin* ECR 1-329, paragraph 20).

22. As the law now stands, however, Turkish nationals are not entitled to move freely within the Community but merely enjoy certain rights in the host Member State whose territory they have lawfully entered and where they have been in legal employment for a specified period (*Tetik*, cited above, paragraph 29).

23. Likewise, the Court has consistently held (see, in particular, Case C-237/91 *Kus* v *Landeshaupstadt Wiesbaden* [1992] ECR 1-6781, paragraph 25) that Decision No 1/80 does not encroach upon the competence retained by the Member States to regulate both the entry into their territories of Turkish nationals and the conditions under which they may take up their first employment, but merely regulates, in Article 6, the situation of Turkish workers already integrated into the labour force of the host Member State.

24. The first point to be noted in that regard is that since the judgment in Case C-192/89 *Sevince* v *Staatssecretaris van Justitie* [1990] ECR 1-3461 the Court has consistently held that Article 6(1) of Decision No 1/80 has direct effect in the Member States and that Turkish nationals who satisfy its conditions may therefore rely directly on the rights given them by the various indents of that provision (Case C-355/93 *Eroglu* v *Land Baden-Württemberg* [1994] ECR 1-5113, paragraph 11).

25. As is clear from the three indents of Article 6(1), those rights themselves

vary and are subject to conditions which differ according to the duration of the legal employment in the relevant Member State (*Eroglu*, paragraph 12).

26.   Second, it should be borne in mind that the Court has consistently held that the rights which the three indents of Article 6(1) confer on Turkish workers in regard to employment necessarily imply the existence of a right of residence for the person concerned, since otherwise the right of access to the labour market and the right to work as an employed person would be deprived of all effect (*Sevince*, paragraph 29, *Kus*, paragraphs 29 and 30, and *Bozkurt*, paragraph 28).

27.   The first question raised by the Bundesverwaltungsgericht must be considered in the light of those principles.

28.   In this regard, it should be noted first that Mr Günaydin, a Turkish migrant worker, was permitted to enter the territory of the Member State concerned and was there lawfully employed under the requisite national permits and without interruption for over three years, in this case as a graduate engineer, by the same employer.

29.   In order to ascertain whether such a worker is duly registered as belonging to the labour force of a Member State for the purposes of Article 6(1) of Decision No 1/80 it must be determined first of all, in accordance with settled case-law (*Bozkurt*, cited above, paragraphs 22 and 23), whether the legal relationship of employment of the person concerned can be located within the territory of a Member State or retains a sufficiently close link with that territory, taking account in particular of the place where the Turkish national was hired, the territory on or form which the paid employment is pursued and the applicable national legislation in the field of employment and social security law.

30.   In a situation such as that of the plaintiff in the main proceedings, that condition is undeniably satisfied.

31.   Next, it should next be ascertained whether the worker is bound by an employment relationship covering a genuine and effective economic activity pursued for the benefit and under the direction of another person for remuneration (Case C-98 *Ertanir v Land Hessen* [1997] ECR 1-0000, paragraph 43).

32.   There is nothing to prevent a Member State from permitting Turkish nationals to enter and reside there only in order to enable them to follow within its territory specific vocational training, in particular in the context of a contract of apprenticeship.

33.   Nevertheless, in a case such as that at issue in the main proceedings, a Turkish worker who, at the end of his vocational training, is in paid employment with the sole purpose of becoming acquainted with and preparing for work in a managerial capacity in one of the subsidiaries of the undertaking which employs him must be considered to be bound by a normal employment relationship where, in genuinely and effectively pursuing an economic activity for the benefit and under the direction of

his employer, he is entitled to the same conditions of work and pay as those which may be claimed by workers who pursue within the undertaking in question identical or similar activities, so that his situation is not objectively different from that of those other workers.

34. In this connection, it is for the national court to determine whether that condition is satisfied and, in particular, whether the worker has been employed on the basis of national legislation derogating from community law and intended specifically to integrate him into the labour force and whether he receives in return for his services remuneration at the level which is usually paid, by the employer concerned or in the sector in question, to persons pursuing identical or comparable activities and which is not preponderantly financed from the public purse in the context of a specific programme for the integration of the person concerned into the workforce.

35. That interpretation is not affected by the fact that, in a situation such as that at issue in the main proceedings, the worker obtained in the host Member State only residence and/or work permits restricted to temporary paid employment by a specific employer and prohibiting that person from changing his employer within the Member State concerned.

36. Admittedly, as the law stands at present, Decision No 1/80 does not encroach upon the competence of the Member States to refuse Turkish nationals the right of entry into their territories and to take up first employment, nor does it preclude those Member States, in principle, from regulating the conditions under which they work for up to one year as provided for in the first indent of Article 6(1) of that decision.

37. None the less, Article 6(1) cannot be construed as permitting a Member State to modify unilaterally the scope of the system of gradual integration of Turkish workers in the host State's labour force, by denying a worker who has been permitted to enter its territory and who has lawfully pursued a genuine and effective economic activity for more than three and a half years the rights which the three indents of that provision confer on him progressively according to the duration of his employment.

38. The effect of such an interpretation would be to render Decision No 1/80 meaningless and deprive it of any practical effect.

39. Accordingly, the Member States have no power to make conditional or restrict the application of the precise and unconditional rights which Decision No 1/80 grants to Turkish nationals who satisfy its conditions (*Sevince*, paragraph 22 and *Kus*, paragraph 31, cited above).

40. Moreover, the wording of Article 6(1) is general and unconditional: it does not permit the Member States to restrict the rights which that provision confers directly on Turkish workers.

41. As regards the question whether a worker such as the appellant in the main proceedings has been legally employed in the host Member State within the meaning of Article 6(1) of Decision 1/80, it is settled case-law

(*Sevince*, paragraph 30, *Kus*, paragraphs 12 and 22, and *Bozkurt*, paragraph 26) that legal employment presupposes a stable and secure situation as a member of the labour force of a Member State and, by virtue of this, implies the existence of an undisputed right of residence.

42.   Thus, in paragraph 31 of the *Sevince* judgment, cited above, the Court stated that a Turkish worker was not in a stable and secure situation as a member of the labour force of a Member State during the period in which he benefited from the suspensory effect of an appeal he had lodged against a decision refusing him a residence permit and had obtained provisional authorization, pending the outcome of the dispute, to reside and be employed in the Member State in question.

43.   Similarly, in *Kuz*, cited above, the Court held that a worker did not fulfil that requirement where a right of residence was conferred on him only by the operation of national legislation permitting residence in the host country pending completion of the procedure for the grant of a residence permit, on the ground that he had been given the right to remain and work in that country only on a provisional basis pending a final decision on his right of residence (paragraph 13).

44.   The Court considered that it was not possible to regard as legal, within the meaning of Article 6(1) of Decision No 1/80, periods in which the worker was employed so long as it was not definitively established that during that period the worker had a legal right of residence, since otherwise a judicial decision finally refusing him that right would be rendered nugatory, and he would thus have been enabled to acquire the rights provided for in Article 6(1) during a period in which he did not fulfil the conditions laid down in that provision (*Kus*, cited above, paragraph 16).

45.   Finally, in Case C-285/95 *Kol* v *Land Berlin* [1997] ECR 1-000, paragraph 27, the Court held that the periods in which a Turkish national was employed under a residence permit which was issued to him only as a result of fraudulent conduct which led to his conviction were not based on a stable situation, and that such employment could not be regarded as having been secure in view of the fact that, during the periods in question, the person concerned was not legally entitled to a residence permit.

46.   By contrast, as regards the case at issue in the main proceedings, the Turkish workers' right to reside in the host Member State was not disputed and his situation was not insecure and thus likely to be called in question at any time, since he had been authorized in November 1986 to pursue genuine and effective paid employment in that State until 30 June 1990 without interruption and therefore his legal situation was secure throughout that period.

47.   A worker employed in such circumstances in a Member State must accordingly be considered to have been legally employed there within the meaning of Article 6(1) of Decision No 1/80 and, provided he satisfied

its conditions, may therefore rely directly o the rights conferred by the various indents of that provision.

48. In that regard, it cannot be argued that the worker's residence and/or work permits in the host Member State were merely provisional and conditional.

49. First, it is settled case-law that the rights conferred on Turkish workers by Article 6(1) are accorded irrespective of whether or not the authorities of the host Member State have issued a specific administrative document, such as a work permit or residence permit (see, to this effect, the judgment in *Bozkurt*, cited above, paragraphs 29 and 30).

50. Second, if conditions or restrictions applied by a Member State to residence and/or work permits for Turkish nationals could result in their lawful employment there being regarded as not legal, Member States would be able to wrongly to deprive Turkish migrant workers whom they permitted to enter their territory and who have been legally employed there for an uninterrupted period of more than three years of rights on which they are entitled to rely directly under Article 6(1) (see paragraphs 37 to 40 of this judgment).

51. Moreover, the fact that, in a case such as that at issue in the main proceedings, the work and residence permits were issued to the worker for a specific purpose, in order to allow him to carry out further vocational training in an undertaking in a Member State with a view to taking up a post subsequently in one of its subsidiaries in Turkey, does not affect that interpretation.

52. Article 6(1) does not make the recognition of the rights it confers on Turkish workers subject to any condition connected with the reason the right to enter, work or reside was initially granted (*Kus*, paragraphs 21 to 23 and, by analogy, *Eroglu*, paragraph 22).

53. The fact that such permits were granted to the person concerned for a specific purpose which genuine and effective paid employment in question sought to achieve is not, therefore, capable of depriving a worker who satisfied the conditions laid down in Article 6(1) of the progressive rights which that provision confers upon him.

54. In the circumstances, the worker cannot be prevented from relying on rights acquired under Decision No 1/80 on the ground that he allegedly stated that he wished to pursue his professional career in his country of origin after being employed for several years in the host Member State with a view to perfecting his vocational skills and that he initially accepted the restriction placed upon his permit to reside in that State.

55. In view of all the foregoing considerations, the answer to the first question must be that Article 6(1) of Decision No 1/80 is to be interpreted as meaning that a Turkish national who has been lawfully employed [inaudible] Member State for an uninterrupted period of more than three years in a genuine and effective economic activity for the same employer and whose employment status is not objectively different to that of other

employees employed by the same employer or in the sector concerned and exercising identical or comparable duties, is duly registered as belonging to the labour force of that State and is legally employed within the meaning of that provision. A Turkish national in that situation may therefore seek the renewal of his permit to reside in the host Member State notwithstanding the fact that he was permitted to take up paid employment there only temporarily with a specific employer for the purpose of acquainting himself with and preparing for employment in one of its subsidiaries in Turkey, and obtained work and residence permits for that purpose only.

The second question

56.   It is apparent from the grounds of the order for reference that, by this question, the Bundesverwaltungsgericht is asking essentially whether the fact that a Turkish worker wishes to extend his stay in the host Member State, although he expressly accepted its restriction and declared his intention of returning to Turkey after having been employed in the Member State concerned for the purpose of perfecting his vocational skills, is such as to deprive the person concerned of the rights deriving from Article 6(1) of Decision No 1/80.

57.   In order to give a reply to that question, it must be stated, first of all, that a Turkish worker such as Mr Günaydin cannot be deprived of the rights acquired under Decision No 1/80 on the sole ground that he is placing reliance in the host Member State on the provisions of Article 6(1) of that decision, whereas he had initially agreed to the restriction of his permit to reside in that Member State (see paragraph 54 of this judgment and the judgment in *Ertanir*, cited above, paragraphs 58 to 61).

58.   Second, an application based on Article 6(1) cannot, in principle, be considered improper because the worker previously expressed his intention to leave the territory of the host Member State upon completion of his preparation for the post which he intended to take up in his country of origin.

59.   As the Commission observed, it is quite possible that Mr Gunaydin first had the firm intention of returning to Turkey after being employed for several years in Germany, but that new and reasonable considerations prompted him to change his mind. Mr Gunaydin points out, first, that his employer's subsidiary in Turkey had informed the parent company in January 1991 that the situation at that time in that country did not make it possible to employ him and, secondly, that the Siemens factory in Amberg strongly wished to keep him as a particularly valued member of staff, *a fortiori* since the competent German authorities had already agreed to extend his work permit.

60.   In such circumstances, it is only if the national court establishes that the Turkish worker made the statement that he wished to leave the host

Member State after a specified period with the sole intention of inducing the competent authorities to issue the requisite permits on false premisses that he can be deprived of the rights flowing from Article 6(1) of Decision No 1/80.

61. In view of the foregoing considerations, the answer to the second question is that the fact that a Turkish worker wishes to extend his stay in the host Member State, although he expressly accepted its restriction, does not constitute an abuse of rights. The fact that he declared his intention of returning to Turkey after having been employed in the Member State for the purpose of perfecting his vocational skills is not such as to deprive him of the rights deriving from Article 6(1) of Decision No 1/80 unless it is established by the national court that that declaration was made with the sold intention of improperly obtaining work and residence permits for the host member state.

Costs

62. The costs incurred by the German, Greek and French Governments and by the Commission of the European Communities, which have submitted observations to the Court, are not recoverable. Since these proceedings are, for the parties to the main proceedings, a step in the proceedings pending before the national court, the decision on costs is a matter for that court.

On those grounds, THE COURT in answer to the questions referred to it by the Bundesverwaltungsgericht by judgment of 24 November 1995, hereby rules:

1. Article 6(1) of Decision No 1/80 of 19 September 1980 on the development of the Association, adopted by the Association Counsel established by the Association Agreement between the European Economic Community and Turkey, is to be interpreted as meaning that a Turkish national who has been lawfully employed in a Member State for an uninterrupted period of more than three years in a genuine and effective economic activity for the same employer and whose employment status is not objectively different to that of other employees employed by the same employer or in the sector concerned and exercising identical or comparable duties, is duly registered as belonging to the labour force of that State and is legally employed within the meaning of that provision. A Turkish national in that situation may therefore seek the renewal of his permit to reside in the host Member State notwithstanding the fact that he was permitted to take up paid employment there only temporarily with a specific employer for the purpose of acquainting himself with and preparing for employment in one of its subsidiaries in Turkey, and obtained work and residence permits for that purpose only.

2. The fact that a Turkish worker wishes to extend his stay in the host Member State, although he expressly accepted its restriction, does not constitute an abuse of rights. The fact that he declared his intention of returning to Turkey after having been employed in the Member State for the purpose of perfecting his vocational skills is not to deprive him of the

rights deriving from Article 6(1) of Decision No 1/80 unless it is established by the national court that that declaration was made with the sole intention of improperly obtaining work and residence permits for the host Member State.

Mancini Murray   Ragnemalm   Schintgen

Delivered in open court in Luxembourg on 30 September 1997

R. Grass   G.F. Mancini
Registrar   President of the Sixth Chamber

Judgment of the Court of Justice of the European Communities

(Sixth Chamber)
5 June 1997

Suat Kol -v- Land Berlin

Case C-285/95,

REFERENCE to the Court under Article 177 of the EC Treaty by the Oberverwaltungsgericht Berlin for a preliminary ruling in the proceedings pending before that court on the interpretation of Articles 6(1) and 14(1) of Decision No 1/80 of 19 September 1980 on the development of the Association, adopted by the Council of Association established by the Association Agreement between the European Economic Community and Turkey,

THE COURT (Sixth Chamber),

composed of: G.F. Mancini, President of the Chamber, C.N. Kakouris, G. Hirsch, H. Ragnemalm and R. Schintgen (Rapporteur), Judges,

Advocate General: M.B. Elmer,
Registrar: D. Louterman-Hubeau, Principal Administrator,

after considering the written observations submitted on behalf of:
- Mr Kol, by C. Rosenkranz, of the Berlin Bar,
- the German Government, by E. Röder, Ministerialrat at the Federal Ministry of Economic Affairs, acting as Agent, assisted by K. Hailbronner, Professor at the University of Konstanz,
- the Spanish Government, by A.J. Navarro González, Director General of Community Legal and Institutional Coordination, and R. Silva de Lapuerta, Abogado del Estado, of the State Legal Service, acting as Agents,
- the French Government, by C. de Salins and A. de Bourgoing, Deputy Director and Special Adviser respectively in the Legal Affairs Directorate, Ministry of Foreign Affairs, acting as Agents,
- the United Kingdom Government, by J.E. Collins, Assistant Treasury Solicitor, acting as Agent, and by E Sharpston, Barrister,
- the Commission of the European Communities, by P. Hillenkamp, Legal Adviser, and P. van Nuffel, of its Legal Service, acting as Agents,

having regard to the Report for the Hearing,

after hearing the oral observations of the German Government, the Spanish Government, the French Government, the United Kingdom Government and the Commission, at the hearing on 23 January 1997, after hearing the Opinion of the Advocate General at the sitting on 6 March 1997, gives the following Judgment

1.   By order of 11 August 1995, which was received at the Court on 28 August 1995, the Oberverwaltungsgericht (Higher Administrative Court) Berlin referred to the Court for a preliminary ruling under Article 177 of the EC Treaty two questions concerning the interpretation of Articles 6(1) and 14(1) of Decision No 1/80 of the Council of Association of 19 September 1980 on the development of the Association (hereinafter "Decision No 1/80"). The Council of Association was established by the Association Agreement between the European Economic Community and Turkey signed on 12 September 1963 in Ankara by the Turkish Republic, on the one hand, and by the Member States of the EEC and the Community, on the other hand; it was concluded, approved and confirmed on behalf of the Community by Council Decision 64/732/EEC of 23 December 1963 (OJ 1973 C 113, p1).

2.   The questions were raised in proceedings between Mr Kol, a Turkish national, and the Land Berlin concerning a decision expelling him from German territory.

3.   The file on the case shows that on 15 February 1988 Mr Kol entered Germany where, on 9 May 1988, he married a German national.

4.   The German authorities, suspecting that it was a marriage of convenience, first issued Mr Kol with a certificate that an application for a residence permit had been lodged, and then with a residence permit of limited duration which was renewed several times.

5.   On 2 May 1991, after he and his spouse had declared that they lived together as man and wife in the marital home, Mr Kol obtained a German residence permit of unlimited duration.

6.   That declaration proved to be false, however. Mr Kol's wife had commenced divorce proceedings in April 1990 and the spouses had ceased to cohabit some time before their declaration of 2 May 1991. The marriage was dissolved by judgment of 14 February 1992.

7.   By judgment of 29 November 1993, the Amtsgericht Berlin Tiergarten fined Mr Kol for having made a false declaration in order to procure a residence permit. His wife was convicted of aiding and abetting him.

8.   Mr Kol has shown that he was employed in Germany from 3 April 1989 to 31 December 1989 and on 7 February 1990 with his first employer, and from 15 June 1990 to 6 July 1993, from 6 September 1993 to 8 February 1994 and from 24 March 1994 onwards with a second employer.

9.   On 7 July 1994 the Landeseinwohneramt Berlin (Residents' Registration Office for the *Land* Berlin) ordered Mr Kol's immediate expulsion. That measure, based on general grounds of a preventative nature, was aimed at deterring other aliens from making false statements in order to obtain a residence permit.

10.   Mr Kol's application for interim relief was rejected by an order of 12 May

1995 of the Verwaltungsgericht (Administrative Court) Berlin, against which he appealed to the Oberverwaltungsgericht Berlin.

11. In support of his appeal Mr Kol claimed that his periods of employment in Germany gave him a right to remain there pursuant to Article 6(1) of Decision No 1/80 and that an expulsion order made solely on general grounds of a preventative nature was incompatible with Article 14(1) of that decision.

12. Although the Oberverwaltungsgericht Berlin found that the expulsion order complied with German law, it raised the question whether a solution more favourable to Mr Kol might not be derived from Articles 6(1) and 14(1) of Decision No 1/80.

13. Article 6(1), which appears in Chapter II (Social provisions), Section 1 (Questions relating to employment and the free movement for workers), is worded as follows:

     "1.   Subject to Article 7 on free access to employment for members of his family, a Turkish worker duly registered as belonging to the labour force of a Member State:

     –   shall be entitled, in that Member State, after one year's legal employment, to the renewal of his permit to work for the same employer, if a job is available;

     –   shall be entitled in that Member State, after three years of legal employment and subject to the priority to be given to workers of Member States of the Community, to respond to another offer of employment, with an employer of his choice, made under normal conditions and registered with the employment services of that State, for the same occupation;

     –   shall enjoy free access in that Member State to any paid employment of his choice, after four years of legal employment."

14. Article 14(1), which forms part of the same section of Chapter II of Decision No 1/80, provides as follows:

     "The provisions of this section shall be applied subject to limitations justified on grounds of public policy, public security or public health."

15. The Oberverwaltungsgericht Berlin had doubts, however, as to the interpretation to be given to the terms "legal employment" and "limitations justified on grounds of public policy, public security or public health" used in those two provisions. It raised the question whether Mr Kol's periods of employment subsequent to the false declaration of 2 May 1991 could be recognised as legal employment within the meaning of the first indent of Article 6(1) of Decision No 1/80. It further sought to ascertain whether the principles governing the free movement of workers who are nationals of a Member State, according to which a deportation order must be based exclusively on the personal conduct of the individual concerned and previous convictions cannot in themselves constitute grounds for making such an order, also apply to Turkish migrant workers.

16. Taking the view that a decision on the case accordingly required an interpretation of the abovementioned provisions, the Oberverwaltungsgericht Berlin stayed proceedings and referred the following two questions to the Court of Justice for a preliminary ruling:
    "1. Are periods of employment spent in a Member State by a Turkish worker on the basis of a residence permit obtained by wilful and criminal deceit to be recognised as legal employment within the meaning of Article 6(1) of Decision No 1/80 of the EEC-Turkey Council of Association?
    2. If Question 1 is answered in the affirmative:
    Is the termination of residence of such a worker by virtue of an expulsion order made solely on general grounds of a preventative nature with a view to deterring other aliens compatible with Article 14(1) of the abovementioned decision?"

First question

17. It should be noted at the outset that, according to the file on the case in the main proceedings, Mr Kol has been convicted of having made a false declaration in order to obtain a German residence permit.

18. In those circumstances, the first question must be understood as seeking to ascertain essentially whether Article 6(1) of Decision No 1/80 must be interpreted as meaning that a Turkish worker satisfies the condition of having been in legal employment, within the meaning of that provision, in the host Member State, where he has been employed there under a residence permit which was issued to him only as a result of fraudulent conduct in respect of which he has been convicted.

19. In order to reply to that question, the first point to note is that the order for reference shows that, on 2 May 1991, the date on which he made an inaccurate declaration in order to obtain a German residence permit of unlimited duration, Mr Kol had not been in legal employment for one year with the same employer, within the meaning of the first indent of Article 6(1) of Decision No 1/80. Mr Kol's two periods of employment in the host Member State prior to that date, the first of nearly nine months and the second of ten and a half months, were for two different employers; as the judgment in Case C-386/95 *Eker* [1997] ECR I-2697 makes clear, the first indent of Article 6(1) presupposes legal employment for an uninterrupted period of one year with the same employer.

20. Consequently Mr Kol cannot avail himself of the rights conferred by the first indent of Article 6(1) unless his periods of employment after 2 May 1991 may be regarded as legal employment within the meaning of that provision.

21. In that connection, the Court has consistently held (Case C-192/89 *Sevince* [1990] ECR I-3461, paragraph 30; Case 237/91 *Kus* [1992] ECR I-6781,

paragraphs 12 and 22; Case C-434/93 *Bozkurt* [1995] ECR I-1475, paragraph 26) that legal employment within the meaning of the first indent of Article 6(1) presupposes a stable and secure situation as a member of the labour force of a Member State and, by virtue of this, implies the existence of an undisputed right of residence.

22. In the *Sevince* judgment, the Court stated that a Turkish worker was not in a stable and secure situation as a member of the labour force of a Member State during the period in which he benefited from the suspensory effect of an appeal he had lodged against a decision refusing him a residence permit and had obtained authorisation, on a provisional basis, pending the outcome of the dispute, to reside and be employed in the Member State in question (paragraph 31).

23. Similarly, in *Kus*, cited above, the Court held that a Turkish worker did not fulfil that requirement where a right of residence was conferred on him only by the operation of national legislation permitting residence in the host country pending completion of the procedure for the grant of a residence permit (paragraph 18), on the ground that the person concerned had been given the right to remain and work in that country only on a provisional basis pending a final decision on his right of residence (paragraph 13).

24. The Court considered that it was not possible to regard as legal, within the meaning of Article 6(1) of Decision No 1/80, periods in which the worker was employed so long as it was not definitively established that during that period the worker had a legal right of residence. Otherwise, a judicial decision finally refusing him that right would be rendered nugatory, and he would thus have been enabled to acquire the rights provided for in Article 6(1) during a period when he did not fulfil the conditions laid down in that provision (*Kus*, cited above, paragraph 16).

25. *A fortiori* that interpretation must apply in a situation such as that in the main proceedings where the Turkish migrant worker obtained a residence permit of unlimited duration in the host Member State only by means of inaccurate declarations in respect of which he was convicted of fraud.

26. Periods of employment after a residence permit has been obtained only by means of fraudulent conduct which has led to a conviction cannot be regarded as legal for the purposes of application of Article 6(1) of Decision No 1/80, since the Turkish national did not fulfil the conditions for the grant of such a permit which was, accordingly, liable to be rescinded when the fraud was discovered.

27. Consequently, the periods in which the Turkish national was employed under a residence permit obtained in those circumstances were not based on a stable situation and such employment cannot be regarded as having been secure in view of the fact that, during the periods in question, the person concerned was not legally entitled to a residence permit.

28. Furthermore, employment under a residence permit issued as a result of

fraudulent conduct which has led, as in this case, to a conviction, cannot give rise to any rights in favour of the Turkish worker, or arouse any legitimate expectation on his part.

29.   In the light of the foregoing considerations, the answer to the first question must be that Article 6(1) of Decision No 1/80 is to be interpreted as meaning that a Turkish worker does not satisfy the condition of having been in legal employment, within the meaning of that provision, in the host Member State, where he has been employed there under a residence permit which was issued to him only as a result of fraudulent conduct in respect of which he has been convicted.

Second question

30.   The national court submitted the second question only in the event of an affirmative answer to the first question.

31.   In view of the negative answer to the first question referred to the Court, therefore, there is no need to rule on the second question.

Costs

32.   The costs incurred by the German, Spanish, French and United Kingdom Government, and the Commission of the European Communities, which have submitted observations to the Court, are not recoverable. Since these proceedings are, for the parties to the main proceedings, a step in the action pending before the national court, the decision on costs is a matter for that court.

On those grounds, THE COURT in answer to the questions referred to it by the Oberverwaltungsgericht Berlin by order of 11 August 1995, hereby rules:

Article 6(1) of Decision No 1/80 of 19 September 1980 on the development of the Association, adopted by the Council of Association established by the Association Agreement between the European Economic Community and Turkey, is to be interpreted as meaning that a Turkish worker does not satisfy the condition of having been in legal employment, within the meaning of that provision, in the host Member State, where he has been employed there under a residence permit which was issued to him only as a result of fraudulent conduct in respect of which he has been convicted.

Mancini   Kakouris   Hirsch

Ragnemalm   Schintgen

Delivered in open court in Luxembourg on 5 June 1997

R. Grass   G.F. Mancini
Registrar   President of the Sixth Chamber

Judgment of the Court of Justice of the European Communities

(Sixth Chamber)

29 May 1997

Case C-386/95,

REFERENCE to the Court under Article 177 of the EC Treaty by the Bundesverwaltungsgericht (Germany) for a preliminary ruling in the proceedings pending before that court. Joined to the proceedings: the Oberbundesanwalt beim Bundesverwaltungsgericht and the Vertreter des öffentlichen Interesses bei den Gerichten der allgemeinen Verwaltungsgerichtsbarkeit in Baden-Württemberg, on the interpretation of the first indent of Article 6(1) of Decision No 1/80 of 19 September 1980 on the development of the Association, adopted by the Council of Association established by the Association Agreement between the European Economic Community and Turkey,

THE COURT (Sixth Chamber),

composed of: G.F. Mancini, President of the Chamber, J.L. Murray, P.J.G. Kapteyn, H. Ragnemalm and R. Schintgen (Rapporteur), Judges,

Advocate General: M.B. Elmer,
Registrar: L. Hewlett, Administrator,

after considering the written observations submitted on behalf of:
- Mr Eker, by Renate Becker, Rechtsanwältin, Titisee-Neustadt,
- Land Baden-Württemberg, by Walter Scheifele, Oberregierungsrat (Landratsamt Waldshut), acting as Agent,
- the Vertreter des öffentlichen Interesses bei den Gerichten der allgemeinen Verwaltungsgerichtsbarkeit in Baden-Württemberg, by Harald Fliegauf, Leitender Oberlandesanwalt, acting as Agent,
- the German Government, by Ernst Röder, Ministerialrat in the Federal Ministry of Economic Affairs, acting as Agent,
- the Greek Government, by Aikaterini Samoni-Rantou, special assistant legal adviser in the Community Legal Affairs Department of the Ministry of Foreign Affairs, acting as Agent, assisted by Lydia Pnevmatikou and Georgios Karipsidais, specialist technical advisers in that department,
- the French Government, by Catherine de Salins, Deputy Director in the Directorate of Legal Affairs of the Ministry of Foreign Affairs, and Claude

Chavance, Secretary for Foreign Affairs in that directorate, acting as Agents,

– the Austrian Government, by Wolf Okresek, Ministerialrat in the Constitutional Service of the Federal Chancellor's Office, acting as Agent,

– the Commission of the European Communities, by Jörn Sack, Legal Adviser, acting as Agent,

having regard to the Report for the Hearing,

after hearing the oral observations of Mr Eker, the Vertreter des öffentlichen Interesses bei den Gerichten der allgemeinen Verwaltungsgerichtsbarkeit in Baden-Württemberg, the German Government, the French Government and the Commission at the hearing on 30 January 1997,

after hearing the Opinion of the Advocate General at the sitting on 6 March 1997, gives the following Judgment

1. By order of 29 September 1995, received at the Court on 11 December 1995, the Bundesverwaltungsgericht (Federal Administrative Court) referred to the Court for a preliminary ruling under Article 177 of the EC Treaty a question on the interpretation of the first indent of Article 6(1) of Decision No 1/80 of the Council of Association of 19 September 1980 on the development of the Association (hereinafter "Decision No 1/80"). The Council of Association was set up by the Agreement establishing an Association between the European Economic Community and Turkey, signed at Ankara on 12 September 1963 by the Republic of Turkey and by the Member States of the EEC and the Community, and concluded, approved and confirmed on behalf of the Community by Council Decision 64/732/EEC of 23 December 1963 (OJ 1973 C 113, p. 1).

2. That question arose in a dispute between Mr Eker, a Turkish national, and the Land Baden-Württemberg concerning the refusal to extend his residence permit for Germany.

3. It appears from the documents in the main proceedings that Mr Eker entered Germany illegally on 1 December 1988 and was expelled on 13 February 1989.

4. On 17 January 1991 Mr Eker married a German national in Turkey, and he returned to Germany on 6 April 1991 with an entry permit.

5. On 17 April 1991 he was granted a work permit with no geographical restrictions and covering all types of employment, and on 24 July 1991 he received a residence permit valid until 24 July 1992.

6. From 15 June to 30 September 1991 Mr Eker was employed at a hotel in Schluchsee (Germany).

7. He then worked in a cure and rehabilitation clinic in Höchenschwand (Germany) from 1 October 1991 to 15 November 1992. He resumed working there on 1 February 1993.

8. According to Mr Eker, the spouses separated on 24 July 1991. In April 1992 he confirmed that divorce proceedings had been initiated.

9.   On 22 July 1992 Mr Eker applied for an extension of his permit to reside in Germany.

10. The Landratsamt Waldshut issued him with a certificate valid until 11 August 1992, while stating that it was minded to refuse his application. By decision of 12 August 1992 the Landratsamt refused to extend Mr Eker's residence permit and ordered him to leave German territory, failing which he would be expelled.

11. Mr Eker's action challenging that decision was upheld at first instance, but dismissed on appeal by the Verwaltungsgerichtshof (Higher Administrative Court), Baden-Württemberg in a judgment dated 30 November 1994. That court considered that there was no basis in German law for conferring on a Turkish national separated from his German spouse an independent right to remain. It further considered that Mr Eker could not rely on the first indent of Article 6(1) of Decision No 1/80, since that provision required the Turkish worker to have had one year's legal employment with the same employer, a condition which Mr Eker had not satisfied at the time when his residence permit expired.

12. Mr Eker then appealed on a point of law to the Bundesverwaltungsgericht. He argued that the first indent of Article 6(1) of Decision No 1/80 merely requires that the renewal of the work and residence permits is applied for with a view to working for the same employer, and that he satisfied that condition when he made the application.

13. The Bundesverwaltungsgericht held that the refusal to renew the residence permit could not be criticized under German law, but was uncertain whether an outcome more favourable to Mr Eker might not ensue from the first indent of Article 6(1) of Decision No 1/80.

14. Article 6(1), which appears in Chapter II ("Social provisions"), Section 1 ("Questions relating to employment and the free movement of workers") of Decision No 1/80, reads as follows:

> "Subject to Article 7 on free access to employment for members of his family, a Turkish worker duly registered as belonging to the labour force of a Member State:
> —   shall be entitled in that Member State, after one year's legal employment, to the renewal of his permit to work for the same employer, if a job is available;
> —   shall be entitled in that Member State, after three years of legal employment and subject to the priority to be given to workers of Member States of the Community, to respond to another offer of employment, with an employer of his choice, made under normal conditions and registered with the employment services of that State, for the same occupation;
> —   shall enjoy free access in that Member State to any paid employment of his choice, after four years of legal employment."

15. In this connection, the Bundesverwaltungsgericht is uncertain whether a Turkish worker may claim an extension of his work and residence permits under the first indent of Article 6(1) of Decision No 1/80 only if he has been legally employed continuously for one year by the same employer, or whether it suffices for the application of that provision that the worker has been employed, for one year continuously and with valid work and residence permits, with several employers and wishes to continue working for the last of his employers.

16. Since it took the view that the resolution of the dispute required an interpretation of that provision, the Bundesverwaltungsgericht stayed the proceedings and referred the following question to the Court for a preliminary ruling:

> "Does a Turkish worker fulfil the requirements of the first indent of Article 6(1) of Decision No 1/80 of the EEC/Turkey Association Council even if during the first year of employment he has, with the permission of the national authorities, worked without interruption but for different employers and wishes to continue employment with his last employer?"

17. By its question the national court is essentially asking whether the first indent of Article 6(1) of Decision No 1/80 is to be interpreted as making extension of a Turkish worker's residence permit in the host Member State subject to his having been legally employed for one year continuously with the same employer, or whether that provision merely requires one year's continuous employment, duly covered by work and residence permits, even for several employers, provided that the worker applies for his residence permit to be extended with a view to continuing working for the employer by whom he is employed.

18. To answer that question, it should be observed, first, that since its judgment in Case C-192/89 *Sevince v Staatssecretaris's van Justitie* [1990] ECR I-3461 the Court has consistently held that Article 6(1) of Decision No 1/80 has direct effect in the Member States, so that Turkish nationals who satisfy its conditions may rely directly on the rights conferred on them by the various indents of that provision (see, most recently, Case C-171/95 *Tetik v Land Berlin* [1997] ECR I-329, paragraph 22).

19. Second, the Court has consistently held that the rights which the three indents of Article 6(1) confer on a Turkish worker in regard to employment necessarily imply the existence of a right of residence for the person concerned, since otherwise the right of access to the labour market and the right to work as an employed person would be deprived of all effect (see, most recently, *Tetik* paragraph 24).

20. Third, the first indent of Article 6(1) of Decision No 1/80 requires, for a Turkish worker to be entitled to renewal of his work permit, the completion of one year's legal employment, without specifying whether this must be a period of employment with the employer for whom renewal of the

permit is sought, or whether it may be a period comprised of employment with different employers.

21. On this point, it should be noted that the three indents of Article 6(1) confer on Turkish workers rights which vary and are subject to conditions which differ according to the duration of legal employment in the relevant Member State (see, most recently, *Tetik*, paragraph 23).

22. Since it requires the completion of one year's continuous employment for there to be a right to renewal of the work permit in respect of the same employer, the first indent of Article 6(1) is based on the premiss that only a contractual relationship which lasts for one year is expressive of employment relations stable enough to guarantee the Turkish worker continuity of his employment with the same employer.

23. The coherence of the system of gradual integration of Turkish workers in the host State's labour force, established by the three indents of Article 6(1), would be disrupted if the worker had the right to enter the service of another employer even before satisfying the condition of one year's legal employment specified in the first indent of Article 6(1). In accordance with the second indent of Article 6(1), it is only after three years of legal employment in the Member State concerned that a Turkish worker is entitled to take up work with a different employer, on condition that the employer is engaged in the same business as the previous employer and respects the priority to be given to workers of the Member States.

24. In those circumstances, the first indent of Article 6(1), which does not confer on the worker the right to choose another employer and does not contain the reservations set out in the second indent, cannot be understood as meaning that a Turkish worker may satisfy its conditions, and therefore exercise the rights it confers, if before completion of the first year of legal employment with a given employer he takes up employment with a new employer.

25. It follows that in a case such as that in point in the main proceedings where the competent national authorities have authorised a Turkish worker to change employers before completing one year of legal employment with the first employer in respect of whom the work and residence permits were issued, the right to renewal of those permits, referred to in the first indent of Article 6(1), arises only on expiry of a further period of one year's legal employment.

26. That interpretation finds support in the Court's case-law.

27. In Case C-355/93 *Eroglu* v *Land Baden-Württemberg* [1994] ECR I-5113 the Court has already interpreted the first indent of Article 6(1) of Decision No 1/80 as not conferring the right to renewal of his permit to work for his first employer on a Turkish national who worked for more than a year for that employer and then for some ten months for another employer.

28. In that judgment the Court pointed out that the aim of that provision is

solely to ensure continuity of employment with the same employer and that the provision is accordingly applicable only where a Turkish worker requests an extension of his work permit in order to continue working for the same employer after the initial period of one year's legal employment (paragraph 13).

29.   The Court then stated that extending the application of that provision to a Turkish worker who, after one year's legal employment, has changed employers and is seeking an extension of his work permit in order to work for the first employer again would allow that worker to change employers under that provision before the expiry of the period of three years prescribed in the second indent and would also deprive workers of the Member States of the priority conferred on them pursuant to that indent when a Turkish worker changes employers (paragraph 14).

30.   While the facts of that case admittedly differ from those of the main proceedings in this case, in that Ms Eroglu had changed employers after one year's legal employment in the host Member State and sought renewal of her work permit in order to work for her first employer again, the Court's interpretation in that judgment of the first indent of Article 6(1) must apply *a fortiori* in a case such as Mr Eker's, where a Turkish worker has changed employers before the end of the first year of employment in the Member State concerned and applies for an extension of his residence permit in order to continue working for his new employer before even completing one year's legal employment with that employer.

Costs

31.   In the light of all the foregoing considerations, the answer to the national court's question must be that the first indent of Article 6(1) of Decision No 1/80 must be interpreted as making the extension of a Turkish worker's residence permit in the host Member State subject to his having been legally employed continuously for one year with the same employer.

32.   The costs incurred by the German, Greek, French and Austrian Governments and by the Commission of the European Communities, which have submitted observations to the Court, are not recoverable. Since these proceedings are, for the parties to the main proceedings, a step in the action pending before the national court, the decision on costs is a matter for that court.

On those grounds, THE COURT in answer to the question referred to it by the Bundesverwaltungsgericht by order of 29 September 1995, hereby rules:

The first indent of Article 6(1) of Decision No 1/80 of 19 September 1980 on the development of the Association adopted by the Council of Association established by the Association Agreement between the European Economic Community and Turkey must be interpreted as making the extension of a Turkish worker's residence permit in the host

Member State subject to his having been legally employed continuously for one year with the same employer.

Mancini   Murray   Kapteyn

Ragnemalm   Schintgen

Delivered in open court in Luxembourg on 29 May 1997.

R. Grass   G.F. Mancini
Registrar   President of the Sixth Chamber

Judgment of the Court of Justice of the European Communities

(Sixth Chamber)

17 April 1997

SELMA KADIMAN V STATE OF BAVARIA

C-351/95,

REFERENCE to the Court under Article 177 of the EC Treaty by the Bayerisches Verwaltungsgericht München (Germany) for a preliminary ruling in the proceedings pending before that court on the interpretation of the first paragraph of Article 7 of Decision No 1/80 of the Association Council of 19 September 1980 on the development of the Association, adopted by the Association Council, established by the Association Agreement between the European Economic Community and Turkey,

THE COURT (Sixth Chamber),

composed of: G.F. Mancini, President of the Chamber, J.L.Murray, P.J.G. Kapteyn, H. Ragnemalm and R.Schintgen (Rapporteur), Judges,

Advocate General: M.B. Elmer,
Registrar: D. Louterman-Hubeau, Principal Administrator,

after considering the written observations submitted on behalf of:

- Mrs Kadiman, by R. Gutmann, Rechtsanwalt, Stuttgart,
- The French Government, by C. De Salins and C. Chavance, respectively Assistant Director and Secretary for Foreign Affairs in the Directorate for Legal Affairs, Ministry of Foreign Affairs, acting as Agents,
- the Netherlands Government, by A. Bos, Legal Adviser in the Ministry of Foreign Affairs, acting as Agent,
- the Commission of the European Communities, by J. Sack, Legal Adviser, acting as Agent, having regard to the Report for the Hearing,

after hearing the oral observations of Mrs Kadiman, represented by R. Gutmann; the German Government, represented by E. Röder, Ministerialrat in the Federal Ministry of Economy, acting as Agent; the French Government, represented by C. Chavance; and the Commission, represented by J. Sack, at the hearing on 14 November 1996,

after hearing the Opinion of the Advocate General at the sitting on 16 January 1997, gives the following Judgment

1. By order of 14 June 1995, received at the Court on 13 November 195, the Bayerisches Verwaltungsgericht München (Administrative Court of

Bavaria, Munich) referred to the Court for a preliminary ruling under Article 177 of the EC Decision No 1/80 of the Association Council, of 19 September 1980, on the development of the Association (hereinafter "Decision No 1/80"). The Association Council was established by the Agreement creating an Association between the European Economic Community and Turkey, signed on 12 September 1963 in Ankara by the Republic of Turkey and the Member States of the EEC and the Community, and concluded, approved and confirmed on behalf of the Community by Council Decision 64/732/EEC of 23 December 1963 (OJ 1973 C 113, p. 1).

2.   Those questions were raised in proceedings brought by Mrs Kadiman, a Turkish national, against the State of Bavaria concerning the latter's refusal to extend her German residence permit.

3.   Article 6(1) of Decision No 1/80 provides as follows:
"1.   Subject to Article 7 on free access to employment for members of his family, a Turkish worker duly registered as belonging to the labour force of a Member State:
–   shall be entitled in that Member State, after one year's legal employment, to the renewal of his permit to work for the same employer, if a job is available;
–   shall be entitled in that Member State, after three years of legal employment and subject to the priority to be given to workers of Member States of the Community, to respond to another offer of employment, with an employer of his choice, made under normal conditions and registered with the employment services of that State, for the same occupation;
–   shall enjoy free access in that Member State to any paid employment of his choice, after four years of legal employment."

4.   Article 7 of Decision 1/80 provides:
"The members of the family of a Turkish worker duly registered as belonging to the labour force of a Member State, who have been authorized to join him:

–   shall be entitled – subject to the priority to be given to workers of Member States of the Community – to respond to any offer of employment after they have been legally resident for at least three years in that Member State;
–   shall enjoy free access to any paid employment of their choice provided they have been legally resident there for at least five years.

5.   Children of Turkish workers who have completed a course of vocational training in the host country may respond to any offer of employment there, irrespective of the length of time they have been resident in that Member State, provided one of their parents has been legally employed in the Member State concerned for at least three years".

6.   Those two provisions are contained in Chapter II (Social provision), Section 1 (Questions relating to employment and the free movement of workers), of Decision No 1/80.

7.   It appears from the documents forwarded by the national court that Mrs Kadiman was married in 1985, when aged 15, to a Turkish national living in Germany and in legal employment there since 1977. In 1988, Mrs Kadiman's husband obtained a permit to reside in that Member State for an unlimited period.

8.   On 17 March 1990 Mrs Kadiman was authorized by the German authorities to join her husband in order to reunite the family; she then established her residence with her husband in Ruhpolding (Germany).

9.   In July 1990, the German authorities granted Mrs Kadiman a residence permit which expired on 14 May 1991; they then extended it until 14 May 1993.

10.   Mrs Kadiman also obtained a work permit for a job in Ruhpolding for the period which expired on 14 May 1991; they then extended it until 14 May 1993.

11.   In September 1991, Mr Kadiman declared to the authorities in Ruhpolding that he had been living apart from his wife for about five months, that he had commenced divorce proceedings in Turkey and that his wife had returned to her country of origin on 7 September 1991.

12.   On 4 February 1992, Mrs Kadiman registered with the authorities in Ruhpolding at an address different from that of her husband. On 1 April 1992, she established her residence at Bad Reichenhall (Germany), where she obtained a further work permit, initially for the period from 6 April 1992 to 5 April 1995; however, its period of validity was amended twice, covering successively the periods from 30 October 1992 to 29 October 1995 and from 1 July 1993 to 30 June 1994, because Mrs Kadiman had on both occasions changed employer.

13.   By decision of 4 May 1992, the Landratsamt Traunstein (Central Administrative Office of the District of Traunstein) reduced the period of validity of Mrs Kadiman's residence permit and ordered her to leave German territory because she was not living with her husband. However, that decision was cancelled on 21 May 1992 on the ground that, because of her move to Bad Reichenhall, Mrs Kadiman came within the jurisdiction of the Landratsamt Berchtesgadener Land.

14.   In July 1992, Mrs Kadiman explained to the latter authority that she had ceased living with her husband because he mistreated her and deceived her. Several attempts to resume life together had failed and her husband had beaten her and ejected her from the matrimonial home. Moreover, Mrs Kadiman had stayed in Turkey from 7 September 1991 for holidays with her husband, but her stay had been involuntarily extended until 1 February 1992 because her husband had concealed her passport from her before returning alone to Germany and she had

not been able to return to Germany until she obtained a visa on 22 January 1992.

15. By decision of 5 January 1993, the Landratsamt Berchtesgadener Land brought forward to 26 January 1993 the expiry date of Mrs Kadiman's residence permit and threatened to deport her if she failed to leave Germany within two months on the ground that she and her husband were no longer living under the same roof.

16. Mr Kadiman then declared that he was prepared to resume living with his wife, whereupon that decision was set aside and on 13 May 1993 Mrs Kadiman obtained a new residence permit valid until 14 May 1994.

17. However, since the spouses were still living apart, the Landratsamt Berchtesgadener Land on 13 October 1993 brought forward to 19 October 1993 the expiry date of Mrs Kadiman's residence permit and ordered her to leave Germany within one month following the date on which its decision became final. The reason given by the Landratsamt for that decision was that, since September 1991, Mrs Kadiman had no longer lived with her husband and, therefore, was no longer entitled to a residence permit granted to her in order to enable the family to be together.

18. Mrs Kadiman lodged an appeal against that decision, which is at present pending before the Bayerisches Verwaltungsgericht München. She then amended her pleadings, and requested that court to the Landratsamt Berchtesgadener Land to extend her German residence permit.

19. In support of her appeal, Mrs Kadiman maintains that she was legally resident in Germany from 17 March 1990, that she was in legal and continuous employment there and that the contested decisions were contrary to the first paragraph of Article 7 of Decision No 1/80.

20. The Bayerisches Verwaltungsgericht München took the view that Mrs Kadiman could not rely on German legislation in order to obtain an extension of her residence permit. Moreover, Article 6 of Decision No 1/80, which granted certain independent employment rights to Turkish workers duly registered as belonging to the labour force of a Member State, was not applicable in this case because Mrs Kadiman had not been legally employed by the same employer for at least one year, as required by that article. Accordingly, Mrs Kadiman's appeal could succeed only on the basis of the first paragraph of Article 7 of Decision No 1/80.

21. In that regard, the Bayerisches Verwaltungsgericht München takes the view that it is necessary, first, to consider whether that provision requires the family member of a Turkish worker employed in a Member State, who is authorized to join him there, to live continuously with that worker as part of his family, in view of the fact that in this case Mr and Mrs Kadiman have not been living under the same roof since September 1991.

22. Second, that court questions the impact of the interruptions in Mrs Kadiman's stay in Germany for the purposes of calculating the period of three years' legal residence in the host Member State referred to in the first indent of the first paragraph of Article 7 of Decision No 1/80: to

arrive, in this case, at a period of three years, it would be necessary to add together the periods for which Mrs Kadiman was legally present in Germany before and after the suspension of her residence permit from 26 January to 13 May 1993 and then to determine whether Mrs Kadiman's involuntary four-month say in Turkey, caused by the removal of her passport by her husband, may be taken into account for the purposes of that calculation.

23. Considering that the decision to be given in the proceedings thus required an interpretation of the first paragraph of Article 7 of Decision No 1/80, the Bayerisches Verwaltungsgericht München referred the following three questions to the Court for a preliminary ruling:

"1.   Does the applicability of the first paragraph of Article 7 of Decision No 1/80 of the EEC/Turkey Association Council on the development of the Association presuppose that the family must still be living together at the time when the other conditions are fulfilled?

2.   Does the applicability of the first indent of the first paragraph of Article 7 of Decision No 1/80 presuppose three years' uninterrupted legal residence in a Member State of the Community?

3.   Is a voluntary or forced intermediate stay of five months in Turkey to be counted towards the period of three years' legal residence within the meaning of the first indent of the first paragraph of Article 7 of Decision No 1/80?"

24. In the first place, it must be observed that the three questions concern the situation of a Turkish national who, as the wife and, therefore, a member of the family of a Turkish migrant worker duly registered as belonging to the labour force of a Member State, was authorized to join him in that State and is seeking extension of her permit to reside there in reliance on the first paragraph of Article 7 of Decision No 1/80. The national court has found that, although legally employed for a particular period in the Member State in question, the person concerned cannot rely on the rights conferred by Article 6 of that decision on Turkish workers integrated into the labour force of a Member State because she does not fulfil the conditions laid down by that provision.

The first question

25. It is apparent from the order for reference that Mr and Mrs Kadiman, who were married in 1985 and lived under the same roof in Germany as from 17 March 1990, ceased cohabiting no later than 4 February 1992, the date on which Mrs Kadiman registered as residing at an address other than that of her husband.

26. In order to give an answer which may be of use to the national court, it must therefore be considered whether the concept of legal residence for at least three years, referred to in the first indent of the first paragraph of Article 7 of Decision No 1/80, presupposes that the Turkish worker

and his spouse have been living together throughout the period mentioned and whether the national authorities are entitled to withdraw the latter's residence permit where the spouses are no longer living together.

27. In those circumstances, the first question must be construed as seeking essentially to ascertain whether the first paragraph of Article 7 of Decision No 1/80 precludes the competent authorities of a Member State from requiring the members of the family of a Turkish worker referred to in that provision to live with him for the period of three years prescribed by the first indent of that article in order to be entitled to a residence permit in that Member State.

28. In order to answer that question, it must first be noted that the first indent of Article 7 of Decision No 1/80, in the same way as Article 6(1) and the second paragraph of Article 7 of that decision, confer, in clear, precise and unconditional terms, the right on the members of the family of a Turkish worker duly registered as belonging to the labour force of the host Member State to respond, subject to priority being granted to workers of the Member States, to any offer of employment after being legally resident there for at least three years, and the right freely to take up paid employment of their choice in the Member State in whose territory they have been legally resident for at least five years.

29. Like Article 6(1) (see in particular Case C-192/89 *Sevince* [1990] ECR I-3461, paragraph 26) and the second paragraph of Article 7 (see Case C-355/93 *Eroglu* v *Land Baden- Württemberg* [1994] ECR I-5113, paragraph 17), the first paragraph of Article 7 of Decision No 1/80 thus has direct effect in the Member States, so that Turkish nationals fulfilling the conditions which it lays down may directly rely on the rights conferred on them by that provision.

30. Next, the specific periods of legal residence referred to in the first paragraph of Article 7 necessarily imply the existence, as regards the members of the family of a Turkish worker who are authorised to join him in the host Member State, of a right of residence during such periods, since the effect of withholding such a right would be to negate the possibility offered to the persons concerned of residing in that Member State. Moreover, without a right of residence, the authorisation granted to the family members concerned in order to join the Turkish worker in the territory of the host Member State would itself be rendered entirely inoperative.

31. Finally, it must be emphasised that, although the social provisions of Decision No 1/80, which include the first paragraph of Article 7, constitute a further stage in securing freedom of movement for workers on the basis of Articles 48, 49 and 50 of the Treaty, and although, therefore, the Court has held that it is essential to transpose, so far as possible, the principles enshrined in those Treaty articles to Turkish workers who enjoy the rights conferred by that decision (see Case C-434/93 *Bozkurt* v *Staatssecretaris van Justitie* [1995] ECR I-1475, paragraphs 14, 19 and

20, and Case C-171/95 *Tetik* [1997] ECR I-0000, paragraph 20), the fact nevertheless remains that, as the law stands at present, Turkish nationals are not entitled to move freely within the Community but benefit only from certain rights in the host Member State whose territory they have lawfully entered and where they have been in legal employment for a specified period (*Tetik*, cited above, paragraph 29) or, in the case of members of a Turkish worker's family, they have been authorised to join him and have been legally resident there for a period laid down in the two indents of the first paragraph of Article 7.

32. It is also apparent from settled case-law (see in particular Case C-237/91 *Kus* v *Landeshauptstadt Wiesbaden* [1992] ECR I-6781, paragraph 25) that Decision No 1/80 does not encroach upon the competence of the Member States to regulate both the entry into their territories of Turkish nationals and the conditions under which they take up their first employment, but merely regulates, in Article 6, the situation of Turkish workers already legally integrated in the labour force of the Member State.

33. Similarly, as regards the first paragraph of Article 7, that decision provides that the members of the family of a Turkish worker duly registered as belonging to the labour force of a Member State are entitled to take up employment in that country after being legally resident there for a specified period, without thereby affecting the power of the Member State concerned to authorise any such persons to join the Turkish worker legally employed there, to regulate their stay until they become entitled to respond to any offer of employment and, if necessary, to allow them, under such conditions as it may specify, to take up employment before the expiry of the initial period of three years laid down by the first indent.

34. With regard more particularly to the residence of a family member during that initial period of three years, at issue in the main proceedings, it must be pointed out that, although, as is apparent from paragraph 29 of this judgment, a Member State which has authorised a person to enter its territory in order to join a Turkish worker cannot then withhold from that person the right to reside there in order to enable the family to be together, that Member State nevertheless retains the power to subject that right of residence to conditions of such a kind as to ensure that the presence of the family member in its territory is in conformity with the spirit and purpose of the first paragraph of Article 7 of Decision No 1/80.

35. In that connection, it must be emphasised that the purpose of that provision is to favour employment and residence of Turkish workers duly registered as belonging to the labour force of a Member State by ensuring that their family links are maintained there.

36. Accordingly, it provides, for the initial stage, that family members of a Turkish worker already duly registered as belonging to the labour force of a Member State may be authorised to join him and take up residence there so as to enable the family to be together. In order to deepen the integration of a migrant Turkish worker's family unit in the host Member

State, it also grants those family members the right, after a specified time, to take up employment in that State.

37.   Thus, the system established by the first paragraph of Article 7 is designed to create conditions conducive to family unity in the host Member State, first by enabling family members to be with a migrant worker and then by consolidating their position by granting them the right to obtain employment in that State.

38.   In view of its meaning and purpose, that provision cannot therefore be interpreted as merely requiring the host Member State to have authorised a family member to enter its territory to join a Turkish worker without at the same time requiring the person concerned to continue actually to reside there with the migrant worker until he or she becomes entitled to enter the labour market.

39.   Such an interpretation would not only seriously undermine the objective of family unity pursued by that provision but would also entail the risk that Turkish nationals might evade the stricter requirements of Article 6 by abusing, in particular by entering into sham marriages, the favourable conditions contained in the first paragraph of Article 7.

40.   Whilst Article 6(1) of Decision No 1/80 makes entitlement to progressive employment rights for Turkish migrant workers subject to the condition that the person concerned must already be duly registered as belonging to the labour force of the Member State concerned, the first paragraph of Article 7 regulates the employment rights of members of the Turkish worker's family exclusively by reference to the duration of their residence in the host Member State. On the other hand, the first paragraph of Article 7 expressly states that the family member must have been author- ised by the Member State concerned to "join" the Turkish worker duly registered as belonging to the labour force of that State, whereas Article 6 does not make recognition of the rights which it confers on the worker dependent upon the circumstances under which the right of entry and residence was obtained (see in particular *Kus*, cited above, paragraph 21).

41.   Where, in circumstances such as those of the main proceedings the Turkish national can rely on his status as a member of the family of a migrant worker within the meaning of the first paragraph of Article 7 because he does not fulfil the conditions for claiming, in his own right, the rights provided for in Article 6(1), the practical effect of Article 7 requires, as emphasised in paragraph 37 of this judgment, that the unity of the family, in pursuit of which the person concerned entered the territory of the Member State concerned, should be evidenced for a specified period by actual cohabitation in a household with the worker.

42.   It follows that Decision 1/80 does not in principle prevent the authorities of a Member State from making extension of the residence permit of a family member authorised to join a Turkish worker in that Member State in order to enable the family to be together subject to the condition that the person concerned actually lives with that worker for the period of

three years prescribed by the first indent of the first paragraph of Article 7 of that decision.

43. As the Commission has convincingly argued, the position would be different only if objective circumstances justified the failure of the migrant worker and the member of his family to live under the same roof in the host Member State. That would be the case in particular if the distance between the worker's residence and the place of employment of the member of his family or a vocational training establishment attended by that person required him or her to live in separate accommodation.

44. In a situation such as that of the Plaintiff in the main proceedings, it is for the national court, which alone has jurisdiction to establish and assess the facts of the case before it, to decide whether objective circumstances exist of such a kind as to justify the fact that the Turkish migrant worker and the family member live apart.

45. In view of the foregoing considerations, the answer to the first question must be that the first paragraph of Article 7 of Decision No 1/80 does not in principle preclude the competent authorities of a Member State from requiring that the family members of a Turkish worker, referred to by that provision, live with him for the period of three years prescribed by the first indent of that article in order to be entitled to reside in that Member State. There may however be objective reasons to justify the family member concerned living apart from the Turkish migrant worker. The second and third questions

46. By its second and third questions, which it is appropriate to consider together, the national court seeks essentially to ascertain whether the first indent of the first paragraph of Article 7 of Decision 1/80 must be interpreted as meaning that the family member concerned is required to reside uninterruptedly for a period of three years in the host Member State. It also seeks to ascertain whether account should be taken, for the purpose of calculating the three year period of legal residence within the meaning of that provision, first of an involuntary stay of some four months by the person concerned in his country of origin and, second of the period during which the validity of his residence permit was suspended in the host Member State.

47. It must be borne in mind in that connection that the first indent of the first paragraph of Article 7 aims to enable the Turkish worker and the members of his family actually to be together in the host Member State, so that the national authorities may in principle require the family members to live under the same roof as the migrant worker for the initial period of three years (see in particular paragraphs 37, 41 and 44 of this judgment).

48. It thus follows from the meaning and purpose of that provision that the family member must in principle reside uninterruptedly during those three years with the Turkish worker.

49. However, that interpretation does not mean that the person concerned

may not be absent from the family residence for a reasonable period and for legitimate reasons, for example in order to take holidays or visit his family in his country of origin. Such short interruptions of cohabitation, not intended to detract from residence together in the host Member State, must be treated as periods in which the family member concerned actually lived with the Turkish worker.

50. The same must apply, *a fortiori*, to a period of less than six months spent by the person concerned in his country of origin for reasons beyond his control.

51. In those circumstances, an intermediate stay of that kind must be taken into account for the purpose of calculating the three-year period of legal residence within the meaning of the first indent of the first paragraph of Article 7 of Decision No 1/80.

52. As regards the limitation of the period of validity of the residence permit held by the Turkish worker's family member in the host Member State, it must be observed that, whilst the Member States retain the power to lay down the conditions under which that family member may enter their territory and reside there until he or she becomes entitled to respond to any offer of employment (see paragraphs 32 and 33 of this judgment), the fact nevertheless remains that the rights conferred by the first paragraph of Article 7 on family members of a Turkish worker are granted by that provision to the persons concerned regardless of the issue by the authorities of the host Member State of specific administrative document, such as a residence permit (see, by analogy with Article 6 of Decision No 1/80, *Bozkurt*, cited above, paragraphs 29 and 30).

53. Moreover, in the case before the national court, the validity of the residence permit issued to the family member concerned was suspended only for a brief period and that limitation was removed by the issue of a new residence permit; nor do the competent authorities of the host Member State claim, on that ground, that the person concerned is not legally resident within national territory.

54. In those circumstances, the period during which the person concerned was not in possession of a residence permit is not such as to affect the running of time for the purposes of the three-year period laid down in the first indent of the first paragraph of Article 7 of Decision No 1/80.

55. In view of the foregoing, the answer to the second and third questions must be that the first indent of the first paragraph of Article 7 of Decision No 1/80 is to be interpreted as meaning that the family member concerned is in principle required to reside uninterruptedly for three years in the host Member State. However, account must be taken, for the purpose of calculating the three-year period of legal residence within the meaning of that provision, of an involuntary stay of less than six months by the person concerned in his country of origin. The same applies to the period during which the person concerned was not in possession of a valid residence permit, where the competent authorities of the host Member

State did not claim on that ground that the person concerned was not legally resident within national territory, but on the contrary issued a new residence permit to him.

Costs

56. The costs incurred by the German, French and Netherlands Governments and by the Commission of the European Communities, which have submitted observations to the Court, are not recoverable. Since these proceedings are, for the parties to the main proceedings, a step in the action pending before the national court, the decision on costs is a matter for that court.

On those grounds, THE COURT, in answer to the questions submitted to it by the Bayerisches Verwaltungsgericht München by order of 14 June 1995, hereby rules:

1. The first paragraph of Article 7 of Decision No 1/80 of 19 September 1980 on the development of the Association, adopted by the Association Council established by the Association Agreement between the European Economic Community and Turkey, does not in principle preclude the competent authorities of a Member State from requiring that the family members of a Turkish worker, referred to by that provision, live with him for the period of three years prescribed by the first indent of that article in order to be entitled to reside in that Member State. There may however be objective reasons to justify the family member concerned living apart from the Turkish migrant worker.

2. The first indent of the first paragraph of Article 7 of Decision No 1/80 is to be interpreted as meaning that the family member concerned is in principle required to reside uninterruptedly for three years in the host Member State. However, account must be taken, for the purpose of calculating the three-year period of legal residence within the meaning of that provision, of an involuntary stay of less than six months by the person concerned in his country or origin. The same applies to the period during which the person concerned was not in possession of a valid residence permit, where the competent authorities of the host Member State did not claim on that ground that the person concerned was not legally resident within national territory, but on the contrary issued a new residence permit to him.

Mancini   Murray   Kapteyn

         Ragnemalm   Schintgen

Delivered in open court in Luxembourg on 17 April 1997.

R. Grass   G.F. Mancini
Registrar   President of the Sixth Chamber

Judgment of the Court of Justice of the European Communities

(Sixth Chamber)
23 January 1997

RECEP TETIK V LAND BERLIN

joined party: the **Oberbundesanwalt beim Bundesverwaltungsgericht** (Federal Attorney attached to the Federal Administrative Court),

Case C-171/95,

REFERENCE to the Court under Article 177 of the EC Treaty by the Bundesverwaltungsgericht (Germany) for a preliminary ruling in the proceedings pending before that court on the interpretation of the third indent of Article 6(1) of Decision No 1/80 of the Council of Association of 19 September 1980 on the development of the Association between the European Economic Community and Turkey,

THE COURT (Sixth Chamber),

composed of: G.F. Mancini, President of the Chamber (Rapporteur), J.L. Murray, C.N. Kakouris, P.J.G. Kapteyn and H. Ragnemalm, Judges,

Advocate General: M.B. Elmer,
Registrar: H.A. Rühl, Principal Administrator,

after considering the written observations submitted on behalf of:
- Mr Tetik, by C. Rosenkranz, Rechtsanwalt. Berlin;
- Land Berlin, by M. Arndt, Rechtsanwältin, Berlin;
- the German Government, by E. Röder and B. Kloke, respectively, Ministerialrat and Oberregierungsrat in the Federal Ministry of Economic Affairs, acting as Agents;
- the French Government, by C. de Salins and C. Chavance, respectively, Assistant Director and Secretary for Foreign Affairs in the Legal Affairs Directorate of the Ministry of Foreign Affairs, acting as Agents;
- the United Kingdom Government, by J.E. Collins, Assistant Treasury Solicitor, acting as Agent, and E. Sharpston, Barrister;
- the Commission of the European Communities, by P. van Nuffel, of its Legal Service, acting as Agent,

having regard to the Report for the Hearing

after hearing the oral observations of the German Government, represented by E. Röder, the French Government, represented by C. Chavance: and the

Commission. represented by U. Wölker, of its Legal Service, acting as Agent, at the hearing on 3 October 1996,

after hearing the Opinion of the Advocate General at the sitting on 14 November 1996, gives the following Judgment

1. By order of 11 April 1995, received at the Court on 7 June 1995, the Bundesverwaltungsgericht (Federal Administrative Court) referred to the Court for a preliminary ruling under Article 177 of the EC Treaty two questions on the interpretation of the third indent of Article 6(1) of Decision No 1/80 of the Council of Association of 19 September 1980 on the development of the Association (hereinafter "Decision No 1/80"). The Council of Association was set up by the Agreement establishing an Association between the European Economic Community and Turkey signed at Ankara on 12 September 1963 by the Republic of Turkey and by the Member States of the EEC and the Community, and concluded, approved and confirmed on behalf of the Community by Council Decision 64/732/EEC of 23 December 1963 (OJ 1973 C 113, P 1, hereinafter "the Agreement").

2. Those questions have arisen in a dispute between Mr Tetik, a Turkish national, and the Land Berlin concerning the rejection of an application for the grant of an unlimited residence permit for Germany.

3. It appears from the documents in the main proceedings that Mr Tetik was legally employed, from September 1980 to 20 July 1988, as a seaman on various German sea-going vessels.

4. For the purpose of that activity, he obtained from the German authorities successive residence permits, on each occasion for a specified period and limited to employment in shipping. Mr Tetik's last residence permit was valid until 4 August 1988 and stated that it would expire upon cessation of his employment in German sea-going shipping.

5. On 20 July 1988, Mr Tetik voluntarily terminated his employment as a seaman.

6. On 1 August 1988, he moved to Berlin, where, on the same day, he applied for an unlimited residence permit for the purpose of engaging in gainful employment on land, stating that he intended to reside in Germany until about 2020.

7. That application was refused by the competent authorities of the *Land* Berlin on 19 January 1989. The legality of that decision was confirmed by the Verwaltungsgericht (Administrative Court) on 10 December 1991 and by the Oberverwaltungsgericht (Higher Administrative Court) Berlin on 24 March 1992.

8. The registration certificate which the German authorities issued to Mr Tetik following his application for an unlimited residence permit was endorsed with the words "not authorized to engage in gainful employment".

9. Mr Tetik, who has been unemployed since his voluntary termination

of employment in German shipping, appealed to the Bundes-verwaltungsgericht.

10. While it found that the refusal to renew the residence permit was in accordance with German law, that court was unsure whether a solution more favourable to Mr Tetik might not follow from Article 6 of Decision No 1/80.

11. Article 6 of Decision No 1/80 provides as follows:
"1. Subject to Article 7 on free access to employment for members of his family, a Turkish worker duly registered as belonging to the labour force of a Member State:
   – shall be entitled in that Member State, after one year's legal employment, to the renewal of his permit to work for the same employer, if a job is available:
   – shall be entitled in that Member State, after three years of legal employment and subject to the priority to be given to workers of Member States of the Community to respond to another offer of employment, with an employer of his choice, made under normal conditions and registered the employment services of that State. for the same occupation,
   – shall enjoy free access in that Member State to any paid employment of his choice, after four years of legal employment.
2. Annual holidays and absences for reasons of maternity or an accident at work or short periods of sickness shall be treated as periods of legal employment. Periods of involuntary unemployment duly certified by the relevant authorities and long absences on account of sickness shall not be treated as periods of legal employment, but shall not affect rights acquired as the result of the preceding period of employment.
3. The procedures for applying paragraphs 1 and 2 shall be those established under national rules."

12. Since it took the view that the resolution of the dispute required an interpretation of Article 6, the Bundesverwaltunusgericht, by order of 11 April 1995, referred the following two questions to the Court for a preliminary ruling:
"1. Is a Turkish seaman, who was employed from 1980 to 1988 on maritime vessels of a Member State, a member of the labour force of that Member State and legally employed there within the meaning of Article 6(1) of Decision No 1/80 of the EEC/Turkey Council of Association on the development of the Association where his employment relationship was governed by national law, and he paid income tax and was affiliated to the social security system in that Member State, but the residence permit issued to him was limited to working in shipping and did not authorize him to take up residence on shore?
   Is it relevant in that connection that under German law that

activity is not subject to the requirement of a work permit and that, to some extent, special statutory arrangements apply to seamen from the point of view of employment law and social security law?

2.   If Question 1 is answered in the affirmative:

Does a Turkish seaman lose his right to be granted a residence permit if he terminates his employment relationship voluntarily, and not, for example, on health grounds, and 11 days later, after the expiry of his residence permit, applies for a residence permit for work on shore and after the refusal to grant the permit is unemployed?"

13.   According to an order made by the Bundesverwaltungsgericht on 30 August 1995 and received at the Court on 25 September 1995, the national court considers that the first question submitted has been adequately settled by the judgment in Case C-434/93 *Bozkurt* v *Staatssecretaris van Justitie* [1995] ECR I-1475. However, the Bundesverwaltungsgericht continues to have doubts as to whether Mr Tetik was entitled to receive a residence permit under the third indent of Article 6(1) of Decision No 1/80 in view of the fact that he had voluntarily terminated his employment as a seaman.

14.   In those circumstances, the Bundesverwaltungsgericht, in its order of 30 August 1995, expressed the view that it was no longer necessary to reply to the first question and requested the Court to rule only on the second question set out in the order of 11 April 1995.

15.   In order to answer that question, it must first be recalled at the outset that, according to Article 12 of the Agreement, "the Contracting Parties agree to be guided by Articles 48, 49 and 50 of the Treaty establishing the Community for the purpose of progressively securing freedom of movement for workers between them".

16.   Article 6 of the Agreement further provides that "to ensure the implementation and the progressive development of the Association, the Contracting Parties shall meet in a Council of Association which shall act within the powers conferred upon it by this Agreement, while Article 22(1) states that "in order to attain the objectives of this Agreement the Council of Association shall have the power to take decisions in the cases provided for therein … ."

17.   Article 36 of the Additional Protocol, signed on 23 November 1970, annexed to the Agreement and concluded by Council Regulation (EEC) No 2760/72 of 19 December 1972 (OJ 1973 C 113, p. 17, hereinafter "the Additional Protocol") provides for progressive stages in securing freedom of movement for workers between Member States of the Community and Turkey and states that "the Council of Association shall decide on the rules necessary to that end".

18.   Pursuant to Article 12 of the Agreement and Article 36 of the Additional Protocol, the Council of Association first adopted, on 20 December 1976, Decision No 2/76, which is described, in Article 1, as constituting a first

stage in securing freedom of movement for workers between the Community and Turkey.

19. According to the third recital in its preamble, Decision No 1/80 on the development of the Association, which the Council of Association subsequently adopted on 19 December 1980, seeks to improve, in the social field, the treatment accorded to workers and members of their families in relation to the arrangements introduced by Decision No 2/76.

20. The provisions of Section 1 ("Questions relating to employment and the free movement of workers") of Chapter II ("Social provisions") of Decision No 1/80, of which Article 6 forms part, thus constitute a further stage in securing, freedom of movement for workers on the basis of Articles 48, 49 and 50 of the Treaty (see paragraphs 14 and 19 of *Bozkurt*, cited above). The Court accordingly considered it essential to transpose, so far as possible, the principles enshrined in those Treaty articles to Turkish workers who enjoy the rights conferred by Decision No 1/80 (see *Bozkurt*, paragraph 20).

21. It must first be noted in this regard that, as the Court has consistently held (see in particular, Case C-237/91 *Kus* v *Landesshauptstadt Wiesbaden* [1992] ECR I-6781, paragraph 25, Decision No 1/80 does not encroach upon the competence retained by the Member States to regulate both the entry into their territories of Turkish nationals and the conditions under which they may take up their first employment, but merely regulates, particularly in Article 6, the situation of Turkish workers already integrated into the labour force of a Member State.

22. Second, it must be pointed out that, since its judgment in Case C-192/89 *Sevince* v *Staatssecretaris van Justitie* [1990] ECR I-3461, the Court has consistently held that Article 6(1) of Decision No 1/80 has direct effect in the Member States and that Turkish nationals who satisfy its conditions may therefore rely directly on the rights given them by the various indents of that provision (Case C-355/93 *Eroglu* v *Land Baden-Württemberg* [1994] ECR I-5113, paragraph 11).

23. As is clear from the three indents of Article 6(1), those rights themselves vary and are subject to conditions which differ according to the duration of legal employment in the relevant Member State (*Eroglu*, paragraph 12).

24. Third, it should also be borne in mind that the Court has consistently held that the rights which the three indents of Article 6(1) confer on a Turkish worker in regard to employment necessarily imply the existence of a right of residence for the person concerned, since otherwise the right of access to the labour market and the right to work as an employed person would be deprived of all effect (*Sevince*, paragraph 29, *Kus*, paragraphs 29 and 30), and *Bozkurt*, paragraph 28).

25. With particular regard to the question submitted for a preliminary ruling, it plainly relates to the situation of a Turkish worker who, by reason of the fact that he was legally employed for almost eight years in a Member State, enjoyed, pursuant to the third indent of Article 6(1) of Decision

No 1/80, "free access... to any paid employment of his choice" in that Member State.

26. In that regard, it is first of all evident from the express terms of Article 6(1) that, in contrast to the first two indents, which merely set out the arrangements under which a Turkish national who has lawfully entered into a territory of a Member State and has been authorised there to engaged in employment may work in the host Member State, by continuing to work for the same employer after one year's legal employment (first indent) or by responding, after three years of legal employment and subject to the priority to be given to workers from the Member States, to an offer of employment made by another employer for the same occupation (second indent), the third indent confers on a Turkish worker not only the right to respond to a prior offer of employment but also the unconditional right to seek and take up any employment freely chosen by the person concerned, without any possibility of this being subject to priority for workers from the Members States.

27. Next, the Court has already held, with regard to the free movement of workers who are nationals of Member States, that Article 48 of the Treaty entails the right for the latter to reside in another Member State for the purpose of seeking employment there and that, while the duration of the stay of a person seeking employment in the Member State concerned may be limited under the relevant national legislation, to give full effect to Article 48 none the less requires that the person concerned be given a reasonable time in which to apprise himself, in the territory of the Member State which he has entered, of offers of employment corresponding to his occupational qualifications and to take, where appropriate, the necessary steps in order to be engaged (see, in this connection, Case C-292/89 *Antonissen* [1991] ECR I-745, paragraphs 13,15 and 16).

28. As pointed out in paragraph 20 of this judgment, the principles enshrined in Articles 48,49 and 50 of the Treaty must, so far as possible, inform the treatment of Turkish workers who enjoy the rights conferred by Decision No 1/80.

29. In contrast to nationals of Member States, Turkish workers are, admittedly, not entitled to move freely within the Community but benefit only from certain rights in the host Member State whose territory they have lawfully entered and where they have been in legal employment for a specified period.

30. Nevertheless, a Turkish worker such as the appellant in the main proceedings must be able, for a reasonable period, to seek effectively new employment in the host Member State and must have a corresponding right of residence during that period, notwithstanding the fact that he himself terminated his previous contract of employment without entering immediately into a new employment relationship.

31. As the Commission has convincingly argued, to give full effect to the third indent of Article 6(1) of Decision No 1/80 a Turkish worker must,

after at least four years of legal employment in a Member State, be entitled to leave his employment on personal grounds and, for a reasonable period, seek new employment in the same Member State, since his right of free access to any paid employment of his choice within the meaning of that provision would otherwise be deprived of its substance.

32. With regard to the reasonable period which the Member State is thus required to allow for the purpose of seeking other employment, it is for the national authorities concerned to determine how long that period should be, in accordance with Article 6(3) of Decision No 1/80. That period must, however, be sufficient not to deprive of its substance the right accorded by the third indent of Article 6(1) by jeopardising in fact the Turkish worker's prospects of finding new employment.

33. In a case such as that at issue in the main proceedings, where the national legislation concerned has not laid down such a period, it is for the national court to determine it in the light of the circumstances put before it.

34. However, a period of a few days, such as that which was in fact available to a Turkish worker such as Mr Tetik between the termination of his employment contract and the expiry of his residence permit, is in any event inadequate to allow him effectively to seek new employment.

35. That interpretation is not invalidated by the arguments of the German and United Kingdom Governments that, in guaranteeing that rights acquired as a result of the preceding period of employment are safeguarded only in the case of involuntary unemployment on the part of the Turkish worker, the second sentence of Article 6(2) of Decision No 1/80 must mean conversely that no acquired right can be relied on where, as in the main proceedings, the worker voluntarily relinquished his employment and definitively left the labour force of the Member State concerned, by reason of the fact that he was unable immediately to enter into a new employment relationship.

36. In that connection, it must first be pointed out that Article 6(2) provides, for the purpose of calculating the periods of legal employment referred to in the three indents of Article 6(1), preferential rules in favour of a Turkish worker who temporarily ceases work, distinguishing those periods of inactivity according to their type and duration.

37. The first sentence of Article 6(2) concerns those periods, in principle of short duration, during which he does not in fact pursue his work (annual holidays, maternity leave, absences because of accidents at work or sickness involving only a brief cessation of work). These absences of the worker from his place of work are, consequently, treated as periods of legal employment for the purposes of Article 6(1).

38. The second sentence of Article 6(2) relates to the period of inactivity due to long-term sickness or involuntary unemployment, that is to say, where the failure to work is not attributable to any misbehaviour on the part of the worker (as also follows from the use of the adjective "unverschuldet" in the German version). It provides that, although periods of inactivity

of this type cannot be treated as periods of legal employment, they do not affect rights which the worker has acquired as the result of preceding periods of legal employment.

39.   The sole purpose of this latter provision is therefore to prevent a Turkish worker who recommences employment after having been forced to stop working because of long-term illness or unemployment through no fault of his own from being required, in the same way as a Turkish national who has never previously been in paid employment in the Member State in question, to recommence the periods of legal employment envisaged by the three indents of Article 6(1).

40.   In circumstances where, as in the main proceedings, a Turkish worker who has already been legally employed for more than four years in the host Member State voluntarily leaves his work to seek other employment in that Member State, that worker cannot automatically be treated as having definitely left the labour force of that State, provided, however, that he continues to be duly registered as belonging to the labour force of the Member State within the meaning of the first Phrase of Article 6(1).

41.   Where a Turkish worker was unable to enter into a new employment relationship immediately after having abandoned his previous employment, as in the main proceedings, that condition continues, in principle, to be satisfied only in so far as the person who finds himself without employment satisfies all the formalities that may be required in the Member State in question, for instance by registering as a person seeking employment and remaining available to the employment authorities of that State for the requisite period.

42.   That requirement also makes it possible to ensure that during the reasonable period which he must be granted in order to allow him to enter into a new employment relationship the Turkish national does not abuse his right of residence in the Member State concerned but does in fact seek new employment.

43.   However, in a case such as that of the appellant in the main proceedings, it is for the national court, which alone has jurisdiction to determine and evaluate the facts of the dispute brought before it, to decide whether the Turkish national concerned was obliged to take the steps which might be required in the Member State concerned to make himself available to the employment authorities, bearing in mind the fact that, following his application for an extension of his residence permit, he was forbidden to engage in any gainful employment (see paragraph 8 of this judgment).

44.   The German and French Governments have also argued that a Turkish national's right of residence in a Member State is no more than the corollary to the right to employment and that, if it follows from the judgment in *Bozkurt* that a Turkish national is not entitled to remain on the territory of the host Member State after he has suffered an accident at work resulting in permanent incapacity for work, this must a fortiori

be the case where the worker has deliberately left the labour force of the Member State concerned by abandoning his employment.

45. It must be noted in that connection that, in *Bozkurt*, at paragraphs 38 and 39, the Court held that, in the absence of any express provision to that end, the Turkish national was not entitled to remain the host Member State after suffering an accident at work which prevents him from engaging in subsequent employment. In such a case the worker is regarded as having definitively ceased to belong to the labour force of that Member State and the right of residence which he seeks has therefore no connection with paid employment, even in the future.

46. On the other hand, in a case such as that at issue in the main proceedings, it follows from paragraphs 40 to 42 of the present judgment that, provided that the Turkish national is genuinely seeking new employment, complying where appropriate with the requirements of the legislation in force in the host Member State, he must be regarded as continuing to be duly registered as belonging to the labour force of that State for the period reasonably necessary for him to find new employment. The argument put forward by the German and French Governments cannot therefore be accepted.

47. Finally, with regard to the German Government's argument that a worker such as Mr Tetik could have taken the steps necessary to seek new employment during the holiday periods to which he was entitled, it must be pointed out that annual holidays serve a purpose different from that of the period which the host Member State is required to grant a Turkish national in order to allow him to seek new employment. Furthermore, the person concerned may already have used up all of his leave for the year in question when he decides to terminate his contract of employment on personal grounds.

48. In view of those considerations, the answer to the second question referred must be that the third indent of Article 6(1) of Decision No 1/80 must be interpreted as meaning that a Turkish worker who has been legally employed for more than four years in a Member State, who decides voluntarily to leave his employment in order to seek new work in the same Member State and is unable immediately to enter into a new employment relationship, enjoys in that State, for a reasonable period, a right of residence for the purpose of seeking new employment there, provided that he continues to be duly registered as belonging to the labour force of the Member State concerned, complying where appropriate with the requirements of the legislation in force in that State, for instance by registering as a person seeking employment and making himself available to the employment authorities. It is for the Member State concerned and, in the absence of legislation to that end, for the national court before which the matter has been brought to fix such a reasonable period, which must, however, be sufficient not to jeopardise in fact the prospects of his finding new employment.

Costs

49.   The costs incurred by the German, French and United Kingdom Governments and the Commission of the European Communities, which have submitted observations to the Court, are not recoverable. Since these proceedings are, for the parties to the main proceedings, a step in the action pending before the national court, the decision on costs is a matter for that court.

On those grounds, THE COURT, in answer to the question referred to it by the Bundesverwaltungsgericht, by order of 11 April 1995, as amended by order of 30 August 1995, hereby rules:

The third indent of Article 6(1) of Decision No 1/80 of the Council of Association of 19 September 1980 on the development of the Association between the European Economic Community and Turkey must be interpreted as meaning that a Turkish worker who has been legally employed for more than four years in a Member State who decides voluntarily to leave his employment in order to seek new work in the same Member State and is unable immediately to enter into a new employment relationship, enjoys in that State, for a reasonable period, a right of residence for the purpose of seeking new paid employment there, provided that he continues to be duly registered as belonging to the labour force of the Member State concerned, complying where appropriate with the requirements of the legislation in force in that State, for instance by registering as a person seeking employment and making himself available to the employment authorities. It is for the Member State concerned and, in the absence of legislation to that end, for the national court before which the matter has been brought to fix such a reasonable period which must, however, be sufficient not to jeopardise in fact the prospects of his finding new employment.

Mancini   Murray   Kakouris

Kapteyn   Ragnemalm

Delivered in open court in Luxembourg on 23 January 1997.

R. Grass   G.F. Mancini
Registrar   President of the Sixth Chamber

Judgment of the Court of Justice of the European Communities
10 September 1996

Z. TAFLAN-MET, S. ALTUN-BASER, E. ANDAL-BUGDAYCI V BESTUUR VAN DE
SOCIALE VERZEKERINGSBANK; O. AKOL -V- BESTUUR VAN DE NIEUWE
ALGEMENE BEDRIJFSVERENIGING

Case C-277/94

REFERENCE to the Court under Article 177 of the EC Treaty by the
Arrondissementsrechtbank, Amsterdam, for a preliminary ruling in the proceedings pending before that court on the interpretation of Articles 12 and 13 of
Decision No 3/80 of the Association Council of 19 September 1980 on the
application of the social security schemes of the Member States of the European
Communities to Turkish workers and members of their families (OJ 1983 C
110, p. 60).

THE COURT

composed of G.C. Rodriguez Iglesias, President, D.A.O. Edward (Rapporteur),
J.-P. Puissochet and G. Hirsch (Presidents of Chambers), G.F. Mancini, J.C.
Moitinho de Almeida, P.J.G. Kapteyn, C. Gulmann and J.L. Murray, Judges,

Advocate General: A. La Pergola
Registrar: H.A. Rühl, Principal Administrator,
- Bestuur van de Sociale Verzekeringsbank, Amsterdam, by E.H.Pijnacker
  Hordijk , of the Amsterdam Bar,
- Bestuur van de Nieuwe Algemene Bedrijfsvereniging, by C.R.J.A.M. Brent,
  Head of the Administration and Legal Affairs Section of the association
  Gemeenschnappelijk Administratiekantoor, acting as Agent,
- the Netherlands Government, by A. Bos, Legal Adviser in the Ministry
  of Foreign Affairs, acting as Agent,
- the German Government, by E. Röder, Ministerialrat in the Federal
  Ministry of Economic Affairs, and G. Thiele, Assessor in that Ministry,
  acting as Agents,
- the Greek Government, by A. Samoni-Radou, Assistant Special Legal
  Adviser in the Department for Community Legal Affairs of the Ministry
  of Foreign Affairs, and L. Pneumatikou, Specialized Academic Adviser
  in that Department, acting as Agents,
- the French Government, by E. Belliard, Deputy Director of the Legal
  Affairs Directorate of the Ministry of Foreign Affairs, and C. Chavance,
  Foreign Affairs Secretary in that Directorate, acing as Agents,

–   the Commission of the European Communities, by P.J. Kuyper, Legal Adviser, and M. Patakia, of its Legal Service, acting as Agents,

having regard to the Report for the Hearing,

after hearing the oral observations of Mrs Altun-Baser, represented by T.A.M. Visser, of the Bar at The Hague; Bestuur van de Sociale Verzekeringsbank, Amsterdam, represented by E.H. Pijnacker Hordijk; Bestuur van de Nieuwe Algemene Bedrijfsvereniging, represented by F.W.M. Keunen, a lawyer in the association Gemeenschappelijk Admnistratiekantoor; the Netherlands Government, represented by M.A. Fierstra, Assistant Legal Adviser in the Ministry of Foreign Affairs, acting as Agent; the German Government, repre-sented by E. Röder; the Greek Government, represented by R. Silva de Lapuerta; the French Government, represented by C. Chavance and J.-F. Dobelle, Deputy Director of the Legal Affairs Directorate of the Ministry of Foreign Affairs, acting as Agent; the United Kingdom Government, represented by E. Sharpston, Barrister, and the Commission, represented by P.J. Kuyper and M. Patakia, at the hearing on 13 February 1996,

after hearing the Opinion of the Advocate General at the sitting on 26 March 1996, gives the following Judgment

1.   By order of 23 August 1994, received at the Court on 12 October 1994, the Arrondissementsrechtbank (District Court), Amsterdam, referred to the Court for a preliminary ruling under Article 177 of the EC Treaty a number of questions on the interpretation of Articles 12 and 13 of Decision No 3/80 of the Association Council of 19 September 1980 on the application of the social security schemes of the Member States of the European Communities to Turkish workers and members of their families (OJ 1983 C 110, p. 60); hereinafter "Decision No 3/80"). The Association Council was set up by the Agreement establishing an associa-tion between the European Economic Community and Turkey, which was signed at Ankara on 12 September 1963 by the Turkish Republic, on the one hand, and by the Member States of the EEC and the Community, on the other, and concluded, approved and confirmed on behalf of the Community by Council Decision 64/732/EEC of 23 December (OJ 1973 C 113, p. 1; hereinafter "the Agreement").

2.   Those questions were raised in proceeding between, Mrs Taflan-Met, Mrs Altun-Baser and Mrs Andal-Bugdayci and Bestuur van de Sociale Verzekeringsbank, Amsterdam, and between Mr Akol and Bestuur van de Nieuwe Algemene Bedrijfsvereniging, relating to the refusal of the competent Netherlands institutions to pay them social security benefits.

3.   Decision No 3/80 sets out to coordinate Member States' social security schemes with a view to enabling Turkish worker employed or formerly employed in the Community, members of their families and their survivors to qualify for benefits in the traditional branches of social security.

4.   To that end, the provisions of Decision No 3/80 refer for the most part

to particular provisions of Council Regulation (EEC) No 1408/71 of 14 June 1971 on the application of social security schemes to employed persons and their families moving within the Community (OJ, English Special Edition 1971 (II)a, p. 461) and, less frequently, to Council Regulation (EEC) No 574/72 of 21 March 1972 laying down the procedure for implementing Regulation (EEC) No 1408/71 (OJ, English Special Edition 1972 (I), p. 159).

5. Title III of Decision No 3/80 consists of coordinating provisions, based on Regulation No 1408/71, relating to sickness and maternity benefits, invalidity benefits, old-age benefits and death benefits (pensions), benefits in respect of accidents at work and occupational diseases, and death grants, together with family benefits and allowances.

6. In particular, Article 12, which constitutes Chapter 2, "Invalidity", of Title III, provides, as follows:

> "The rights to benefits of a worker who has successively or alternately been subject to the legislation of two or more Member States shall be established in accordance with Article 37(1), first sentence, and (2), Articles 38 to 40, Article 41(1)(a), (b), (c) and (e) and (2), and Articles 42 and 43 of Regulation (EEC) No 1408/71.

However:

(a) for the purpose of applying Article 39(4) of Regulation (EEC) No 1408/71, all the members of the family, including children, residing in the Community or in Turkey, shall be taken into account;

(b) the reference in Article 40(1) of this Regulation to the provisions of Title III, Chapter 3, of Regulation (EEC) No 1408/71 shall be replaced by a reference to the provisions of Title III, Chapter 3 of this Decision."

7. Article 13, which forms part of Chapter 3, "Old age and death benefits (pensions)", of Title III of Decision No 3/80, provides that:

> "The rights to benefits of a worker who has been subject to the legislation of two or more Member States, or of his survivors, shall be established in accordance with Article 44(2), first sentence, Articles 45, 46(2), Articles 47, 48, 49 and 51 of Regulation (EEC) No 1408/71.

However:

(a) Article 46(2) of Regulation (EEC) No 1408/71 shall apply even if the conditions for acquiring entitlement to benefits are satisfied without the need to have recourse to Article 45 of the said Regulation;

(b) for the purposes of applying Article 47(3) of Regulation (EEC) No 1408/71, all the members of the family, including children, residing in the Community or in Turkey shall be taken into account;

(c) for the purpose of applying Article 49(1)(a) and (2) and Article 51 of Regulation (EEC) No 1408/71, the reference to Article 46 shall be replaced by a reference to Article 46(2)."

8.   Unlike the other two decisions adopted on the same date by the EEC-Turkey Association Council (Decision No 1/80 on the development of the Association and Decision No 2/80 determining the conditions for implementing the special aid to Turkey (not published)), Decision No 3/80 does not specify on what date it should enter into force.

9.   It appears from the order for reference that the plaintiffs in the first three actions before the national court are Turkish nationals, residing in Turkey, who are widows of Turkish workers who were in gainful employment in various Member States, including the Netherlands. After their husbands' death, they applied for widows' pensions in the Member States where their husbands had worked. The competent Belgian and German institutions granted those applications. Their applications were however rejected by the Netherlands authorities on the ground that their husbands had died in Turkey, whereas, under the Netherlands legislation, the insured person or his successors are entitled to claim benefit only if the insured risk materializes at a time when the person concerned is covered by that legislation.

10.   The plaintiff in the fourth action before the national court is a Turkish national, residing in Germany, who worked first in the Netherlands and subsequently in Germany, where he became incapable of work. He therefore applied for an invalidity pension both in Germany and in the Netherlands. Unlike the German institution, the competent Netherlands institution refused to grant the application on the ground that Mr Akol's incapacity for work had occurred at a time when he was no longer working in the Netherlands and, as a result, was not covered by the Netherlands legislation.

11.   Taking the view that the plaintiffs in the main proceedings could qualify for the benefits sought in the Netherlands only under Decision No 3/80, in particular Articles 12 and 13 thereof, the Arrondissementsrechtbank, Amsterdam, decided to stay proceedings and refer the following questions to the Court for a preliminary ruling:

"1.   Is Decision No 3/80 of the EEC-Turkey Association Council on the application of social security schemes of the Member States of the European Communities to Turkish workers and members of their families applicable in the Community without an implementation procedure having taken place, as laid down in Article 2(1) of the Agreement creating an association between the European Economic Community and Turkey?

2.   (a)   If Decision No 3/80 is not (yet) applicable in the Community, can that decision nevertheless in certain circumstances have legal consequences, in so far as its provisions are capable of being applied directly?

   (b)   If the first question is answered in the affirmative, are Articles

12 and 13 of Decision No 3/80 sufficiently clear and precise
to be capable of being applied directly without the need for
further implementing measures, as provided for in Article 32
of Decision No 3/80?

3.   (a)   If Article 13 of Decision No 3/80 can be applied in cases such
as these, should the articles of Regulation (EEC) No 1408/71
referred to in Article 13 be applied as they were worded at
the time when the Association Council adopted that decision
on 19 September 1980, or should subsequent amendments to
the relevant articles of Regulation No 1408/71 also be taken
into account?

(b)   Is it also relevant in that regard whether the amendments
made after 19 September 1980 have resulted in parts of the
relevant provisions subsequently being set out in more detail
in other articles of or in annexes to Regulation No 1408/71?"

First question

12.   The first question, on the applicability of Decision No 3/80 in the
Community, must be construed as seeking to establish whether, and if so
at what date, that decision has entered into force.

13.   Since Decision No 3/80 contains no provision on its entry into force, the
question is whether such effect can result from the Agreement on which
that decision is based.

14.   The Agreement provides in Article 6, which forms part of Title I,
"Principles", that "To ensure the implementation and the progressive
development of the Association, the Contracting Parties shall meet in a
Council of Association, which shall act within the powers conferred upon
it by this Agreement".

15.   Article 22(1), which comes under Title III on the general and final
provisions of the Agreement, provides as follows:

"In order to attain the objectives of this Agreement the Council
of Association shall have the power to take decisions in the cases
provided for therein. Each of the Parties shall take the measures
necessary to implement the decisions taken. [...]"

16.   Lastly, under Article 23, which also forms part of Title III of the
Agreement:

"The Council of Association shall consist of members of the
Governments of the Member States and members of the Council
and of the Commission of the Community on the one hand and of
members of the Turkish Government on the other.
...
The Council of Association shall act unanimously."

17.   It follows from all those provisions that decisions of the EEC-Turkey Association Council are measures adopted by a body provided for by the Agreement and empowered by the Contracting Parties to adopt such measures.

18.   In so far as they implement the objectives set by the Agreement, such decisions are directly connected with the Agreement and, as a result of the second sentence of Article 22(1) thereof, have the effect of binding the Contracting Parties.

19.   By virtue of the Agreement, the Contracting Parties agreed to be bound by such decisions and if those parties were to withdraw from that commitment, that would constitute a breach of the Agreement itself.

20.   Consequently, contrary to the contention of the defendants in the main proceedings and the Governments of the Member States which have submitted observations to the Court, the binding effect of decisions of the Association Council cannot depend on whether implementing measures have in fact been adopted by the Contracting Parties.

21.   In those circumstances, in the absence of any provision on its entry into force, it follows from the binding character which the Agreement attaches to decisions of the EEC-Turkey Association Council that Decision No 3/80 entered into force on the date on which it was adopted, that is to say, 19 September 1980, and that, since then, the Contracting Parties have been bound by that decision.

22.   The reply to be given to the national court's first question must therefore be that Decision No 3/80 entered into force on the date on which it was adopted, namely 19 September 1980, and has been binding on the Contracting Parties since then.

Second question

23.   By its second question, the national court essentially seeks to establish whether the provisions of Decision No 3/80, and more specifically Articles 12 and 13 thereof, have direct effect in the territory of the Member States and are therefore such as to entitle individuals to rely on them before the national court

24.   In that regard, it should be recalled that the Court has consistently held (see, in particular, Case 12/86 *Demirel* v *Stadt Schwäbisch Gmünd* [1987] ECR 3719, paragraph 14) that a provision of an agreement concluded by the Community with non-member countries must be regarded as being directly applicable when, regard being had to its wording and the purpose and nature of the agreement itself, the provision contains a clear and precise obligation which is not subject, in its implementation or effects, to the adoption of any subsequent measure.

25.   In Case C-192/89 *Sevince* v *Staatssecretaris van Justitie* [1990] ECR I-3461, paragraphs 14 and 15, the Court held that the same criteria apply

in determining whether the provisions of a decision of the EEC-Turkey Association Council can have direct effect.

26. As has been observed above, the purpose of Decision No 3/80 is to coordinate the Member States' social security schemes with a view to enabling Turkish workers employed or formerly employed in the Community, members of their families and their survivors to qualify for benefits in the traditional branches of social security.

27. Regulation No 1408/71, to which Decision No 3/80 refers, is also intended to coordinate, within the Community, the various laws of the Member States.

28. However, the practical application of Regulation No 1408/71 necessitated the adoption of implementing measures, set out in the voluminous Regulation No 574/72.

29. As already mentioned, Decision No 3/80 refers in terms to certain provisions of Regulation No 1408/71 and Regulation No 574/72, while taking account, for the purposes of the implementation of those provisions, of the specific situation of Turkish workers who are or have been subject to the legislation of one or more Member States and of members of their families residing in the territory of one of the Member States.

30. However, comparison of Regulations Nos 1408/71 and 574/72, on the one hand, and Decision No 3/80, on the other, shows however, that the latter does not contain a large number of precise, detailed provisions, even though such were deemed indispensable for the purpose of implementing Regulation No 1408/71 within the Community.

31. Thus, Regulation No 1408/71, which the Council adopted on the basis of Article 51 of the Treaty, implements the fundamental principle enshrined in that provision, which consists in securing, for migrant workers and those entitled under them, aggregation, for the purpose of acquiring and retaining the right to benefit and of calculating the amount of benefit, of all periods taken into account under the various laws of the Member States. Nevertheless, in order to give practical effect to the aggregation rules set out in Regulation No 1408/71, it was necessary to adopt Article 15 of Regulation No 574/72.

32. Similarly, whilst Decision No 3/80 does indeed refer to the provisions of Regulation No 1408/71 setting forth the principle of aggregation for the branches sickness and maternity, invalidity, old age, death grants and family benefits, supplementary implementing measures of the kind set out in Article 15 of Regulation No 574/72 must be adopted before that principle can be applied.

33. In those circumstances, it must be held that, by its nature, Decision No 3/80 is intended to be supplemented and implemented in the Community by a subsequent act of the Council.

34. Thus, on 8 February 1983 the Commission submitted a proposal for a Council Regulation implementing within the European Economic Community Decision No 3/80 (OJ 1983 C 110, p. 1).

35.   That proposal for a regulation states that it is a measure intended to implement Decision No 3/80 in the Community. Article 1 provides that "Decision No 3/80 of the EEC-Turkey Association Council … , annexed to this Regulation, shall be applicable within the Community". To that end, it embodies some 80 articles and seven annexes containing "supplementary detailed rules for implementing Decision No 3/80", which lay down detailed rules with a view to the application of the provisions of the Decision in respect of each category of benefits coming within its scope. They also contain particulars relating, among other things, to prevention of overlapping benefits, determining the applicable legislation and aggregation of periods, together with financial and transitional provisions. Those provisions implementing Decision No 3/80 are based to a large degree on those contained in Regulation No 574/72. Thus, as far as the principle of aggregation is concerned, the content of Article 13 of the proposal for a regulation corresponds closely to that of Article 15 of Regulation No 574/72.

36.   However, that proposal for a regulation has not yet been adopted by the Council.

37.   It follows from all the foregoing considerations that, even though some of its provisions are clear and precise, Decision No 3/80 cannot be applied so long as supplementary implementing measures have not been adopted by the Council.

38.   The reply to be given to the national court's second question must therefore be that, so long as the supplementary measures essential for implementing Decision No 3/80 have not been adopted by the Council, Articles 12 and 13 of that decision do not have direct effect in the territory of the Member States and are therefore not such as to entitle individuals to rely on them before the national courts.

Third question

39.   In view of the replies given to the first and second questions, there is no need to consider the third question.

Costs

40.   The costs incurred by the Netherlands, German, Greek, Spanish, French and United Kingdom Governments and by the Commission of the European Communities, which have submitted observations to the Court, are not recoverable. Since these proceedings are, for the parties to the main proceedings, a step in the proceedings pending before the national court, the decision on costs is a matter for that court.

On those grounds, THE COURT, in answer to the questions referred to it by the Arrondissementsrechtbank, Amsterdam, by order of 23 August 1994, hereby rules:

1. Decision No 3/80 of the Association Council of 19 September 1980 on the application of the social security schemes of the Member States of the European Communities to Turkish workers and members of their families entered into force on the date on which it was adopted, namely 19 September 1980, and has been binding on the Contracting Parties since then.

2. So long as the supplementary measures essential for implementing Decision No 3/80 have not been adopted by the Council, Articles 12 and 13 of that decision do not have a direct effect in the territory of the Member States and are therefore not such as to entitle individuals to rely on them before the national courts.

Rodriguez Iglesias	Edward	Puissochet
Hirsch	Mancini	Moitinho de Almeida
Kapteyn	Gulmann	Murray

Delivered in open court in Luxembourg on 10 September 1996.

R. Grass   G.C. Rodriguez Iglesias
Registrar   President

Judgment of the Court of Justice of the European Communities

6 June 1995

Aʜᴍᴇᴛ Bᴏᴢᴋᴜʀᴛ -v- Sᴛᴀᴀᴛssᴇᴄʀᴇᴛᴀʀɪs ᴠᴀɴ Jᴜsᴛɪᴛɪᴇ

Case C-434/93

Reference to the Court under Article 177 of the EEC Treaty by the Raad van State (Council of state, Netherlands) for a preliminary ruling in the proceedings pending before that court on the interpretation of Article 2 of Decision No 2/76 of 20 December 1976 and Article 6 of Decison No 1/80 of 19 September 1980 of the Association Council established by the agreement establishing an Association between the European Economic Community and Turkey, signed on 12 September 1963 in Ankara and approved on behalf of the Community by Council Decision 64/732/EEC of 23 December 1963 (OJ, English Special Edition 1973 C 113, p. 1),

THE COURT,

composed of: G.C. Rodriguez Iglesias, President, F.A. Schockweiler (Rapporteur), P.J.G. Kapteyn and C. Gulmann (Presidents of Chambers), G.F. Mancini, C.N. Kakouris, J.C. Moitinho de Almeida, J.L. Murray, D.A.O. Edward, J.P. Puissochet and G.Hirsch, Judges.

Advocate General: M.B. Elmer,
Registrar: H. Von Holstein, Deputy Registrar

after considering the written observations submitted on behalf of:
— the applicant, by Dr Schaap, of the Rotterdam Bar,
— the Netherlands Government, by J.G. Lammers, Legal Adviser seconded to the Ministry of Foreign Affairs, acting as Agent,
— the German Government, by E. Roder, Ministerialrat in the Federal Ministry of Economic Affairs, and B. Kloke, Regierungsrat at the same Ministry, acting as Agents,
— the Greek Government, by N. Mavrikas, Deputy Legal Adviser in the State Legal Service, and C. Sitara, Legal Representative of the State Legal Service, acting as Agents,
— the United Kingdom, by E. Sharpston, Barrister and J.D. Holahan of the Treasury Solicitor's Department, acting as Agent,
— the Commission of the European Communities, by P. van Nuffel of its Legal Service, acting as Agents,

having regard to the Report for the Hearing.

After hearing the oral observations of Mr Bozkurt, of the Netherlands Government, represented by J W de Zwaan, Deputy Legal Adviser in the Ministry of Foreign Affairs, acting as Agent, of the German Government, of the Greek Government, represented by M Apessos, Deputy Legal Adviser in the State Legal Service, acting as Agent, of the United Kingdom and of the Commission of the European Communities at the hearing on 17 January 1995,

after hearing the Opinion of the Advocate General at the sitting on 28 March 1995, gives the following Judgment

1.   By interlocutory judgment of 24 September 1993, received at the Court on 4 November 1993, the Raad van State der Nederlanden (Council of State of the Netherlands) referred to the Court for a preliminary ruling under Article 177 of the EC Treaty four questions on the interpretation of Article 2 of Decision No 2/76 of 20 December 1976 and Article 6 of Decision No 1/80 of 19 September 1980 of the Association Council established by the Agreement establishing an Association between the European Economic Community and Turkey, signed on 12 September 1963 in Ankara and approved on behalf of the Community by Council Decision 64/732/EEC of 23 December 1963 (OJ, English Special Edition 1973 C 113, p. 1, "the Agreement").

2.   Those questions were raised in proceedings between Ahmet Bozkurt, a Turkish national, and the Netherlands Ministry of Justice, concerning a request for the grant of a permit, unrestricted as to time, to reside in the territory of the Netherlands.

3.   Mr Bozkurt was employed, from at least 21 August 1979, as an international lorry-driver on routes to the Middle East by Rynart Transport b.V., a company incorporated under Netherlands law, with its head office at Klundert in the Netherlands. His contract of employment was concluded under Netherlands law. In the periods between his journeys and during his periods of leave he lived in the Netherlands.

4.   A work permit issued by the Ministry of Social Affairs was not required for work carried out by Mr Bozkurt because, for the purposes of the application of the Wet Arbeid Buitenlandse Werknemers of 9 November 1978 (Law on Work by Foreign Employees, Staatsblad 1978, 737, "the WABW"), international lorry-drivers are not, by virtue of the Decree of 25 October 1979 adopting a general administrative measure pursuant to Article 2(1)(c) of the WABW (Staatsblad 1979, 574), regarded as foreigners.

5.   Nor did Mr Bozkurt, the holder of a visa valid for multiple journeys, require a residence permit under Articles 9 and 10 of the Vreemdelingwet of 13 January 1965 (Law on Aliens, Staatsblad 1965, 40) in order to be able to work as an international driver and to stay in the Netherlands during the periods between his journeys, described as "free periods", the duration of which is stated on the visa. In the Netherlands international lorry-drivers are not covered by the general policy on aliens, as is apparent from the 1982 circular regarding aliens.

6. In June 1988 Mr Bozkurt was the victim of an accident at work. The degree of his incapacity for work was determined at between 80 and 100%. For that reason he receives benefits under the Wet op de Arbeidsongeschiktheids-verzekering (Law on Insurance against Incapacity for Work) and the Algemene Arbeidsongeschiktheidswet (General Law of Incapacity for Work).

7. On 6 March 1991 the chief of the municipal police of Rotterdam rejected Mr Bozkurt's request for an unrestricted residence permit. On 18 March 1991 the applicant submitted to the Minister of Justice a request that that decision be reviewed. That request was also rejected. On 16 July 1991 Mr Bozkurt made an application to the Raad van State for annulment of the decision, claiming that Article 2 of Decision No 2/76 and Article 2 of Decision No 1/80 conferred on him the right to stay in the Netherlands.

8. Decisions No 2/76 and No 1/80 implement Article 12 of the Agreement, a provision which appears in the last chapter of Title II, concerning "Other Economic Provisions". Under that article the Contracting Parties agree "to be guided by Articles 48, 49 and 50 of the Treaty establishing the Community for the purpose of progressively securing freedom of movement for workers between them".

9. Article 2(1) of Decision No 2/76 provides as follows:

    "(a) After three years of legal employment in a Member State of the Community, a Turkish worker shall be entitled, subject to the priority to be given to workers of Member States of the Community, to respond to an offer of employment, made under normal conditions and registered with the employment services of that State, for the same occupation, branch of activity and region.

    (b) After five years of legal employment in a Member State of the Community, a Turkish worker shall enjoy free access in that country to any paid employment of his choice".

10. Article 6(1) of Decision No 1/80 provides as follows:

    "Subject to Article 7 on free access to employment for members of his family, a Turkish worker duly registered as belonging to the labour force of a Member State:
    – shall be entitled in that Member State, after one year's legal employment, to the renewal of his permit to work for the same employer, if a job is available;
    – shall be entitled in that Member State, after three years of legal employment and subject to the priority to be given to workers of Member States of the Community, to respond to another offer of employment, with an employer of his choice, made under normal conditions and registered with the employment services of that State, for the same occupation;
    – shall enjoy free access in that Member State to any paid employment of his choice, after four years of legal employment".

11.   Article 2(1)(c) of Decision No 2/76 provides:

"Annual holidays and short absences for reasons of sickness, maternity or an accident at work shall be treated as periods of legal employment. Periods of involuntary unemployment duly certified by the relevant authorities and long absences on account of sickness shall not be treated as periods of legal employment, but shall not affect rights acquired as the result of the preceding period of employment".

12.   The wording of Article 6(2) of Decision No 1/80 is slightly different:

"Annual holidays and absences for reasons of maternity or an accident at work or short periods of sickness shall be treated as periods of legal employment. Periods of involuntary unemployment duly certified by the relevant authorities and long absences on account of sickness shall not be treated as periods of legal employment, but shall not affect rights acquired as a result of the preceding period of employment".

13.   Considering that an interpretation of the provisions quoted above was necessary to its decision in the proceedings, the Raad van State referred to the Court the following questions for a preliminary ruling:

1.   Is the criterion laid down in the judgment of the Court of Justice in Case 9/88 *Lopes da Veiga* v *Staatsecretaris van Justitie* [1989] ECR 2989 also to be applied in resolving the question of whether work carried out by a Turkish worker pursuant to an employment contract under Netherlands law as international lorry-driver in the service of a Netherlands company established in the Netherlands can be regarded as (legal) employment in a Member State within the meaning of Article 2 of Decision No 2/76 and/or Article 6 of Decision No 1/80, and in that respect are the same circumstances to be taken into account *mutatis mutandis* by the national courts?

2.   Is there a situation of legal employment in a Member State within the meaning of Article 2 of Decision No 2/76 and/or Article 6 of Decision No 1/80 where a Turkish worker does not need to hold a work permit or a residence permit in order to carry out his work as an international lorry-driver because of the usually short periods that he remains in the Netherlands between his journeys, but cannot in principle acquire a right of long-term residence on the basis of that work under Netherlands legislation and Netherlands policy with regard to immigration?

3.   If the answers to Questions 1 and 2 are in the affirmative, does it follow from Article 2 of Decision No 2/76 and/or Article 6 of Decision No 1/80 that a Turkish worker has a right of residence at least for so long as he is in legal employment within the meaning of those Decisions?

4.   If the answer to Question 3 is affirmative, does the Turkish worker

retain that right of residence ensuing from Article 2 of Decision No 2/76 and/or Article 6 of Decision No 1/80 if he becomes permanently and completely incapable of working?"

14.   It should first be noted that Decision No 2/76 is presented, in Article 1 thereof, as constituting a first stage in securing freedom of movement for workers between the Community and Turkey which was to last for four years as from 1 December 1976. Section 1 of Chapter II, headed "Social Provisions", of Decision No 1/80, which includes Article 6, constitutes a further stage in securing freedom of movement for workers and has applied, pursuant to Article 16, since 1 December 1980. As from that date, Article 6 of Decision No 1/80 has replaced the corresponding, less favourable, provisions of Decision No 2/76. That being so, for the purposes of giving a helpful answer to the questions submitted to the Court, and having regard to the times at which the facts summarized above occurred, it is solely to Article 6 of Decision No 1/80 that reference should be made.

The first question

15.   By means of this question the national court seeks essentially to ascertain what criteria should be used to determine whether a Turkish worker employed as an international lorry-driver belongs to the legitimate labour force of a Member State for the purposes of Article 6 of Decision No 1/80.

16.   In its judgment in Case 9/88 *Lopes da Veiga* v *Staatssecretaris van Justitie* [1989] ECR 2989, paragraph 17, the Court ruled that in the case of a worker who is a national of a Member State and who is permanently employed on board a ship flying the flag of another Member State, in that instance the Netherlands, in deciding whether the legal relationship of employment could be located within the territory, for the purposes of the application of Council Regulation (EEC) No 1612/68 of 15 October 1968 on freedom of movement for workers within the Community (OJ, English Special Edition 1968 (II), p. 475), it was for the national court to take into account the following circumstances apparent from the case-file before the Court: the fact that the applicant worked on board a vessel registered in the Netherlands in the employment of a shipping company established in the Netherlands, that he was hired in the Netherlands, that the employment relationship between him and his employer was subject to Netherlands law and, finally that he was insured under the social security system of the Netherlands and paid income tax there.

17.   Mr Bozkurt and the Commission consider that the same criteria should be applied in this case. The Commission maintains, in particular, that the Court's decision in Lopes da Veiga falls to be applied because Article 12 of the Agreement requires the contracting parties to be guided by Articles 48, 49 and 50 of the EEC Treaty for the purpose of progressively securing freedom of movement for workers between them.

18.   In contrast, the German, Greek and Netherlands Governments and the

United Kingdom consider that the *Lopes da Veiga* judgment is concerned with the interpretation of a fundamental concept of Community law in the field of freedom of movement for workers and they oppose the view that the judgment can be used to interpret provisions in an association agreement, with its more modest objectives, governing the situation of a national of a non-member country in the labour force of a Member State.

19.   On that point, it should first be noted that, when the Association Council adopted the social provisions in Decision No 1/80, its aim was to go one stage further, guided by Articles 48, 49 and 50 of the Treaty, towards securing freedom of movement for workers.

20.   In order to ensure compliance with that objective, it would seem to be essential to transpose, so far as is possible, the principles enshrined in those articles to Turkish workers who enjoy the rights conferred by Decision No 1/80.

21.   Article 6(1) is confined to regulating, so far as access to employment is concerned, the situation of a Turkish worker who already belongs to the legitimate labour force of a Member State.

22.   In order to determine, for the purposes of the application of Article 6(1), whether a Turkish worker is to be regarded as belonging to the labour force of a Member State, it must, in accordance with the principle laid down in Article 12 of the Agreement and by analogy with the situation of a worker who is a national of a Member State employed in another Member State, be ascertained, as the Court has held, in particular in the *Lopes da Veiga* judgment, whether the legal relationship of employment can be located within the territory of a Member State or retains a sufficiently close link with that territory.

23.   It is for the national court to determine whether the employment relationship of the applicant in the main proceedings as an international lorry-driver retained a sufficiently close link with the territory of the Netherlands, and, in so doing, to take account in particular of the place where he was hired, the territory on which the paid employment was based and the applicable national legislation in the field of employment and social security law.

24.   The answer to the first question must therefore be that, in order to ascertain whether a Turkish worker employed as an international lorry-driver belongs to the legitimate labour force of a Member State, for the purposes of Article 6(1) of Decision No 1/80, it is for the national court to determine whether the applicant's employment relationship retains a sufficiently close link with the territory of the Member State and, in so doing, to take account in particular of the place where he was hired, the territory on which the paid employment was based and the applicable national legislation in the field of employment and social security law.

The second and third questions

25.   By means of its second and third questions the national court seeks

essentially to ascertain whether the existence of legal employment in a Member State can be established in the case of a Turkish worker who was not required under national legislation to hold a work permit or a residence permit issued by the authorities of the host State in order to carry out his work and, if so, whether that worker may claim a right of residence for so long as he is in legal employment.

26. It should be borne in mind, as the Court pointed out in its judgment in Case C-192/89 *Servince* v *Staatssecretaris van Justitie* [1990] ECR I-3461, paragraph 30, that legality of employment for the purposes of Article 6(1) presupposes a stable and secure situation as a member of the labour force of a Member State.

27. The legality of employment engaged in over a certain period must be determined in the light of the legislation of the host State governing the conditions under which the Turkish worker entered the national territory and is employed there.

28. Where those conditions are satisfied, Article 6(1) of Decision No 1/80, which grants Turkish workers the right, after specified periods of legal employment, to continue working for the same employer or in the same occupation for an employer of his choice, or to enjoy free access to any paid employment of his choice, necessarily implies the existence of a right of residence for the person concerned, since otherwise the right of access to the labour force and the right to work as an employed person would be deprived of all effect (see, to that effect, the judgments in *Sevince*, cited above, paragraph 29, and Case C-237/91 *Kus* v *Landeshaupstradt Weisbaden* [1992] ECR I- 6781, paragraphs 29 and 30).

29. Article 6(1) of Decision No 1/80 does not subject recognition of those rights to the condition that Turkish nationals must establish the legality of their employment by possession of any specific administrative document, such as a work permit or residence permit, issued by the authorities of the host country.

30. It follows that the rights conferred under Article 6(1) on Turkish nationals who are already duly integrated into the labour force of a Member State are accorded to such nationals irrespective of whether or not the competent authorities have issued administrative documents which, in this context, can only be declaratory of the existence of those rights and cannot constitute a condition for their existence.

31. The answer to the second and third questions must therefore be that the existence of legal employment in a Member State within the meaning of Article 6(I) of Decision No 1/80 can be established in the case of a Turkish worker who was not required under the national legislation concerned to hold a work permit or a residence permit issued by the authorities of the host State in order to carry out his work and that the existence of such employment necessarily implies the recognition of a right of residence for the person concerned.

The fourth question

32.   By means of this question the Raad van State seeks to ascertain whether, where it has been established that a Turkish worker such as Mr Bozkurt duly belongs to the legitimate labour force of the Netherlands because he is employed as an international driver, Article 6(I) of Decision No 1/80 entitles him to remain in the territory of the host State following an accident at work which rendered him permanently incapacitated for work.

33.   Mr Bozkurt considers that he can derive a right to remain in the Netherlands from the second sentence of Article 6(2) of Decision No 1/80, inasmuch as it refers to long absences on account of sickness, taking into account the preceding period of employment.

34.   The Commission shares that view, drawing support from the wording of the first sentence of Article 6(2) of Decision No 1/80, which treats certain periods of absence as periods of legal employment. It therefore considers that a period of permanent incapacity for work resulting from an accident at work must be treated in the same way as permanent legal employment, which implies the existence of a right of residence for the person concerned.

35.   In contrast, the German, Greek and Netherlands Governments and the United Kingdom are at one in considering that, in the absence of any express provision on the subject, along the lines of Article 48(3)(d) of the Treaty and Commission Regulation (EEC) No 1251/70 of 29 June 1970 on the rights of workers to remain in the territory of a Member State after having been employed in that State (OJ, English Special Edition 1970 (II), p. 402), Turkish workers must be regarded as not entitled to claim the right to remain. The consequences of any permanent incapacity for work from which they may suffer are therefore, from the point of view of their right of residence in a Member State, governed exclusively by the national law of the Member State concerned.

36.   The German Government adds that, taking into account the objective of Decision No 1/80, which it maintains is to consolidate the situation of Turkish workers who are already in employment, the right of residence must remain a corollary of the worker's employment so that, where there is a break in employment, the right of residence can subsist only if that break is of limited duration. That interpretation is in conformity with the wording of Article 6(2) of Decision No 1/80, which refers only to temporary absences which would not as a rule affect the worker's subsequent participation in working life. In contrast, in the case of long-lasting incapacity for work, the worker is no longer available as a member of the labour force at all and there is no objectively justified reason for guaranteeing him the right of access to the labour force and an ancillary right of residence. To maintain in being a right of residence in the event of permanent incapacity for work would, according to the German Government, amount to conferring on it an independent character, contrary to the purpose of Decision No 1/80. The observations of the United Kingdom are to the same effects.

37.   As the provisions adopted by the Association Council for the purpose of progressively securing freedom of movement for workers between the Member States of the Community and Turkey, in accordance with the principle stated in Article 12 of the Agreement, now stand, the argument set out in the preceding paragraph must be accepted.

38.   Article 6(2) is intended only to regulate the consequences, for the application of Article 6(1), of certain breaks in employment. Accordingly, annual holidays and absences for reasons of maternity or an accident at work or short periods of sickness are treated as periods of legal employment, particularly in calculating the length of the period of legal employment required in order to acquire the right of free access to any paid employment. Periods of unemployment and long absences on account of sickness, which are not treated as periods of legal employment, are taken into account only in order to ensure that rights acquired by the worker as the result of preceding periods of employment are preserved. Consequently, the provisions of Article 6(2) merely ensure the continuation of the right to employment and necessarily presuppose fitness to continue working, even if only after a temporary interruption.

39.   It follows that Article 6 of Decision No 1/80 covers the situation of Turkish workers who are working or are temporarily incapacitated for work. It does not, on the other hand, cover the situation of a Turkish worker who has definitely ceased to belong to the labour force of a Member State because he has, for example, reached retirement age or, as in the present case, become totally and permanently incapacitated for work.

40.   Consequently, in the absence of any specific provision conferring on Turkish workers a right to remain in the territory of a Member State after working there, a Turkish national's right of residence, as implicitly but necessarily guaranteed by Article 6 of Decision No 1/80 as a corollary of legal employment, ceases to exist if the person concerned becomes totally and permanently incapacitated for work.

41.   Furthermore, as far as Community workers are concerned, the conditions under which such a right to remain may be exercised were, under Article 48(3)(d) of the Treaty, made subject to regulations to be drawn up by the Commission, with the result that the rules applicable under Article 48 cannot simply be transposed to Turkish workers.

42.   The answer to the fourth question must therefore be that Article 6(2) of Decision No 1/80 does not confer on a Turkish national who has belonged to the legitimate labour force of a Member State the right to remain in the territory of that State following an accident at work rendering him permanently incapacitated for work.

Costs

43.   The costs incurred by the German, Greek and Netherlands Governments, the United Kingdom and the Commission of the European Communities,

which have submitted observations to the Court, are not recoverable. Since these proceedings are, for the parties to the main proceedings, a step in the proceedings pending before the national court, the decision on costs is a matter for that court.

On those grounds, THE COURT, in answer to the question referred to it by the Rad van State der Nederlanden by interlocutory judgment of 24 September 1993, hereby rules:

1.   In order to ascertain whether a Turkish worker employed as an international lorry-driver belongs to the legitimate labour force of a Member State, for the purposes of Article 6(1) of Decision No 1/80 of 19 September 1980 of the Association Council established by the agreement establishing an Association between the European Economic Community and Turkey, signed on 12 September 1963 in Ankara and approved on behalf of the Community by Council Decision 64/732/EEC of 23 December 1963, it is for the national court to determine whether the applicant's employment relationship retained a sufficiently close link with the territory of the Member State and, in so doing, to take account, in particular, of the place where he was hired, the territory on which the paid employment is based and the applicable national legislation in the field of employment and social security law.

2.   The existence of legal employment in a Member State within the meaning of Article 6(1) of Decision No 1/80, cited above, can be established in the case of a Turkish worker who was not required by the national legislation concerned to hold a work permit or a residence permit issued by the authorities in the host State in order to carry out his work. The fact that such employment exists necessarily implies the recognition of a right of residence for the person concerned.

3.   Article 6(2) of Decision No 1/80 does not confer on a Turkish national who has belonged to the legitimate labour force of a Member State the right to remain in the territory of that State following an accident at work rendering him permanently incapacitated for work.

Rodriquez Iglesias	Schockweiler	Kapteyn
Gulmann	Mancini	Kakouris
Moitinho de Almeida	Murray	Edward
Puissochet		Hirsch

Delivered in open court in Luxembourg on 6 June 1995.

R. Grass	G.C. Rodriguez Iglesias
Registrar	President

Judgment of the Court of Justice of the European Communities
(Sixth Chamber)
5 October 1994

HAYRIYE EROGLU V LAND BADEN-WÜRTTEMBERG

Case C-355/93

REFERENCE to the Court under Article 177 of the EEC Treaty by the Verwaltungsgericht Karlsruhe (Germany) for a preliminary ruling in the proceedings pending before that court before that court on the interpretation of Articles 6 and 7 of Decision No 1/80 of the Association Council established by the Association Agreement between the European Economic Community and Turkey, of 19 September 1980, on the development of the Association,

THE COURT (Sixth Chamber),

composed of: G.F. Mancini, President of the Chamber, C.N. Kakouris, F.A. Schockweiler (Rapporteur), P.J.G. Kapteyn and J.L. Murray, Judges,

Advocate General: M. Darmon,
Registrar: H.A. Rühl, Principal Administrator,

after considering the written observations submitted on behalf of:
– Mrs Hayriye Eroglu, by H. Lichtenberg Professor at the University of Bremen,
– the German Government, by E. Röder, Ministerialrat in the Federal Ministry of Economic Affairs, acting as Agent,
– the Commission of the European Communities, by J. Pipkorn, Legal Adviser, and H. Kreppel, a national civil servant seconded to the Commission, acting as Agents,

having regard to the Report for the Hearing,

after hearing the oral observations of Mrs Hayriye Eroglu, the German Government and the Commission at the hearing on 5 May 1994,

after hearing the Opinion of the Advocate General at the sitting on 12 July 1994, gives the following

Judgment

1. By order of 26 May 1993, received at the Court Registry on 14 July 1993, the Verwaltungsgericht (Administrative Court) Karlsruhe (Germany)

referred to the Court for a preliminary ruling under Article 177 of the EEC Treaty two questions on the interpretation of Articles 6 and 7 of Decision No 1/80 of the Association Council established by the Association Agreement between the European Economic Community and Turkey, of 19 September 1980, on the development of the Association ("Decision No 1/80").

2.   Those questions were raised in proceedings between Mrs Hayriye Eroglu, a Turkish national, and the Land Baden-Württemberg, concerning the refusal to extend the residence permit allowing her to stay in the Federal Republic of Germany.

3.   It is apparent from the order for reference that in April 1980 Mrs Eroglu, who was born in Turkey on 12 May 1960, entered into the Federal Republic of Germany where her father had been living and working quite lawfully without interruption since 4 May 1976, in order to take a business administration course at the University of Hamburg. She completed those studies in 1987 and obtained a diploma in further business studies, then began to study for a doctorate. During her studies, and until October 1989, she was granted several residence permits, all limited to one year and marked "valid only for the purposes of study ....".

4.   In October 1989, Mrs Eroglu moved to Hardheim. At her request, the Landratsamt Neckar-Odenwald-Kreis (the Nekar-Odenwald Rural District Central Administrative Office) issued her with residence permits on 15 January 1990 and 27 June 1990 valid initially until 1 March 1991, and containing the proviso: "Gainful employment not permitted; valid only for the "hotel project" activity with company B. in Hardheim". On 7 February 1991 she received a conditional residence authorisation valid until 1 March 1992, allowing her to undertake practical training with company B. At the same time, she was told that it would not be possible to renew the residence authorisation beyond 1 March 1992. In a decision of 9 April 1991, the conditions attached to the authorisation were changed so as to permit Mrs Eroglu thereafter to pursue "activity as a trainee (marketing assistant) at company F. GmbH in Tauberbischofsheim".

5.   For all those activities Mrs Eroglu was issued with corresponding work permits. Those which were valid from 6 February 1990 to 14 January 1991 and from 25 April 1991 to 1 March 1992 respectively authorised her in general and without further restriction to carry on certain occupational activities, the one as Commercial Management Assistant and the other as Marketing Assistant, in the employment of a certain company. The permit applying from 15 January 1991 to 14 April 1991, on the other hand, was limited to carrying on "occupational activity as a trainee". As a matter of fact, Mrs Eroglu was employed from 1 March 1990 to 15 April 1991 by company B., then from 15 April 1991 to 18 May 1992 by company F. Both employers paid her a monthly gross salary of more than DM 3,000.

6.   On 24 February 1992 Mrs Eroglu applied to the Landratsamt Neckar-
Odenwald-Kreis for an extension of her residence permit to allow her to
continue her activity with her last employer, company F. That application
and her subsequent complaint to the Regierungspräsidium Karlsruhe
(Chief Executive's Office of Karlsruhe District) were rejected, whereupon
Mrs Eroglu brought proceedings before the Verwaltungsgericht
Karlsruhe. In that court Mrs Eroglu, who had in the meantime again
been offered employment with her first employer, company B., claimed
that she had a right of residence by virtue of the first indent of Article 6(1)
and the second paragraph of Article 7 of Decision NO 1/80, which
provides as follows:

Article 6

1.   Subject to Article 7 on free access to employment for members of his
family, a Turkish worker duly registered as belonging to the labour force
of a Member State:
  —   shall be entitled in that Member State, after one year's legal employ-
       ment, to the renewal of his permit to work for the same employer,
       if a job is available;
  —   shall be entitled in that Member State, after three years of legal
       employment and subject to the priority to be given to workers of
       Member States of the Community, to respond to another offer of
       employment, with an employer of his choice, made under normal
       conditions and registered with the employment services of that
       State, for the same occupation;
  —   shall enjoy free access in that Member State to any paid employment
       of his choice, after four years of legal employment.

Article 7

The members of the family of a Turkish worker duly registered as belonging
to the labour force of a Member State, who have been authorised to join him:
  —   shall be entitled – subject to the priority to be given to workers of
       Member States of a Community – to respond to any offer of
       employment after they have been legally resident for at least three
       years in that Member State;
  —   shall enjoy free access to any paid employment of their choice
       provided that they have been legally resident there for at least
       five years.
Children of Turkish workers who have completed a course of vocational
training in the host country may respond to any offer of employment there,
irrespective of the length of time they have been resident in that Member State,

provided one of their parents have been legally employed in the Member State concerned for at least there years."

7.   The Verwaltungsgericht Karlsruhe found that the refusal to renew the residence permit was in accordance with German law but was uncertain whether a solution more favourable to Mrs Eroglu might not follow from the abovementioned provisions of Decision No 1/80, with particular regard to the Court's judgments in Case C-192/89 *Sevince* v *Staatssecretaris van Justitie* [1990] ECR I-3461 and Case C-237/91 *Kus* v *Landeshauptstadt Wiesbaden* [1992] ECR I-6781.

8.   Consequently, it decided to stay the proceedings until the Court of Justice had given a ruling on the following questions:

"1.   Does a Turkish national satisfy the conditions of the first indent of Article 6(1) of Decision No 1/80 of the Association Council of the Association between the European Economic Community and Turkey on the development of the Association if under national law she was granted, as a graduate of a German university, a conditional residence authorisation for two years and corresponding work permits for the purpose of deepening her knowledge by pursuing an occupational activity or a period of specialised practical training and if she initially worked for more than a year for one employer (gross monthly earnings: approximately DM 3,000) and immediately afterwards worked, with the authorities' permission, for some ten months for another employer, after which she was offered work by her first employer?

2.   May a Turkish national who, as a graduate of a German university, satisfies the conditions set out in the second paragraph of Article 7 of the aforementioned decision and who may therefore "respond to any offer of employment", demand the extension of her residence permit on the basis thereof, or does the second paragraph of Article 7 of the decision govern exclusively the position under employment law of children of Turkish workers who have been legally employed in the host Member State for at least three years?"

Question 1

9.   In its first question, the national court asks whether the first indent of Article 6(1) of Decision No 1/80 is to be construed as giving the right to the renewal of his permit to work for his first employer to a Turkish national who is a university graduate and who worked for more than one year for his first employer and for some ten months for another employer, having been issued with a two-year conditional residence authorisation and corresponding work permits in order to allow him to deepen his knowledge by pursuing an occupational activity for specialised training.

10.   Decision No 1/80 does not encroach upon the power of the Member

States to regulate both the entry into their territory of Turkish nationals and the conditions of their first employment, but makes provision exclusively, particularly in Article 6, for the case of Turkish workers who are already duly registered as belonging to the labour force of the Member States (see judgment in *Kus*, cited above, at paragraph 25).

11. In *Sevince*, cited above, the Court held that Article 6(1) of Decision No 1/80 has direct effect in the Member States of the European Community (paragraph 2 of the operative part). Turkish nationals who satisfy its conditions may thus rely directly on the rights given them by the various indents of that provision.

12. Those rights themselves vary and are subject to conditions which vary according to the length of time that legal employment in the relevant Member State has lasted. After four years of legal employment, he is entitled to free access to any paid employment of his choice (third indent).

13. The aim of the first indent of Article 6(1) of Decision No 1/80 is to ensure solely continuity of employment with the same employer and is, accordingly, applicable only where a Turkish worker requests an extension of his work permit in order to continue working for the same employer after the initial period of one year's legal employment.

14. Extending the application of that provision to a Turkish worker who, after one year's legal employment, changed employers and is seeking an extension of his work permit in order to work for the first employer again would allow that worker to change employers under that provision before the expiry of the three years prescribed in the second indent and would also deprive workers of the Member States of the priority conferred on them pursuant to that indent when a Turkish worker changes employers.

15. It is sufficiently clear from the foregoing that the answer to the first question must be that the first indent of Article 6(1) of Decision No 1/80 of Decision No 1/80 is to be construed as not giving the right to the renewal of his permit to work for his first employer to a Turkish national who is a university graduate and who worked for more than one year for his first employer and for some ten months for another employer, having been issued with a two-year conditional residence authorisation and corresponding work permits in order to allow him to deepen his knowledge by pursuing an occupational activity or specialised practical training.

Question 2

16. In its second question, the national court seeks to ascertain whether a Turkish national who satisfies the conditions set out in the second paragraph of Article 7 of Decision 1/80 and may therefore respond to any offer of employment in the Member State concerned may, by the same token, also rely on that provision to obtain the extension of his residence permit.

17.   Like Article 6(1) of Decision No 1/80, Article 7 clearly, precisely and unconditionally embodies the rights of those children of Turkish workers who have completed a course of vocational training in the host country to respond to any offer of employment there, irrespective of the length of time they have been resident in the Member State, provided one of their parents has been legally employed in the Member State concerned for at least three years. Like Article 6(1), the second paragraph of Article 7 has direct effect in the Member States of the European Community

18.   It is noteworthy that in *Sevince*, in the context of the third indent of Article 6(1) of Decision No 1/80, the Court held that even if that provision merely governs the circumstances of the Turkish worker as regards employment and makes no reference to the right of residence, those two aspects of the personal situation of a Turkish worker are closely linked and that by granting to such a worker, after a specified period of legal employment in the Member State, access to any paid employment of his choice, the provision in question necessarily implies – since otherwise the right granted by it to the Turkish worker would be deprived of any effect – the existence, at least at that time, of a right of residence for the person concerned (paragraph 29).

19.   In *Kus*, the Court applied the same reasoning to the first indent of Article 6(1) of Decision No 1/80, since, without a right of residence the grant to a Turkish worker of the right to renewal of his permit to work for the same employer after one year's legal employment would likewise be deprived of any effect (paragraph 30).

20.   Since the right of residence is essential to access to and the pursuit of any paid employment, whether for the same employer in connection with renewal of a work permit or for another employer, chosen freely or subject to the priority given to workers of the Member States of the Community, it must also be accepted that the right conferred on a person by the second paragraph of Article 7 of Decision No 1/80 to respond to any offer of employment necessarily implies the recognition of a right of residence for that person.

21.   No argument to the contrary can be based on Article 48(3) of the Treaty which, in the field of freedom of movement for workers within the Community, explicitly sets out, in addition to the right to accept offers actually made, the right to stay in a Member State for the purpose of employment. Article 48(3) enumerates in a non-exhaustive way certain rights benefiting nationals of Member States in the context of the free movement of workers (Case C-292/89 *Antonissen* [1991] ECR I-745, paragraph 13), and that freedom entails the right for Community nationals to stay in the Member States not only in order to accept offers actually made there, but also to look for employment there (*Kus*, paragraph 35).

22.   Contrary to the assertions of the German Government, the right to respond to any offer of employment, conferred by the second paragraph of Article 7 of Decision No 1/80 on children of Turkish workers who

have completed a course of vocational training in the host country is not subject to any condition concerning the ground on which a right to enter and to stay was originally granted. The fact that that right was not given them with a view to reuniting the family but, for example, for the purposes of study does not, therefore, deprive the child of a Turkish worker who satisfies the conditions of the second paragraph of Article 7 of the enjoyment of the rights conferred thereunder.

23.   In view of the foregoing, the answer to the second question must be that a Turkish national who satisfies the conditions set out in the second paragraph of Article 7 of Decision No 1/80 and may therefore respond to any offer of employment in the Member State concerned may, by the same token, also rely on that provision to obtain the extension of his residence permit.

Costs

24.   The costs incurred by the German Government and the Commission of the European Communities, which have submitted observations to the Court, are not recoverable. Since these proceedings are, for the parties to the main proceedings, a step in the action pending before the national court, the decision on costs is a matter for that court.

On those grounds, THE COURT, in answer to the questions referred to it by the Verwaltungsgericht Karlsruhe, by order of 26 May 1993, hereby rules:

1.   The first indent of Article 6(1) of Decision No 1/80 of the Association Council established by the Association Agreement between the European Economic Community and Turkey, of 19 September 1980, on the development of the Association is to be construed as not giving the right to the renewal of his permit to work for his first employer to a Turkish national who is a university graduate and who worked for more than one year for his first employer and for some ten months for another employer, having been issued with a two-year conditional residence authorisation and corresponding work permits in order to allow him to deepen his knowledge by pursuing an occupational activity or specialised practical training.

2.   A Turkish national who satisfies the conditions set out in the second paragraph of Article 7 of Decision No 1/80 and may therefore respond to any offer of employment in the Member State concerned may, by the same token, rely on that provision to obtain the extension of his residence permit.

Mancini   Kakouris   Schockweiler   Kapteyn   Murray

Delivered in open court in Luxembourg on 5 October 1994.

R. Grass   G.F. Mancini
Registrar   President of the Sixth Chamber

Judgment of the Court of Justice of the European Communities
16 December 1992

Kazim Kus v Landeshauptstadt Wiesbaden

Case C-237/91

REFERENCE to the Court under Article 177 of the EEC Treaty by the Hessischer Verwaltungsgerichtshof (Germany) for a preliminary ruling in the proceeding pending before that court on the interpretation of Article 6(1) of Decision No 1/80 of the Association Council of 19 September 1980 on the development of the Association, adopted by the Association Council, established by the Association Agreement between The European Economic Community and Turkey,

THE COURT

composed of: Rodriguez la lesias President Zuleeg and Murray (Presidents of the Chambers), Mancini, Juliet, Schoctweiler, Moitinho de Almeida, Grévisse and Kapteyn

Advocate General: M. Daiman

after considering the written observations submitted on behalf of:
- Reinhold Wendl, of the Wiesbaden Bar and Hagen Lichtenberg, professor at the University of Bremen, for the Plaintiff.
- Ernst Röder, Ministerialrat in the German Ministry of Economic Affairs, and JoachimKark. Regierungsdirektor in the same Ministry, for the German government as amicus curiae.
- J.W. de Zwaan, Deputy Legal Adviser in the Ministry of Forcign Affairs, for the Dutch government as amicus curiae.
- Richard Plender Q.C, instructed by *Sue Cochrane*, of the Treasury Solicitor's Department, for the United Kingdom government as *amicus curiae.*
- Jörn Pipkorn, Legal Adviser, and Pieter Jason Kuyper, of the Commission's Legal Service, for the E.C. Commission as amicus curiae.

gives the following Judgment
1. By order of 12 August 1991, received by the Court on 18 September following, the Hessischer Verwaltungsgerlcht referred to the Court for a preliminary ruling under Article 177 EEC three questions on the interpretation of Article 6 of Decision 1/80 of 19 September 1980 of the Council of Association established by the Agreement establishing an

219

association between the European Economic Community and Turkey, relating to the development of the Association ("Decision 1/80").

2.   The questions have arisen in the context of an action brought by Mr Kazim Kus, a Turkish national, against Landeshauptstadt Wiesbaden, represented by the Mayor, concerning a refusal to extend a permit to reside in Germany.

3.   It appears from the order making the reference that Mr Kus entered Germany on 24 August 1980 in order to marry a German national on 16 April 1981. It also appears that he has been continuously employed there since 1 April 1982 on the basis of a work permit in due legal form. First he worked for approximately seven years for the same enterprise and then changed his employer twice.

4.   By decision of 6 August 1984 the Mayor of Landeshauptstadt Wiesbaden refused to extend the residence permit which Mr Kus had held since 27 April 1981 as the husband of a German citizen and which had expired on 17 August 1983, on the ground that the original reason for Mr Kus to reside in Germany had ceased to exist, as a divorce between Mr and Mrs. Kus had been granted by decree of 18 October 1983 which became final on 26 April 1984.

5.   As the complaint against the Mayor's decision of 6 August 1984 was unsuccessful, Mr Kus brought an action before the Verwaltungsgericht Wlesbaden which, by order of 23 May 1985, provisionally suspended with retrospective effect the contested decision and, by judgment of 30 October 1987, rescinded the decision and ordered the defendant to extend the residence permit held by Mr Kus.

6.   The defendant appealed to the Hessischer Verwaltungsgerichtshof, which, although it found that Mr Kus was not entitled to a residence permit on the basis of German law, raised the question of whether a more favourable outcome for Mr Kus could follow from Article 6(1) of Decision 1/80, which is worded as follows:

1.   Subject to Article 7 on free access to employment for members of his of family, a Turkish worker duly registered as belonging to the labour force of a Member State:

–   shall be entitled in that Member State, after one year's legal employment, to the renewal of his permit to work for the same employer, if a job is available;

–   shall be entitled in that Member State, after three years of legal employment and subject to the priority to be given to workers of Member States of the Community, to respond to another offer of employment, with an employer of his choice, made under normal conditions and registered with the employment services of that State, for the same occupation;

–   shall enjoy free access in that Member State to any paid employment of his choice, after four years of legal employment.

2. The procedures for applying paragraphs 1 and 2 shall be those established under national rules.

7. Therefore the Hessischer Verwaltungsgerichtshof decided to stay the proceedings until the Court of Justice had given a ruling on the following questions:

    1. Does a Turkish worker meet the conditions of the third indent of Article 6(1) of Decision 1/80 of the EEC-Turkey Association Council on the development of the Association if under national law his residence is deemed to be authorised pending the completion of the procedure for granting a residence permit and if on the basis of that right of residence and a concomitant work permit he has been employed for over four years?

    2. Do the provisions of the first indent of Article 6(1) of the abovementioned Decision apply if a Turkish national, who entered Germany in order to marry a German national and whose marriage was terminated by divorce after three years, applies after his divorce for a residence permit for the purpose of engaging in employment and if at the time when that application is refused he has already been employed for two and a half years by the same employer under a valid work permit?

    3. Does a Turkish worker in the circumstances described in 1 or 2 above have a right, directly on the basis of the first or third indent of Article 6(1) of the abovementioned Decision, to the renewal of this residence permit in addition to the renewal of his work permit, or do the rules governing the effects on rights of residence of the decisions of the EEC-Turkey Association Council concerning rights of employment fall within the implementing provisions which under Article 6(3) of that Decision are to be adopted by the Member States on their own responsibility without being bound by Community law?

8. Reference is made to the Report for the Hearing for a fuller account of the facts of the case, the course of the procedure and the observations submitted to the Court, which are mentioned or discussed hereinafter only in so far as is necessary for the reasoning of the Court.

9. As the German Government has expressly asked the Court to reconsider its jurisdiction to give rulings pursuant to Article 177 EEC on the interpretation of decisions adopted by an organ established by an association agreement to ensure the implementation of that agreement, the Court wishes to point out that the observations submitted in the framework of the present case have not yielded any new factor for assessment likely to lead the Court to go back on its findings in Case C-192/89, SEVINCE.

10. It should be noted at the outset that the three questions submitted all refer to the situation of a Turkish worker who is already authorised to reside in a Member State.

The first question

10. The national court's first question is essentially whether the third indent of Article 6(1) of Decision 1/80 must be interpreted as meaning that a Turkish worker fulfils the condition of at least four years' legal employment laid down by that provision if he has been employed on the basis of a right of residence which was recognised only by virtue of a national measure which permits residence in the host country during the procedure for the grant of the residence permit.

11. On this point it should be observed that it follows from SEVINCE cited above that the legality of employment, within the meaning of the third indent of Article 6(1) of Decision 1/80, presupposes a stable and secure situation as a member of the labour force and that this is not the situation of a Turkish worker while he benefits from the suspensory effect deriving from his appeal against a decision refusing him a right of residence and while he is authorised provisionally, pending the outcome of the dispute, to reside and to be employed in the member- State in question.

12. This must also apply in a case such as the present, where the suspensory effect does not attach automatically by law to the appeal, but where it is granted retrospectively by a court. In both cases, as the Advocate General observes, suspension is effective only for the duration of the appeal proceedings and it has the effect of permitting the plaintiff to reside and work provisionally pending a final decision on his right of residence.

13. This conclusion cannot be altered by the fact that, as in the present case, the plaintiff has obtained a first-instance judgment which upholds his right of residence but which, as it has been appealed against, can still be set aside and does not therefore finally regulate his situation with regard to a right of residence.

14. The reason why the court refused, in paragraph 31 of SEVINCE, to recognise as periods of legal employment the periods during which the person concerned benefited from the suspensory effect deriving from his appeal against a decision refusing him a right of residence was to prevent a Turkish worker from contriving to fulfil that condition and consequently from being recognised as possession the right of residence inherent in the freedom of access to any paid employment, as provided for by the third indent of Article 6(1) of Decision 1/80, during a period when he had only a provisional right of residence pending the outcome of the dispute.

15. This reason remains valid until it is finally established that, during the period concerned, the person in question had a legal right of residence, otherwise a judicial decision finally refusing such right will have no effect whatever and the person in question will be enabled to contrive to obtain the rights provided for by the third indent of Article 6(1) during a period when he did not fulfil the requisite conditions.

16. The argument by Mr Kus that failure to take account of a first-instance judgment upholding a Turkish national's right of residence would mean that a refusal, even if it were illegal, to extend a residence permit would be likely to deprive the person concerned of rights which he is capable of deriving from Article 6(1) of Decision 1/80 is not relevant because, if such a right is finally granted, he must be deemed retrospectively to have had during the period in question a right of residence which was not provisional and therefore also to have had a stable situation as a member of the labour force.

17. Therefore the reply to the first question must be that the third indent of Article 6(1) of Decision 1/80 must be interpreted as meaning that a Turkish worker does not fulfil the condition of at least four years legal employment merit laid down by that provision if he has been employed oil the basis of a right of residence conferred upon him only by the effect of a national provision permitting residence in the host country during the procedure for the grant of a residence permit, even if the legality of his right of residence has been confirmed by a judgment of a first-instance court against which an appeal is lodged.

The second question

18. The national court's second question seeks to determine whether the first indent of Article 6(1) of Decision 1/80 must be interpreted as meaning that a Turkish national who obtains a residence permit in a Member State in order to marry a national of that State and who works there for more than one year for the same employer on the basis of a valid work permit is entitled to the renewal of his work permit pursuant to that provision even if his marriage has been dissolved at the date of the decision on the application for renewal.

19. In this connection it should be observed firstly that Article 6(1) of Decision 1/80 merely governs the circumstances of the Turkish worker as regards employment, and makes no reference to his circumstances concerning the right of residence.

20. Secondly, according to the wording of the provision, it applies to Turkish workers duly registered as belonging to the labour force of a Member State and, in particular, pursuant to the first indent of Article 6(1), it is sufficient if a Turkish worker has had legal employment for more than one year for him to be entitled to the renewal of his work permit with the same employer. Therefore this provision does not make recognition of that right dependent on any other condition, particularly the conditions under which the right of entry and residence was obtained.

21. Consequently, even if the legality of employment for the purpose of these provisions presupposes a stable and secure situation as a member of the labour force and thereby implies the existence of an undisputed right of residence and even possession of a legal residence permit, if necessary,

the reasons why such right is recognised or such permit granted are not decisive for the purpose of their application.

22. It follows that, if a Turkish worker has been employed for more than one year on the basis of a valid work permit, he must be regarded as fulfilling the conditions laid down by the first indent of Article 6(1) of Decision 1/80, even if his residence permit was originally issued for purposes other than that of paid employment.

23. At the hearing the United Kingdom Government argued that this approach could have the effect that Turkish nationals would be treated differently depending on whether the national law of the Member State where they reside permits them to work or not if the original reason for residence was not to take up paid employment.

24. However, it should be observed that such a situation would only be a consequence of the fact that Decision 1/80 does not encroach on the power of the Member States to regulate the entry of Turkish nationals into their territory and the conditions of their first employment. Article 6 of the Decision only regulates the situation of Turkish workers who are already duly registered as belonging to the labour force of the Member States. Therefore it cannot justify depriving Turkish workers of the rights laid down by Article 6(1) of Decision 1/80 if they already hold, from the viewpoint of the law of a Member State, a work permit and a right of residence, if the latter is required.

25. Consequently the reply to the second question should be that the first indent of Article 6(1) of Decision 1/80 must be interpreted as meaning that a Turkish national who has obtained a permit to reside in a Member State in order to marry a national of that State and who has worked there for more than one year for the same employer on the basis of a valid work permit has a right to the renewal of his work permit under that provision even if his marriage has been dissolved at the date of the decision on the application for renewal.

The third question

26. The national court's third question is essentially whether a Turkish worker who fulfils the conditions of the first or third indents of Article 6(1) of Decision 1/80 can rely directly on those provisions to obtain the extension of his residence permit in addition to that of his work permit.

27. On this point it should be observed that, firstly, in SEVINCE cited above, the Court held that Article 6(1) of Decision 1/80 has direct effect in the Member States of the European Community.

28. Secondly, in the same judgment the Court found, in the context of the third indent of Article 6(1) of Decision 1/80, that although that provision only governs the circumstances of the Turkish worker as regards employment and not as regards the right of residence, those two aspects of the personal situation of a Turkish worker are closely linked and by granting

to such a worker, after a specified period of legal employment in the Member State, access to any paid employment of his choice, the provisions in question necessarily imply – since otherwise the right granted by them to the Turkish worker would be deprived of any effect – the existence, at least at that time, of a right of residence for the person concerned.

29. This finding applies also to the first indent of Article 6(1) of Decision 1/80 because, without a right of residence, the grant to a Turkish worker, after one year's employment, of a right to the renewal of his work permit with the same employer would be of no effect either.

30. This conclusion cannot be altered by the fact that, pursuant to Article 6(3) of Decision 1/80, the procedures for applying paragraph (1) are established by national rules. As the Court pointed out in SEVINCE at paragraph 22, Article 6(3) of Decision 1/80 merely clarifies the obligation of the Member States to take such administrative measures as may be necessary for the implementation of those provisions, without empowering the Member States to make conditional or restrict the application of the precise and unconditional right which it grants to Turkish workers.

31. In its observations to the Court, the German Government expressly disputes that there is necessarily a link between the right of access to the labour force and the right of residence because, even with regard to the freedom of movement of workers in the Community, situations may arise where the two aspects do not necessarily coincide. By way of example, the German Government refers, firstly, to Council Directive 64/221 for the co-ordination of special measures for aliens in relation to travel and residence, which are justified on grounds of public policy, public security and public health," Articles 3(2) and 4(1) of which are said to permit the right of residence to be withdrawn or refused by reason of certain offences or certain diseases and, secondly, to Case C-292/89, ANTONISSEN, from which it is said to follow that the right of residence of a Community national who has searched for employment unsuccessfully could be limited in time, without him losing his unlimited right of access to the labour force.

32. Neither of these examples is relevant, however. Far from proving that an individual can have a right of access to the labour force without a right of residence, they show, on the contrary, that the right of residence is essential for taking up and pursuing paid employment.

33. Firstly, it is in order to prevent such a fundamental right as that of the freedom of movement for workers being unduly restricted that Article 3(2) of Directive 64/221 provides that the mere existence of criminal convictions cannot automatically Justify measures of public policy or public security, and that Article 4(1) provides that only certain diseases, also listed exhaustively in an annex, can justify the refusal of entry to a Member State or the issue of the first residence permit. It should also be observed that Article 14(1) of Decision 1/80, like Article 48(3) EEC and the abovementioned Directive 64/221, permits the rights for which it

provides to be restricted on grounds of public policy, public security and public health.

34. Secondly, in ANTONISSEN cited above, the Court found, on the basis of the Treaty provisions concerning the freedom of movement for workers, that Community nationals have a right of residence in the Member States not only in order to accept offers of employment actually made, but also to seek employment.

35. Therefore the reply to the third question must be that a Turkish worker who fulfils the conditions of the first or third indent of Article 6(1) of Decision 1/80 may rely directly on those provisions to obtain an extension of his residence permit, in addition to that of his work permit.

Costs

36. The costs incurred by the German, Dutch and United Kingdom Governments, which have submitted observations to the Court, are not recoverable. As these proceedings are, in so far as the parties to the main proceedings are concerned, in the nature of a step in the proceedings pending before the national court, the decision on costs is a matter for that court.

On those grounds, THE COURT, in answer to the questions submitted to it by the Hessischer Verwaltungsgerichtshof by order of 12 August 1991, hereby rules:

1. The third indent of Article 6(1) of Decision 1/80 of the Council of Association established by the Agreement establishing an Association between the European Economic Community and Turkey of 19 September 1980 on the development of the Association must be interpreted as meaning that a Turkish worker does not fulfil the condition of having been engaged in legal employment for at least four years laid down by that provision where he engaged in that employment on the basis of a right of residence which was recognised only by virtue of national rules authorising residence in the host country pending the procedure for the grant of a residence permit, if the lawfulness of his right of residence has been even confirmed by a judgment of a court sitting at first instance against which an appeal was lodged.

2. The first indent of Article 6(1) of the abovementioned Decision 1/80 must be interpreted as meaning, that a Turkish national who has obtained a permit to reside on the territory of a Member State in order to marry there a national of that Member State and who has worked for more -than one year with the same employer on the basis of a valid work permit is entitled to have his work permit renewed under that provision, even if at the time when a decision on his application for renewal of his work permit is taken his marriage has been dissolved.

3. A Turkish worker who fulfils the conditions under the first or third

indents of Article 6(1) of Decision 1/80 may rely directly on those provisions in order to obtain the extension of his residence permit as well as that of his work permit.

Rodríguez Iglesias   Zuleeg   Murray

Mancini   Juliet   Schockweiler

Moitinho de Almeida   Grevisse

Kapleyn

Delivered in open court in Luxembourg 16 December 1992

R. Grass   Rodríguez Iglesias
Registrar   President of the Chamber

Judgment of the Court of Justice of the European Communities

20 September 1990

S.Z. Sevince v Staatssecretaris Van Justitie

Case C-192/89

REFERENCE to the Court under Article 177 of the EEC Treaty by the Raad van State (Netherlands) on the interpretation of Decision No 1/80 of the Association Council of 19 September 1980 on the development of the Association, adopted by the Association Council, established by the Association Agreement between the European Economic Community and Turkey

THE COURT

composed of: O. Due President of the Court, Slynn, Kakouris Schockweiler and Zuleeg, Presidents of the Chambers, Mancini, O'Higgins, Moitinho de Almeida, Rodríguez Iglesias, Grévisse and Díez de Velasco, Judges

Advocate General: M. Darmon

after considering the written observations submitted on behalf of:
- A.W.M. Willems, of the Amsterdam Bar, for the Plaintiff.
- B.R. Bot, Secretary General of the Dutch Ministry of Foreign Affairs, for the Dutch Government.
- Ernst Röder, Reigierungsdirektor, Bundesministerium für Wirtschaft, for the German Government as amicus curiae.
- Pieter Jan Kuijper, of the Commission's Legal Department, for the E.C. Commission as amicus curiae.

1. By decision of 1 June 1989, which was received at the Court on 8 June 1989, the Raad van State (Dutch court of last instance in administrative matters) referred to the Court for a preliminary ruling under **Article 177** EEC three questions on the interpretation of certain provisions of Decisions 2/76 of 20 December 1976 and 1/80 of 19 September 1980 of the Council of Association established by the Agreement establishing an Association between the European Economic Community and Turkey, signed in Ankara on 12 September 1963, concluded on behalf of the Community by Council Decision 64/732/EEC of 23 December 1963, (hereinafter referred to as "the Agreement").

2. The questions were raised in proceedings brought by Mr S Z Sevince, a Turkish national, against the Staatssecretaris van Justitie (State Secretary of Justice) concerning the latter's refusal to grant him a permit allowing him to reside in the Netherlands.

3.   It is apparent from the documents before the Court that on 11 September 1980 Mr Sevince was refused an extension to the residence permit which had been granted to him on 22 February 1979 on the ground that the family circumstances which had justified the grant of the permit no longer existed. The appeal lodged against that decision, which had full suspensive effect, was definitively dismissed by the Raad van State on 12 June 1986. During the period in which he benefited from the suspensory effect of the appeal, Mr Sevince obtained an employment certificate which remained valid until the abovementioned judgment of the Raad van State was delivered on 12 June 1986.

4.   Claiming that he had been in paid employment for a number of years in the Netherlands, on 13 April 1987 Mr Sevince applied for a residence permit. In support of his application, he relied on Article 2(1)(b) of Decision 2/76, according to which a Turkish worker who has been in legal employment for five years in a Member State of the Community is to enjoy free access in that Member State to any paid employment of his choice, and on the third indent of Article 6(1) of Decision 1/80, according to which a Turkish worker duly registered as belonging to the labour force of a Member State is to enjoy free access in that Member State to any paid employment of his choice after four years' legal employment. His application was rejected, by implication, by the Dutch authorities.

5.   An appeal against that decision was brought before the Raad van State, which decided to stay the proceedings until the Court of Justice had given a ruling on the following questions:

1.   Is Article 177 EEC to be interpreted as meaning that a court or tribunal of a Member State may (and, in this case, must) refer to the Court of Justice for a preliminary ruling a question concerning the interpretation of the decisions of the Council of Association at issue in this case, that is to say, Decision 2/76 and/or Decision 1/80, if such a question is raised before it and it considers that a decision on the question is necessary to enable it to give judgment?

2.   If Question 1 is answered in the affirmative: Are the following to be regarded as provisions applicable in the countries of the European Community to legal disputes: Article 2(1)(b) of Decision 2/76 and/or Article 6(1) of Decision 1/80, and Article 7 of Decision 2/76 and/or Article 13 of Decision 1/80?

3.   If Question 2 is answered in the affirmative: What is to be understood by the term "legal employment" in Article 2(1)(b) of Decision 2/76 and/or Article 6(1) of Decision 1/80 (in the light of Article 7 of Decision 2/76 and/or Article 13 of Decision 1/80)? Is it to be understood as referring to employment while the person concerned was in possession of a residence permit in compliance with the laws relating to aliens – with the subsidiary question whether, more broadly, it includes employment which that person could have had while he was waiting for the decision concerning his residence permit to become final and irreversible – or solely to employment which

may be regarded as lawful employment within the terms of the legislation governing the employment of aliens?

6. Reference is made to the Report for the Hearing for a fuller account of the facts of the case, the course of the procedure and the submissions and arguments of the parties, which are mentioned or discussed hereinafter only in so far as is necessary for the reasoning, of the Court.

The first question

7. The national court's first question is essentially whether an interpretation of Decisions 2/76 and 1/80 may be given under Article 177 EEC.

8. By way of a preliminary observation, it should be borne in mind that, as the Court has consistently held, the provisions of an agreement concluded by the Council under Articles 228 and 238 EEC form an integral part of the Community legal system as from the entry into force of that agreement: Case 12/86 *Demirel* [1987] ECR 3719 and Case 30/88 *Greece v EC Commission* [1989] ECR 3711.

9. The Court has also held that, since they are directly connected with the Agreement to which they give effect, the decisions of the Council of Association, in the same way as the Agreement itself, form an integral part, as from their entry into force, of the Community legal system: see Case 30/88 *Greece* v *EC Commission* [1989] ECR 449.

10. Since the Court has jurisdiction to give preliminary rulings on the Agreement, in so far as it is an act adopted by one of the institutions of the Community: see Case 181/73 Haegeman, [1974] ECR 449 it also has jurisdiction to give rulings on the interpretation of the decisions adopted by the authority established by the Agreement and entrusted with responsibility for its implementation.

11. That finding is reinforced by the fact that the function of Article 177 EEC is to ensure the uniform application throughout the Community of all provisions forming part of the Community legal system and to ensure that the interpretation thereof does not vary according to the interpretation accorded to them by the various Member States: see Case 104/81 *Kupferberg* [1982] ECR 3641 and Joined Cases 267-269/81 *Spi and Sami* [1983] ECR 801.

12. It must therefore be stated in reply to the first question submitted by the Raad van State that the interpretation of Decisions 2/76 and 1/80 falls within the scope of Article 177 EEC.

The second question

13. The second question submitted by the Raad van State is whether Articles 2(1)(b) and 7 of Decision 2/76 and Articles 6(1) and 13 of Decision 1/80 have direct effect in the territory of the Member States.

14. In order to be recognised as having direct effect, the provisions of a

decision of the Council of Association must satisfy the same conditions as those applicable to the provisions of the Agreement itself.

15. In *Demirel (supra)* the Court held that a provision in an agreement concluded by the Community with non-member countries must be regarded as being directly applicable when, regard being had to its wording and the purpose and nature of the agreement itself, the provision contains a clear and precise obligation which is not subject, in its implementation or effects, to the adoption of any subsequent measure. The same criteria apply in determining whether the provisions of a decision of the Council of Association can have direct effect.

16. In order to determine whether the relevant provisions of Decisions 2/76 and 1/80 satisfy those criteria, it is first necessary to examine their terms.

17. Article 2(1)(b) of Decision 2/76 and the third indent of Article 6(1) of Decision 1/80 uphold, in clear, precise and unconditional terms, the right of a Turkish worker, after a number of years' legal employment in a Member State, to enjoy free access to any paid employment of his choice.

18. Similarly, Article 7 of Decision 2/76 and Article 13 of Decision 1/80 contain an unequivocal "standstill" clause regarding the introduction of new restrictions on access to the employment of workers legally resident and employed in the territory of the contracting States.

19. The finding that the provisions of the decisions of Council of European Association at issue in the main proceedings are capable of direct Court of application to the situation of Turkish workers duly registered as belonging to the labour force of a Member State is confirmed by the Judgment purpose and nature of the decisions of which those provisions form part and of the Agreement to which they relate.

20. According to Article 2(1) of the Agreement, its purpose is to promote the continuous and balanced strengthening of trade and economic relations between the parties, and it establishes between the European Economic Community and Turkey an association which provides for a preparatory stage to enable Turkey to strengthen its economy with aid from the Community, a transitional stage for the progressive establishment of a customs union and for the alignment of economic policies, and a final stage based on the customs union and entailing close coordination of economic policies: see Case 12/86 *Demirel (supra)*. As far as freedom of movement for workers is concerned, Article 12 of the Agreement, forming part of Title II concerning implementation of the transitional stage, provides that the contracting parties agree to be guided by Article 48, 49 and 50 EEC for the purpose of progressively securing freedom of movement for workers between them. Article 36 of the Additional Protocol signed on 23 November 1970, annexed to the Agreement establishing an association between the European Economic Community and Turkey, concluded by Council Regulation 2760/72 (hereinafter referred to as the "Additional Protocol") lays down the time-limits for the progressive attainment of such freedom of movement and provides that the Council of Association is to decide on the rules necessary to that end.

21.   Decisions 2/76 and 1/80 were adopted by the Council of Association in order to implement Article 12 of the Agreement and Article 36 of the Additional Protocol which, in its Judgment in *Demirel (supra)* the Court recognised as being intended essentially to set out a programme. Thus, in the preamble to Decision 2/76 reference is expressly made to Article 12 of the Agreement and Article 36 of the Additional Protocol and Article 1 of the decision lays down the detailed arrangements for the first stage of implementation of Article 36 of the Additional Protocol. The third recital in the preamble to Decision 1/80 refers to improving, in the social sphere, the conditions available to workers and members of their families in relation to the arrangements introduced by Decision 2/76. The fact that the abovementioned provisions of the Agreement and the Additional Protocol essentially set out a programme does not prevent the decisions of the Council of Association which give effect in specific respects to the programmes envisaged in the Agreement from having direct effect.

22.   The conclusion that the articles of Decisions 2/76 and 1/80 mentioned in the second question referred to the Court can have direct effect cannot be affected by the fact that Article 2(2) of Decision 2/76 and Article 6(3) of Decision 1/80 provide that the procedures for applying the rights conferred on Turkish workers are to be established under national rules. Those provisions merely clarify the obligation of the Member States to take such administrative measures as may be necessary for the implementation of those provisions, without empowering the Member States to make conditional or restrict the application of the precise and unconditional right which the decisions of the Council of Association grant to Turkish workers.

23.   Similarly, Article 12 of Decision 2/76 and Article 29 of Decision 1/80, which provide that the contracting parties are, each for its own part, to take any measures required for the purposes of implementing the provisions of the decision, merely lay emphasis on the obligation to implement in good faith an international agreement, an obligation which, moreover, is referred to in Article 7 of the Agreement itself.

24.   The direct effect of the provisions at issue in the main proceedings cannot, furthermore, be contested merely because Decisions 2/76 and 1/80 were not published. Although non-publication of those decisions may prevent their being applied to a private individual, a private individual is not thereby deprived of the power to invoke, in dealings with a public authority, the rights which those decisions confer on him.

25.   As regards the safeguard clauses which enable the contracting parties to derogate from the provisions granting certain rights to Turkish workers duly registered as belonging to the labour force of a Member State, it must be observed that they apply only to specific situations. Otherwise than in the specific situations which may give rise to their application, the existence of such clauses is not in itself liable to affect the direct applicability inherent in the provisions from which they allow derogations: see Case 104/81 *Kupferberg (supra)*.

26.   It follows from the foregoing considerations that it must be stated in reply to the second question submitted by the Raad van State that Article 2(1)(b) of the Decision 2/76 and/or Article 6(1) of Decision 1/80 and Article 7 of Decision 2/76 and/or Article 13 of Decision 1/80 have direct effect in the Member States of the European Community.

The third question

27.   The national court's third question seeks to determine whether the expression "legal employment" contained in Article 2(1)(b) of Decision 2/76 and in the third indent of Article 6(1) of Decision 1/80 covers a situation where a Turkish worker is authorised to work during the period for which the operation is suspended of a decision refusing him a right of residence, against which he has appealed.

28.   In replying to that question it must first be stated that the abovementioned provisions merely govern the circumstances of the Turkish worker as regards employment, and make no reference to his circumstances concerning the right of residence.

29.   The fact nevertheless remains that those two aspects of the personal situation of a Turkish worker are closely linked and that by granting to such a worker, after a specified period of legal employment in the Member State, access to any paid employment of his choice, the provisions in question necessarily imply – since otherwise the right granted by them to the Turkish worker would be deprived of any effect – the existence, at least at that time, of a right of residence for the person concerned.

30.   The legality of the employment within the meaning of those provisions, even assuming that it is not necessarily conditional upon possession of a properly issued residence permit, nevertheless presupposes a stable and secure situation as a member of the labour force.

31.   In particular, although legal employment over a given period gives rise, at the end of that period; to recognition of a right of residence, it is inconceivable that a Turkish worker could contrive to fulfil that condition, and consequently be recognised as being vested with that right, merely because, having been refused a valid residence permit by the national authorities during that period and having exercised the rights of appeal provided for by national law against such refusal, he benefited from the suspensory effect deriving from his appeal and was therefore able to obtain authorisation, on a provisional basis pending the outcome of the dispute, to reside and be employed inthe Member State in question.

32.   Consequently, the expression "legal employment" contained in Article 2(1)(b) of Decision 2/76 and in the third indent of Article 6(1) of Decision 1/80 cannot cover the situation of a Turkish worker who has been legally able to continue in employment only by reason of the suspensory effect deriving from his appeal pending a final decision by the

national court thereon, provided always, however, that that court dismisses his appeal.

33. It must therefore be stated in reply to the third question submitted by the national court that the term "legal employment" in Article 2(1)(b) of Decision 2176 and the third indent of Article 6(1) of Decision 1/80 does not cover the situation of a Turkish worker authorised to engage in employment for such time as the effect of a decision refusing him a right of residence, against which he has lodged an appeal which has been dismissed, is suspended.

Costs

34. The costs incurred by the Government of the Federal Republic off Germany, the Government of the Kingdom of the Netherlands and the Commission, which have submitted observations to the Court, are not recoverable. Since these proceedings are, in so far as the parties to the main proceedings are concerned, in the nature of a step in the action pending before the national court, the decision on costs is a Court of matter for that court.

On those grounds, THE COURT, in reply to the questions submitted to it by the Raad van State of the Netherlands by decision of 1 June 1989, hereby rules:

1. The interpretation of Decision 2/76 of 20 December 1976 and Decision 1/80 of 19 September 1980 of the Association Council set up by the Agreement establishing an Association between the European Economic Community and Turkey falls within the scope of Article 177 EEC.

2. Article 2(1)(b) of Decision 2/76, cited above, and Article 6(1) of Decision 1/80, cited above, and Article 7 of Directive 2/76 and Article 13 of Decision 1/80 have direct effect in the Member States of the European Community.

3. The term "legal employment" in Article 2(1)(b) of Decision No. 2/76, cited above, and the third indent of Article 6(1) of Decision No. 1180, cited above, does not cover the situation of a Turkish worker authorised to engage in employment for such time as the effect of a decision refusing him a right of residence, against which he has lodged an appeal which has been dismissed, is suspended.

Due	Slynn	Kakouris
Schockweiler	Zuleeg	Mancini
	O'Higgins	Moitinho de Almeida
	Rodríguez Iglesias	Grévisse Díez de Velasco

Delivered and open court in Luxembourg on 20 September 1990

R. Grass
Registrar

O. Due
President

Judgment of the Court of Justice of the European Communities

30 September 1987

MERYEM DEMIREL V STADT SCHWÄBISCH GMÜND

Case-12/86

REFERENCE to the Court under Article 177 of the EEC Treaty by the Verwaltungsgericht Stuttgart (Germany) for a preliminary ruling in the proceedings pending before that court on the interpretation of Article 12 of the Association Agreement between the EEC and Turkey of 12 September 1963 and Article 36 of the Additional Protocol to that Agreement of 23 November 1970.

THE COURT

composed of Lord MacKenzie Stuart, President of the Court, Galmot, O'Higgins and Schockweiler, Presidents of the Chambers, Basco, Koopmans, Everling, Bahlmann, Joliet, Mointinho de Almeida and Rodríguez Iglesias, Judges,

Advocate General: M. Darmon

after considering the written observations submitted on behalf of: Dieter Schädel, of the Legal Deapartment of the City of Schwäbisch Gmünd, for the defendant City in the written proceedings only. Professor Harald Fliegauf, Leitender Oberlandesanwalt (Senior Regional Prosecutor), for the Vertreter des Offentlichen Interesses (Representative of the Public Interest) (interventor in the main proceedings).

Martin Seidel, Principal at the Federal Ministry of Economics, with him in the written proceedings only Jochim Sedemund, of the Cologne Bar, for the German Government as *amicus curiae*.

Gilbert Guillaume, Director of Legal Affairs at the Ministry of Foreign Affairs, in the written proceedings, and Philippe Pouzoulet, Secretary for Foreign Affairs at the Legal Department of the Ministry of Foreign Affairs, in the oral proceedings, for the French Government as *amicus curiae*.

Stelios Perrakis, Legal Adviser in the European Communities Section of the Ministry of Foreign Affairs, alone in the oral proceedings and assisting Iannos Kranidiotis, Secretary at the Ministry of Foreign Affairs, in the written proceedings, for the Greek Government as *amicus curiae*.

B.E. McHenry, of the Treasury Solicitor's Deapartment, in the written proceedings, and Professor David Edward, of the Scottish Bar, in the oral proceedings, for the United Kingdom Government as *amicus curiae*

Peter Gilsdorf, Legal Adviser to the E.C. Commisssion, for the Commission as *amicus curiae.*

having regard to the Report for the Hearing and after hearing the Opinion of the Advocate General at the sitting on 19 May 1987,

gives the following Judgment

1. By an order of 11 December 1985 lodged at the Court Registry on 17 January 1986, the Verwaltungsgericht (Administrative Court) referred to the Court for a preliminary ruling under Article 177 EEC two questions concerning the interpretation of Articles 7 and 11 of the Agreement establishing an Association between the European Economic Community and Turkey (hereinafter referred to as "the Agreement"), signed at Ankara on 12 September 1963) and concluded on behalf of the Community by a decision of the Council of 13 December 1963, and of Article 36 of the Additional Protocol (hereinafter referred to as "the Protocol") signed at Brussels on 23 November 1970 and concluded on behalf of the Community by Council Regulation 2760/72 of 19 December 1972.

2. The questions arose in the course of an action for the annulment of an order to leave the country, accompanied by the threat of expulsion, which the City of Schwäbisch Gmünd had issued against Mrs Meryem Demirel, a Turkish national, on the expiry of her visa. Mrs Demirel is the wife of a Turkish national who had been living and working in the Federal Republic of Germany since entering that country in 1979 for the purpose rejoining his family. She had come to rejoin her husband holding a visa which was valid only for the purposes of a visit and was not issued for family reunification.

3. It appears from the order of the Verwaltungsgericht that the conditions for family reunification in the case of nationals of non-member countries who have themselves entered the Federal Republic of Germany for the purposes of family reunification were tightened in 1982 and 1984 by amendments to a circular issued for the *Land* of Baden- Württemberg by the Minister of the Interior of *Land* pursuant to the Ausldndergesetz (Aliens Act); those amendments raised from three to eight years the period during which the foreign national was required to have resided continuously and lawfully on German territory. Mrs Demirel's husband did not fulfil that condition at the time of the events which led to the main proceedings.

4. The Verwaltungsgericht Stuttgart, to which application was made for annulment of the order that Mrs Demirel leave the country, referred the following questions to the Court of Justice:

    1. Do Article 12 of the Association Agreement between the European

Economic Community and Turkey and Article 36 of the Additional Protocol thereto, in conjunction with Article 7 of the Association Agreement, already lay down a prohibition that under Community law is directly applicable in the Member States on the introduction law is directly applicable in the Member States on the introduction of further restrictions on freedom of movement applicable to Turkish workers lawfully resident in a member-State in the form of a modification of an existing administrative practice?

2. Is the expression "freedom of movement" in the Association Agreement to be understood as giving Turkish workers residing in a Member State the right to bring children under the age of majority and spouses to live with them?

5. Reference is made to the Report for the Hearing for a fuller account of the facts in the main proceedings, the provisions of German legislation, the Agreement and the Protocol thereto, the course of the procedure and the observations submitted under Article 20 of the Protocol on the Statute of the Court of Justice of the EEC, which are mentioned or discussed hereinafter only in so far as is necessary for the reasoning of the Court.

Jurisdiction of the Court

6. Since, in their written observations, the Government of the Federal Republic of Germany and the United Kingdom call in question the Jurisdiction of the Court to interpret the provisions of the Agreement and the Protocol regarding the freedom of movement for workers, it is appropriate to consider the issue of the Court's Jurisdiction before ruling on the questions submitted by the national court.

7. It should first be pointed out that, as the Court held in Case 181/73, *Haegeman v Belgium* [1974] ECR 449, an agreement concluded by the council under Articles 228 and 238 of the Treaty is, as far as the community is concerned, an act of one of the institutions of the Community within the meaning of Article 177(b), and, as from its entry into force, the provisions of such an agreement form an integral part of the Community legal system; within the framework of that system the Court has jurisdiction to give preliminary rulings concerning the interpretation of such an agreement.

8. However, the German Government and the United Kingdom take the view that, in the case of "mixed" agreements such as the Agreement and the Protocol at issue here, the Court's interpretative jurisdiction does not extend to provisions whereby Member States have entered into commitments with regard to Turkey in the exercise of their own powers which is the case of the provisions on freedom of movement for workers.

9. In that connection it is sufficient to state that that is precisely not the case in this instance. Since the agreement in question is an association

agreement creating special, privileged links with a non-member country which must, at least to a certain extent, take part in the Community system, Article 238 must necessarily empower the Community to guarantee commitments towards non-member countries in all the fields covered by the Treaty. Since freedom of movement for workers is, by virtue of Article 48 et seq. of the EEC Treaty, one of the fields covered by that Treaty, it follows that commitments regarding freedom of movement fall within the powers conferred on the Community by Article 238. Thus the question whether the Court has jurisdiction to rule on the interpretation of a provision in a mixed agreement containing a commitment which only the Member States could enter into in the sphere of their own powers does not arise.

10.   Furthermore, the jurisdiction of the Court cannot be called in question by virtue of the fact that In the field of freedom of movement for workers, as Community law now stands, it is for the Member States to lay down the rules which are necessary to give effect in their territory to the provisions of the Agreement or the decisions to be adopted by the Association Council.

11.   As the Court held in Case 104/81, *Hauptzollamt Mainz* v *Kupferberg* [1982] ECR 3641, in ensuring respect for commitments arising from an agreement concluded by the Community institutions the Member States fulfil, within the Community system, an obligation in relation to the Community, which has assumed responsibility for the due of performance of the agreement.

12.   Consequently, the Court does have Jurisdiction to interpret the provisions on freedom of movement for workers contained in the Agreement and the Protocol.

The questions referred to the Court

13.   The Verwaltungsgericht's first question seeks essentially to establish whether Article 12 of the Agreement and Article 36 of the Protocol, read in conjunction with Article 7 of the Agreement, constitute rules of Community law which are directly applicable in the internal legal order of the Member States.

14.   A provision in an agreement concluded by the Community with non-member countries must be regarded as being directly applicable when, regard being had to its wording and the purpose and nature of the agreement itself, the provision contains a clear and precise obligation which is not subject, in its implementation or effects, to the adoption of any subsequent measure.

15.   According to Articles 2 to 5 thereof, the Agreement provides for a preparatory stage to enable Turkey to strengthen its economy with aid from the Community, a transitional stage for the progressive establishment of a customs union and for the alignment of economic policies, and a final

stage based on the customs union and entailing closer co-ordination of economic policies.

16. In structure, and content, the Agreement is characterised by the fact that, in general, it sets out the aims of the association and lays down guidelines for the attainment of those aims without itself establishing the detailed rules for doing so. Only in respect of certain specific matters are detailed rules laid down by the protocols annexed to the Agreement, later replaced by the Additional Protocol.

17. In order to achieve the aims set out in the Agreement. Article 22 confers decision- making powers on the Council of Association which consists of members of the Governments of the Member States and members of the Council and Commission, on the one hand, and members of the Turkish Government, on the other.

18. Title II of the Agreement, which deals with the implementation of the transitional stage, includes two chapters on the customs union and agriculture together with a third chapter containing other economic provisions, of which Article 12 on the freedom of movement for workers forms part.

19. Article 12 of the Agreement provides that the Contracting Parties agree to be guided by Articles 48, 49 and 50 of the Treaty establishing the Community for the purpose of progressively securing freedom of movement for workers between them.

20. Article 36 of the Protocol provides that freedom of movement shall be secured by progressive stages in accordance with the principles set out in Article 12 of the Agreement between the end of the 12th and the 22nd year after the entry into force of that Agreement, and that the Council of Association is to decide on the rules necessary to that end.

21. Article 36 of the Protocol gives the Council of Association exclusive powers to lay down detailed rules for the progressive attainment of freedom of movement for workers in accordance with political and economic considerations arising in particular out of the progressive establishment of the customs union and the alignment of economic policies, pursuant to such arrangements as the Council of Association may deem necessary.

22. The only decision which the Council of Association adopted on the matter was Decision 1/80 of 19 September 1980 which, with regard to Turkish workers who are already duly integrated in the labour force of a Member State, prohibits any further restrictions on the conditions governing access to employment. In the sphere of family reunification, on the other hand, no decision of that kind was adopted.

23. Examination of Article 12 of the Agreement and Article 36 of the Protocol therefore reveals that they are essentially serve to set out a programme and are not sufficiently precise and unconditional to be capable of governing directly the movement of workers.

24. Accordingly, it is not possible to infer from Article 7 of the Agreement a

prohibition on the introduction of further restrictions on family reunification. Article 7, which forms part of Title I of the Agreement dealing with the principles of the Association, provides in very general terms that the Contracting Parties are to take all appropriate measures, whether general or particular, to ensure fulfilment of the obligations arising from the agreement and that they are to refrain from any measures liable to jeopardise the attainment of the objectives of the Agreement. That provision does no more than impose on the Contracting Parties a general obligation to co-operate in order to achieve the aims of the Agreement and it cannot directly confer on individuals rights which are not already vested in them by other provisions of the Agreement.

25.   Consequently, the answer to be given to the first question is that Article 12 of the Agreement and Article 36 of the Protocol, read in conjunction with Article 7 of the Agreement, do not constitute rules of the Community law which are directly applicable in the internal legal order of the Member States.

26.   By its second question the national court wishes to establish whether the conditions subject to which the spouse and minor children of a Turkish worker established within the Community may join him are covered by the concept of "freedom of movement" within the meaning of the Agreement.

27.   In the light of the answer to the first question, the second question does not not call for an answer.

28.   As to the point whether Article 8 of the European Convention on Human Rights has any bearing on the answer to that question, it must be observed that, as the Court ruled in Joined Cases 60-61/84, *Cinetheque Federation Nationale Des Cinemas Francais* [1985] ECR 2605, although it is the duty of the Court to ensure observance of fundamental rights in the field of Community law, it has no power to examine the compatibility with the European Convention on Human Rights of national legislation lying outside the scope of Community law. In this case, however, as is apparent from the answer to the first question, there is at present no provision of Community law defining the conditions in which Member States must permit the family reunification of Turkish workers lawfully settled in the Community. It follows that the national rules at issue in the main proceedings did not have to implement a provision of Community law. In those circumstances, the Court does not have jurisdiction to determine whether national rules such as those at issue are compatible with the principles enshrined in Article 8 of the European Convention on Human Rights.

Costs

29.   The costs incurred by the Government of the Federal Republic of Germany, the Government of the French Republic, the Government of the Hellenic Republic, the United Kingdom and the Commission of the

European Communities, which have submitted observations to the Court, are not recoverable. As these proceedings are, in so far as the parties to the main action are concerned, in the nature of a step in the proceedings before the national court, the decision on costs is a matter for that court.

On those grounds, THE COURT, in answer to the questions referred to by the Verwaltungsgericht Stuttgart by an order of 11 December 1985 hereby rules:

> Article 12 of the Agreement establishing an Association between the European Economic Community and Turkey, signed in Ankara on 12 September 1963 and concluded on behalf of the Community by a Council Decision of 23 December 1963, and Article 36 of the Additional Protocol, signed at Brussels on 23 November 1970 and concluded on behalf of the Community by Council Regulation 2760/72 of 19 December 1972, read in conjunction with Article 7 of the Agreement, do not constitute rules of Community law which are directly applicable in the internal legal order of the Member States.

Lord MacKenzie Stuart   Galmot

O'Higgins   Schockweiler   Bahlmann

Joliet

Delivered in open court in Luxembourg on 30 September 1987

R. Grass   Lord MacKenzie Stuart
Registrar   President
April 28, 1999

Index